CHRIST AND CAESAR

DATE DUE

# CHRIST AND CAESAR

*The Gospel and the Roman Empire
in the Writings of Paul and Luke*

Seyoon Kim

WILLIAM B. EERDMANS PUBLISHING COMPANY
GRAND RAPIDS, MICHIGAN / CAMBRIDGE, U.K.

Published 2008 by
Wm. B. Eerdmans Publishing Co.
2140 Oak Industrial Drive N.E., Grand Rapids, Michigan 49505 /
P.O. Box 163, Cambridge CB3 9PU U.K.

Printed in the United States of America

14 13 12 11 10 09 08      7 6 5 4 3 2 1

**Library of Congress Cataloging-in-Publication Data**

Kim, Seyoon.
    Christ and Caesar: the Gospel and the Roman Empire in the writings
of Paul and Luke / Seyoon Kim.
       p.      cm.
    Includes bibliographical references and index.
    ISBN 978-0-8028-6008-8 (pbk.: alk. paper)
    1. Bible. N.T. Epistles of Paul — Criticism, interpretation, etc.
    2. Bible. N.T. Luke — Criticism, interpretation, etc.
    3. Bible. N.T. Acts — Criticism, interpretation, etc.
    4. Rome.    I. Title.

BS2650.52.K56   2008
227′.067 — dc22

                        2008031706

www.eerdmans.com

*For Professor Martin and Frau Marianne Hengel*
*on his eightieth birthday*

# Contents

# Preface

This book has grown out of an intended excursus to my commentary on 1 and 2 Thessalonians. Since the call for an interpretation of Paul in connection with the Roman imperial cult and ideology is getting ever louder these days and 1 Thessalonians is treated by many scholars as a test case for such an interpretation, I felt the need to have a clear understanding of how much Paul interacts with those realities of the Roman Empire and to what extent he formulates his preaching and teaching in conscious reaction to them. Initially impressed by the assumption of the prevalent imperial cult in the Roman East as well as by the parallelism between terms for imperial propaganda and the Pauline gospel, I started my investigation sympathetic to a counter-imperial interpretation of Paul and even anticipated a more integrated understanding of Paul based on a full consideration of the neglected political dimension of his missionary context. I planned to attach the results of my investigation to my commentary and reflect them in the relevant sections of the Thessalonian epistles. But the investigation grew larger than anticipated. Then I thought that it would be useful to examine the Lucan witness, too, as in his Acts of the Apostles he purports to report on Paul's actual encounters with Greco-Roman cities and Roman officials. This decision has naturally involved studying the whole of the Lucan writings, as the Gospel of Luke and the Acts of the Apostles have to be seen together.

This brief account of the book's *Werdegang* explains why it is limited in scope. However, it does not excuse its deficiency in thoroughness, which has more to do with the lack of my ability and time than anything else. Therefore, I would like to beg indulgence of those colleagues whose contributions are inadequately reflected or sometimes even go unnoticed. Having wondered why recent commentaries on Pauline epistles do not deal much with the imperial cult and ideology or interact with those scholars who make these issues central in Pauline studies, I could have found Robert Jewett's commentary on Romans in the Hermeneia series (Minneapolis: Fortress, 2007) useful for this book, as it is written specifically from the perspective of anti-Roman imperial cult and ideology. But unfortunately it came out too late for any serious consultation for this book. I am well aware of some areas in which a deeper and wider reflection would have made the book more complete. Even so, I hope that this book may be found to make some contributions to a better understanding of the gospel that Paul and Luke preached. It will be very gratifying to me if it can also help some readers, including laypeople, think about effective ways of preaching the gospel today as well as about proper Christian discipleship in the political sphere.

I would like to thank Fuller Theological Seminary for granting me a sabbatical quarter during the fall of 2006 which, added to the summer recess, has enabled me to write this book. I would like to express my gratitude also to the staff of Fuller Seminary library and to my secretary, Grace Bong, for their help with literature procurement. Steve Young, a Ph.D. candidate, has been a most reliable assistant, and I would like to thank him especially for his help with obtaining literature and compiling the bibliography and indices. I am very grateful to Susan Carlson Wood of Faculty Publications Service, School of Theology, Fuller Theological Seminary, for her fine job of editing the book and improving its style. It is very gratifying once more to appreciate the warm and faithful friendship of Bill and Sam Eerdmans and thank their colleagues for their efficient labor in the publishing of this book. I must thank also the editors of the Word Biblical Commentary series (especially my senior colleague Ralph P. Martin) as well as Thomas Nelson Publishers for their patience with my work on the Thessalonian epistles which has had to be further delayed because of this book. Last but not least, I record affectionately my debt of gratitude to my wife, Yea Sun, and my daughters, Songi and Hahni, for their love and encouragement.

It gives me great pleasure to dedicate this book to Professor Martin and Frau Marianne Hengel on his eightieth birthday. I hope that they would accept it as a token, inadequate as it is, of my gratitude to them for all their help since my student days as well as of my appreciation of his model scholarship. Three years ago I spoke at the party celebrating his seventy-seventh birthday, explaining what special meaning the seventy-seventh birthday has for Koreans *(hesoo)* and wishing that the Lord would preserve him in good health to labor fruitfully for the church of Christ worldwide at least until his ninetieth birthday. That prayer is renewed on this occasion of his eightieth birthday.

SEYOON KIM
*Pasadena, California*
*Thanksgiving 2006*

# Introduction

Recently the movement to read out of the New Testament efforts to counter the Roman imperial cult and subvert the Roman imperial order has been gaining significant momentum. No doubt, this state of affairs reflects the spirit of the times, which is still concerned with various problems of imperialism in this supposedly "post-colonial" age. Did Paul and other preachers of the gospel in the first century A.D. formulate their message in conscious reaction to the imperial cult and ideology of Rome? Did they present Christ as an antithesis to Caesar? This question is important not only for a proper contextual interpretation of their writings in the New Testament but also for wisdom that the church can derive from them for proper ministry today.

The movement is especially strong in the field of Pauline studies. Besides many monographs and articles, three symposium volumes have been produced under the editorship of Richard A. Horsley, the leader of the movement, to explain Paul comprehensively in terms of anti-Roman struggles.[1] John Dominic Crossan and Jonathan L. Reed have produced a monograph to recover, by the integrated approach of archeology and exegesis, "the actual and historical Paul" who "opposed Rome with Christ against Caesar."[2] In a recent book N. T. Wright makes the anti-Roman po-

---

1. The three volumes are all edited by R. A. Horsley and published by Trinity Press International, Harrisburg, Pennsylvania: *Paul and Empire: Religion and Power in Roman Imperial Society* (1997); *Paul and Politics: Ekklesia, Israel, Imperium, Interpretation: Essays in Honor of Krister Stendahl* (2000); and *Paul and the Roman Imperial Order* (2004).

2. J. D. Crossan and J. L. Reed, *In Search of Paul: How Jesus' Apostle Opposed Rome's Empire with God's Kingdom* (San Francisco: HarperSanFrancisco, 2004), xiii.

litical reading of Paul an essential component of the "fresh perspective" that he is now proposing for Pauline studies.[3] As the editor of *Journal for the Study of the New Testament,* David G. Horrell, with a group of scholars, has devoted a whole issue of the journal to a critical examination of the topic of the New Testament and the Roman imperial cult.[4] Thus, these scholars bear clear witness to the importance that the anti-imperial reading of Paul has acquired in Pauline scholarship today.

Of course, there are also attempts to read Lucan writings (the Gospel of Luke and the Acts of the Apostles) in terms of anti-imperialism, but those attempts are less prominent. This may be because although Luke's well-known concern for the poor and the oppressed seems to invite such attempts, another feature of his writings, often designated as his apologetic for the church and the Roman Empire toward each other, seems to make him appear ambivalent. Nevertheless, Lucan writings occupy a pivotal place for our question because in his second volume he, like no other author in the New Testament, describes direct encounters of Christian missionaries with Greco-Roman cities and Roman officials. Adolf Deissmann, a pioneer of the movement to read Paul in the light of the imperial cult, wrote: "It must not be supposed that St. Paul and his fellow believers went through the world blindfolded, unaffected by what was then moving the minds of men in great cities," namely, the imperial cult.[5] This famous statement must apply to Luke as much as to Paul. It is not just because he may have been a companion of Paul on certain stretches of Paul's missionary journeys (cf. the famous "we" sections: Acts 16:10-17; 20:5-15; 21:1-18; 27:1–28:16). It is essentially because with his two-volume work, Luke was also concerned to present the gospel to the same Roman world as Paul was. In fact, Deissmann's words should apply to Luke even more than to Paul, since Luke wrote a couple of decades later, during which time the imperial cult grew stronger. Luke also reported that Paul and his fellow missionaries traveled on the streets of Hellenistic cities, not "blindfolded" but with eyes wide open, the streets adorned with imperial statues and other symbols of the empire, and that they proclaimed the gospel of the Lord Jesus Christ in

---

3. N. T. Wright, *Paul: In Fresh Perspective* (Minneapolis: Fortress, 2005).

4. *JSNT* 27 (2005).

5. A. Deissmann, *Light from the Ancient East: The New Testament Illustrated by Recently Discovered Texts of the Graeco-Roman World* (New York: George H. Doran, 1927; ET of the 4th German ed. [1923]), 340.

the centers of those cities where often the temples of Caesar prominently stood.[6]

Does then Luke show his reaction to those symbols of the imperial cult himself, or at least indirectly by describing Paul's reaction to them? Luke says that at Athens Paul "was provoked within him as he saw that the city was full of idols" (Acts 17:16) and that at the Areopagus Paul proclaimed the true God and his agent (Jesus Christ), chiding his Athenian audience for their ignorance of the true God in spite of their great religiosity expressed through multiple statues, including an altar dedicated to "an unknown god" (Acts 17:22-31). But in this account of Paul's mission to Athens as in the accounts of his mission in other cities, Luke does not refer to the imperial cult and Paul's reaction to it — or so it appears on the surface.

We find the same phenomenon in the Pauline Epistles. While criticizing pagan idolatry (e.g., Rom 1:18-31; 1 Cor 8–10), Paul does not refer to the imperial cult. Again, this appears so at least on the surface. Thus we will have to inquire deeper to see whether both Paul and Luke do in fact criticize the imperial cult and fight imperial oppression in indirect, oblique, or otherwise hidden ways, and whether they formulate the gospel of the Kingdom of God and the Lord Jesus Christ in conscious antithesis to the imperial ideology of Rome. If our investigation turns up a negative answer to this question, we will have to ask why they do not do that. We will study Paul and Luke separately and then compare them and see to what extent they corroborate each other.

---

6. Because of this feature of the Acts of the Apostles, this study has been expanded to examine the Lucan writings as well as the Pauline. For the attempts to interpret other New Testament books (besides Revelation and Pauline and Lucan books) in anti-imperial terms, see, e.g., W. Carter, *Matthew and Empire: Initial Explorations* (Harrisburg, Pa.: Trinity Press International, 2001); J. K. Riches and D. C. Sim, eds., *The Gospel of Matthew in Its Roman Imperial Context*, Early Christianity in Context/JSNTSup 276 (London and New York: T&T Clark, 2005); T. S. Caulley, "Rereading 1 Peter in Light of the Roman Imperial Cult" (paper presented at the Kolloquium für Graduierte, University of Tübingen, October 24, 2005; the author kindly sent me a copy of it along with some helpful bibliography).

PART ONE   *The Epistles of Paul*

# 1. Reading 1 and 2 Thessalonians in Terms of the Imperial Cult

## Luke's Testimony in Acts 17:1-9

In his account of Paul's mission to Thessalonica in Acts 17:1-9, Luke provides a very strong impetus for interpreting 1 and 2 Thessalonians in terms of the imperial ideology and cult. According to Luke, during the mission Paul and Silas were accused before the *politarchs* of the city for being revolutionaries, "acting against the decrees of Caesar, saying that there is another king, Jesus" (Acts 17:6-7). In light of this account, Paul's use in the Thessalonian epistles of terminology from the imperial cult and propaganda seems to demand an anti-imperial reading of these texts, and several scholars have taken up this challenge.

Much of the recent work was anticipated by Edwin A. Judge's seminal paper in 1971.[1] After quickly dismissing the possibility that "the decrees of Caesar" in Acts 16:7 could refer to the law of treason *(maiestas)*,[2] Judge considers whether it refers then to the edicts of Augustus (A.D. 11) and Tiberius (A.D. 16), as Paul's proclamation of the future *parousia* of the Lord Jesus Christ could have been seen as transgressing the edicts' ban of prediction on the death of the ruler and therefore a change of ruler.[3] But since the accusation against Paul is said to have been taken up by the Thessalonian *politarchs* rather than the Roman proconsul of Macedonia,

---

1. E. A. Judge, "The Decrees of Caesar at Thessalonica," *RTR* 30 (1971): 1-7.

2. Judge, "Decrees of Caesar at Thessalonica," 2.

3. Judge, "Decrees of Caesar at Thessalonica," 3-5, referring to Cassius Dio, *Roman History* 56.25.5, 6; 57.15.8.

Judge concludes that "the decrees of Caesar" probably refers to the provincial oaths of personal loyalty to the Caesarean house administered by the provincial authorities, like the oath that the Paphlagonians swore to the emperor and his descendents, pledging to hunt down offenders of the oath (A.D. 3).[4]

## The Imperial Cult in Thessalonica

Karl P. Donfried and other scholars support Judge's conclusion by showing the Thessalonians' deep commitment to the imperial cult.[5] Appealing to the fundamental research of Holland L. Hendrix on the Thessalonian practices of honoring Romans,[6] Donfried and others point to the following salient features to illustrate what they consider to be the prevalent imperial cult in the city.[7] From the middle of the second century B.C. the Thessalonians' fortunes were determined by Roman interests and hence the Thessalonians were eager to develop ways to honor their Roman benefactors in order to sustain and increase their beneficence. So the Roman benefactors were included as objects of honor alongside the gods. During 42-41 B.C. the cult of the goddess Roma and the Roman benefactors was es-

4. Judge, "Decrees of Caesar at Thessalonica," 5-7.

5. K. P. Donfried, "The Imperial Cults of Thessalonica and Political Conflict in 1 Thessalonians," in *Paul and Empire*, ed. R. A. Horsley (Harrisburg, Pa.: Trinity Press International, 1997), 215-19; C. S. de Vos, *Church and Community Conflicts: The Relationships of the Thessalonian, Corinthian, and Philippian Churches with Their Wider Civic Communities*, SBLDS 168 (Atlanta: Scholars Press, 1999), 156; J. R. Harrison, "Paul and the Imperial Gospel at Thessaloniki," *JSNT* 25 (2002): 79-80; cf. also M. Tellbe, *Paul between Synagogue and State: Christians, Jews, and Civic Authorities in 1 Thessalonians, Romans, and Philippians*, CBNT 34 (Stockholm: Almqvist & Wiksell International, 2001), 119-23. However, J. K. Hardin, "Decrees and Drachmas at Thessalonica: An Illegal Assembly in Jason's House (Acts 17.1-10a)," *NTS* 52 (2006): 29-49, rejects Judge's thesis and argues instead that "both the charges and the seizure of payment in this judicial episode relate to the imperial laws representing Graeco-Roman voluntary associations" (p. 29).

6. H. L. Hendrix, "Thessalonicans Honor Romans," Th.D. diss. (Harvard University, 1984).

7. Donfried, "Imperial Cults of Thessalonica," 217-19; de Vos, *Church and Community Conflicts*, 142; Tellbe, *Paul between Synagogue and State*, 83-86; Harrison, "Paul and the Imperial Gospel," 81-82; cf. also J. D. Crossan and J. L. Reed, *In Search of Paul: How Jesus' Apostle Opposed Rome's Empire with God's Kingdom* (San Francisco: HarperSanFrancisco, 2004), 154-60.

tablished, replete with a special priesthood. Thus, in the cultic practices of the city, honoring the gods, Roma, and the Roman benefactors became increasingly intermixed.[8] In the reign of Augustus a temple of Caesar was built and a "priest and ago[nothete of the Im]perator Caesar Augustus son [of God]" was attached to it, who apparently took priority over the other priesthoods (*IG* 10.2.1.31, 130-33, 226).[9] The coins minted in Thessalonica ca. 27 B.C. had the image of Julius with the legend "god" (θεός) on the obverse side and that of Octavian/Augustus on the reverse side, thus giving the impression of the latter being "son of god" (υἱὸς θεοῦ/*divi filius*).[10] Such a deification of the emperor was expressed also in the replacement of the head of Zeus on the earlier issues of Thessalonian coins with that of Augustus on the later issues.[11] This practice of honoring the emperor continued with Tiberius and Gaius.[12]

## Parallelism of Terms

Having painted this situation of Thessalonica during Paul's mission, Donfried and other scholars point to Paul's employment of a series of terms that were prominent in the imperial cult and imperial ideology:[13] Paul proclaims Jesus Christ as "Lord" (κύριος, *kyrios*) and "Son of God," thus attributing to him the titles that were used for the emperor. He announces the future coming of Jesus the *kyrios* and Son of God, and he does that using the word *parousia* (παρουσία; 1 Thess 2:19; 4:15; 2 Thess 2:8),

---

8. Hendrix, "Thessalonicans Honor Romans," 19-61.

9. Cf. Hendrix, "Thessalonicans Honor Romans," 99-139, 312.

10. Hendrix, "Thessalonicans Honor Romans," 170-73.

11. Hendrix, "Thessalonicans Honor Romans," 179.

12. Hendrix, "Thessalonicans Honor Romans," 310.

13. Donfried, "Imperial Cults of Thessalonica," 216-17; de Vos, *Church and Community Conflicts*, 156; Tellbe, *Paul between Synagogue and State*, 123-30; Harrison, "Paul and the Imperial Gospel," 82-88; A. Smith, "'Unmasking the Powers': Toward a Postcolonial Analysis of 1 Thessalonians," in *Paul and the Roman Imperial Order*, ed. R. A. Horsley (Harrisburg, Pa.: Trinity Press International, 2004), 57-65; Crossan and Reed, *In Search of Paul*, 165-68. See further H. Koester, "Imperial Ideology and Paul's Eschatology in 1 Thessalonians," in *Paul and Empire*, ed. R. A. Horsley (Harrisburg, Pa.: Trinity Press International, 1997), 158-66. For a comprehensive and critical discussion of the Roman imperial ideology and propaganda of *pax Romana*, see K. Wengst, *Pax Romana and the Peace of Jesus Christ*, trans. J. Bowden (Philadelphia: Fortress, 1987), 7-54.

which was regularly used for the official visit of an emperor or a ruler to his provincial city, or the word *epiphaneia* (ἐπιφάνεια, "manifestation"; 2 Thess 2:8), which also evoked the imperial aura as its adjectival cognate *epiphanēs* (ἐπιφανής) was regularly applied to Julius Caesar and his successors.[14] In the Hellenistic world, the word *apantēsis* (ἀπάντησις) was used for the leading citizens of a city going out to welcome a ruler coming to visit their city (i.e., *parousia*). Paul employs the word in 1 Thess 4:17 in connection with the *parousia* of the *kyrios*: the *kyrios* Jesus Christ will descend from heaven to make his *parousia* and the believers will be lifted up for *apantēsis* of him in the air. This gives a strong impression that Paul wants to depict Christ's future coming in terms of the majestic ceremony of an imperial visit. Further, there is a general agreement among commentators that with his critical remark on "peace and security" (εἰρήνη καὶ ἀσφάλεια) in 1 Thess 5:3 Paul is expressing his disapproval of the central slogan of the Roman imperial propaganda, *pax et securitas* (peace and security), or *pax Romana*.[15] So, when Paul says we should be awake for the day of the Lord, or the *parousia* of the *kyrios* Jesus, with the "hope of salvation" (ἐλπίδα σωτηρίας; 1 Thess 5:8-10), he must be presenting Christ as the true "Savior" (σωτήρ, *sōtēr*) in deliberate antithesis to Augustus and his successors who were so hailed. In view of all this, Paul's use of the word "gospel" (εὐαγγέλιον, *euangelion*) seems to be related to its usage in the celebration of the emperor's birthday or accession as the beginning of a new auspicious age,[16] as well as rooted in Deutero-Isaianic proclamation of God's liberation (Isa 52:7; 61:1-2).[17] Further, Paul's designation of the church as *ekklēsia* (ἐκκλησία) seems to have a political connotation, as the word typically referred to the assembly of the citizens of a *polis*. With his

14. See G. H. R. Horsley, *New Documents Illustrating Early Christianity*, vol. 4 (Macquarie University: Ancient History Documentary Research Centre, 1987), no. 52. Note esp. Julius Caesar as "the god manifest" (θεὸν ἐπιφανῆ) and "the general saviour (σωτῆρα) of human life" (*I. Eph.* II.251).

15. For the nature of the slogan and Paul's criticism of it, see especially Wengst, *Pax Romana*, 19-21, 37-38, 77-78.

16. See below, p. 79, n. 6.

17. In his latest study on the origin of the Christian usage of "gospel," G. N. Stanton, *Jesus and Gospel* (Cambridge: Cambridge University Press, 2004), 9-62, argues that although Jesus used the verb "to proclaim God's good news" under the influence of Isa 61:1-2 he did not use the noun "gospel" and that the earliest Christian usage of the noun "developed in rivalry with the prominent use in the propaganda and ideology of the imperial cult of this word group and a clutch of associated themes" (p. 11).

unusual way of describing the Thessalonian church as "the *ekklēsia* of the Thessalonians in God the Father and the Lord Jesus Christ" (1 Thess 1:1; 2 Thess 1:1), Paul may be expressing his belief in the assembly of the Christian Thessalonians in contrast to that of the Thessalonian citizens under the Roman regime.

## Paul's Counter-Imperial Message in 1 Thessalonians?

For their claim that Paul proclaimed the gospel in Thessalonica in deliberate antithesis to the imperial gospel, many scholars point merely to the prevalent imperial cult there and the presence in 1 and 2 Thessalonians of terms prominent in the imperial ideology, as well as to Acts 17:1-9.[18] But some scholars go further, attempting to read Paul's teachings as anti-imperial. So, for example, Donfried thinks that the dead believers about whom the Thessalonian Christians were grieving (1 Thess 4:13-18) were victims of persecution (1 Thess 2:14) for transgressing the oath of loyalty to the Caesarean house by following Paul's "'political preaching' and his direct attack on the *Pax et Securitas* emphasis of the early principate."[19] So, in 4:13-18, "Paul attempts to assure the community that those who have died will not be forgotten and that those who are alive at the parousia will not have precedence."[20] But if such Christian martyrdom was the issue that

---

18. Even Crossan and Reed, *In Search of Paul*, 125-77, fail to make clear what anti-Roman or anti-imperial message Paul is imparting in 1 Thessalonians by his deliberate application of those imperial terms to Christ. Or is his exhortation for his readers to form an assembly of loving and sharing to be understood as such a message, because Paul must be giving it over against "the normalcy of a greed-world" (p. 176)? In the rest of their book, Crossan and Reed's surveys of Galatians, Philippians, Philemon, 1 and 2 Corinthians, and Romans also show Paul not as resisting specifically the Roman imperial cult and oppression but as trying to establish the ethos of God's Kingdom or Christ's Lordship in opposition to "the normalcy of civilization itself" (see esp. pp. x, 404-13). Therefore, their book makes one wonder not only how the vast amount of information about the Roman Empire that they provide is related to their brief summaries of the contents of those Pauline epistles, but more fundamentally whether the book should not bear the subtitle "How Jesus' Apostle Opposed the World (or Civilization) with God's Kingdom," instead of "How Jesus' Apostle Opposed Rome's Empire with God's Kingdom."

19. Donfried, "Imperial Cults of Thessalonica," 222; cf. also Crossan and Reed, *In Search of Paul*, 168.

20. Donfried, "Imperial Cults of Thessalonica," 223.

Paul was addressing, he did a poor job with his argument that those martyrs would not suffer disadvantage over against the surviving believers at the *parousia* of the Lord Jesus. He failed to make it clear that the martyrs would be rewarded when Jesus, the true *kyrios* and *sōtēr*, made *parousia* to lay claim on their city, Thessalonica, destroying the rule of Caesar, the false *kyrios* and *sōtēr*.

According to J. R. Harrison, the use of imperial terminology in the Thessalonian epistles suggests that Paul is countering specifically the eschatology of the imperial gospel that presented Augustus as having inaugurated the eschatological age of bliss, as well as the belief in the apotheosized Augustus.[21] The need to counter these ideas has led Paul to give a more pronounced eschatological and apocalyptic response in 1 and 2 Thessalonians than in his other epistles.[22] Then, observing that many imperial terms were used in Jewish apocalyptic as well as imperial ideological contexts,[23] Harrison concludes that "the apostle was summoning his Gentile converts [in Thessalonica] back to the Jewish roots of their faith, which had found its eschatological fulfillment in the house of David and not in the house of the Caesars."[24] But this is a strange view. To begin with, in these epistles nothing is said explicitly about the Jewish roots of the Christian faith, let alone the house of David. Instead, Paul strongly condemns the Jews for having "killed both the Lord Jesus and the prophets," for persecuting the church and hindering his Gentile mission, and for displeasing God and filling up "the measure of their sins"; he even delivers the fateful word, "But God's wrath has come upon them for good and all!" (1 Thess 2:14-16).[25] These are the only remarks that Paul makes about the Jews and Judaism in the two epistles. More seriously, for Harrison as for Donfried, it is problematic that in the crucial eschatological sections of 1 Thess 4:13–5:11 Paul argues mainly that the believers should not worry about the fate of the dead believers, nor be anxious to know about the ex-

---

21. Harrison, "Paul and the Imperial Gospel," 88-95.
22. Harrison, "Paul and the Imperial Gospel," 78.
23. Harrison, "Paul and the Imperial Gospel," 76, 96.
24. Harrison, "Paul and the Imperial Gospel," 96.
25. For the authenticity of the passage, see S. Kim, "The Structure and Function of 1 Thessalonians 1–3," in *History and Exegesis: New Testament Essays in Honor of Dr. E. Earle Ellis*, ed. Sang-Won (Aaron) Son (New York and London: T&T Clark, 2006), 177-83; cf. also C. J. Schlueter, *Filling Up the Measure: Polemical Hyperbole in 1 Thessalonians 2.14-16*, JSNTSup 98 (Sheffield: Sheffield Academic Press, 1994).

act date of the day of the Lord, yet fails to stress that not Caesar but Christ is the real *kyrios* who will bring about the real eschatological salvation. Further, it is quite doubtful whether Harrison's view is justified that more prominently (if not for the first time) in 1 Thessalonians than in his other epistles Paul formulated his gospel and eschatology using imperial terminology because of the prevalence of the imperial cult in Thessalonica.

Abraham Smith seeks to outdo Donfried and Harrison in going against the grain of the text to read 1 Thessalonians as anti-Roman. According to Smith, in 1 Thess 2:13-16 Paul is really "criticizing the pro-Roman aristocracy in Thessalonica by way of an analogy with the pro-Roman rulers of Judea."[26] This interpretation makes Paul's extended charges of the Jews quite incomprehensible. Why does he expand his condemnation of them for killing the Lord Jesus and the prophets, displeasing God and being contrary to all human beings, and preventing Paul from preaching the gospel to the Gentiles, which are all meaningful only as charges specifically concerned with the Jews? It is remarkable enough that Smith thinks that because of "the repressive character of the imperial order" and Paul's recent experience of it in Philippi (1 Thess 2:2), he chose to use such "indirect critique in order not to offend the Roman authorities in a blunt fashion."[27] But this view contradicts his own claim that the "key terms" such as *parousia, apantēsis,* and *asphaleia* (ἀσφάλεια, "security") which Paul uses "were not politically innocuous."[28] Since Smith has argued for an anti-Roman interpretation of 1 Thessalonians precisely by pointing to the presence of such politically evocative terms as well as the prevalence of the imperial ideology in Thessalonica, how can he now suggest that Paul sought "subtle or indirect ways" to criticize the imperial order?[29] Smith's suggestion of "indirect critique" also contradicts his own interpretation of 1 Thess 5:1-11, where he sees Paul attacking a key imperial slogan of "peace and security," or *pax Romana,* and urging the Thessalonian church to wage war on the Roman Empire with "weaponry for the eschatological battle," namely faith, love, and hope.[30] Unfortunately, Smith fails to clarify what concrete shape the "battle" was to take when the church was to fight against the Roman Empire with such "weap-

---

26. Smith, "Unmasking the Powers," 60.
27. Smith, "Unmasking the Powers," 54.
28. Smith, "Unmasking the Powers," 48.
29. Smith, "Unmasking the Powers," 54.
30. Smith, "Unmasking the Powers," 63-65.

onry." All this seems to make Smith's projection of "indirect critique" tantamount to an admission of arbitrariness in his reading of the text. It goes without saying that, like other "political" interpreters, Smith also bypasses the chief concerns of 1 Thess 4:13–5:11, namely, the fate of the dead believers and the date of the *parousia.*

Helmut Koester tries to explain the "battle" of 1 Thess 5:1-11 a little more concretely. In view of the Qumran literature as well as Paul's reference to the weaponry in 5:8, Koester interprets the "children of light" (5:5) as God's people prepared for the eschatological battle against the kingdom of Belial.[31] He does note the defensive nature of the Christian weaponry (faith, love, and hope). Nevertheless, he interprets Paul as saying that with such weaponry the church is to make "'the day' [of the Lord] a reality in the present, or to [build up] the community that is equal to the presence of the future,"[32] and to "present a utopian alternative to the prevailing eschatological ideology of Rome."[33] Koester claims that in this way Paul is obliterating the distance between present and future, "mak[ing] traditional apocalyptic postures irrelevant."[34] But it is difficult to see how such a fashionable meaning can be read out of 5:1-11 where, as throughout the epistle, Paul calls the church to *wait* for the day of the Lord or the *parousia* of the Lord Jesus, the Son of God, with faith, love, and hope, not succumbing to the *Zeitgeist* of the Roman Empire and the contemporary Hellenism (1:10; 2:19; 3:13; 4:13-18).

31. Koester, "Imperial Ideology and Paul's Eschatology," 162-63.
32. Koester, "Imperial Ideology and Paul's Eschatology," 163.
33. Koester, "Imperial Ideology and Paul's Eschatology," 166.
34. Koester, "Imperial Ideology and Paul's Eschatology," 166.

## 2. Anti-Imperial Interpretation of Other Pauline Epistles

### Philippians

Along with 1 Thessalonians, Philippians is a favorite epistle among the so-called political interpreters because in at least two passages (2:6-11; 3:20-21) it seems to draw a direct and explicit contrast between Caesar and Jesus Christ as Lord and Savior. The passages not only apply to Christ the titles *kyrios* and *sōtēr* but also employ the politically evocative term *politeuma* (πολίτευμα, "commonwealth") and the equally evocative imagery of the *kyrios/sōtēr* coming to deliver the believers as the Roman emperor might come to a provincial city to rescue his beleaguered subjects with his overwhelming forces. So, on the basis of the two passages, N. T. Wright attempts to interpret the whole epistle, or at least chapters 2–3, as Paul's call for the Philippians to render loyalty to Jesus the true Lord rather than Caesar, his mere parody.[1] Wright starts from the assumption that, in the light of the Jewish narratives of creation and covenant as well as Jewish apocalypticism, the apostolic proclamation of Jesus as the Messiah meant Jesus was the king of Israel and the lord of the whole world.[2] So Wright characterizes Paul's missionary work as follows:

> [It] must be conceived not simply in terms of a traveling evangelist offering people a new religious experience, but of an ambassador for a

1. N. T. Wright, "Paul's Gospel and Caesar's Empire," in *Paul and Politics,* ed. R. A. Horsley (Harrisburg, Pa.: Trinity Press International, 2000), 160-83 (quotation p. 174).

2. Wright, "Paul's Gospel and Caesar's Empire," 166-67; more fully in N. T. Wright, *Paul: In Fresh Perspective* (Minneapolis: Fortress, 2005), 40-58.

king-in-waiting, establishing cells of people loyal to this new king, and ordering their lives according to his story, his symbols, and his praxis, and their minds according to his truth. This could not but be construed as deeply counterimperial, as subversive to the whole edifice of the Roman Empire; and there is in fact plenty of evidence that Paul intended it to be so construed, and that when he ended up in prison as a result he took it as a sign that he had been doing his job properly.[3]

Wright finds Phil 2 and 3 along with Romans supporting this understanding deduced from the apostolic "gospel" of Jesus as the Messiah and Lord.

According to Wright, in Phil 3:20-21 Paul clearly proclaims: Jesus is Lord, and Caesar is not. In this passage, Paul reveals an understanding of Caesar's empire and Philippi, its colonial outpost, as a parody of Jesus' empire and the Philippian church, its colonial outpost. And he describes Jesus and his eschatological saving work in analogy to the emperor's coming from the mother city to a colonial outpost in order to rescue his loyal subjects from troubles. So "Paul's description of Jesus, and his future saving activity, thus echoes what can be called imperial eschatology, even while being obviously derived from the same Jewish sources as was 1 Cor 15:25-28."[4] Peter Oakes strengthens this interpretation of Phil 3:20-21 by observing the political sound of the phrase "according to the working of the power to subject all things to him": "In the first century A.D., the one whom most people would see as saving in accordance with his power to subject all things to himself was the Emperor."[5]

As widely recognized, Phil 3:20-21 is closely related to the Christ hymn of 2:6-11. So Wright proceeds to interpret the latter in the light of the former, explicitly drawing on the work of his former student, Peter Oakes.[6] Having found a close parallel between the conceptions of 2:9-11 and those of the Roman imperial ideology, Oakes concludes that hearers in a Roman context would have recognized "the imperial shape of the events" in these verses ("raised to power on account of deeds, universal submission, universal acclamation as Lord").[7] Looking at the passage from the viewpoint

---

3. Wright, "Paul's Gospel and Caesar's Empire," 161-62.

4. Wright, "Paul's Gospel and Caesar's Empire," 173-74.

5. P. Oakes, *Philippians: From People to Letter*, SNTSMS 110 (Cambridge: Cambridge University Press, 2001), 140-45 (quotation p. 145).

6. Wright, "Paul's Gospel and Caesar's Empire," 173; *Paul: In Fresh Perspective*, 72.

7. Oakes, *Philippians*, 147-74.

of how it would have been heard in that Roman society, Oakes thinks the Philippians would have heard a comparison between Christ and the emperor,[8] and Jesus as having an authority that eclipsed that of the emperor.[9] Then Oakes argues that Paul is placing Christ above the emperor in order to offer the Philippian Christians security and to move them toward obedient suffering and unity by reinforcing "the value and authority of Christ's norms of behavior over against those of society."[10] Therefore Oakes rejects Gordon Fee's suggestion[11] that with this comparison Paul was reacting to the Roman authorities' persecution of the Philippian Christians for not participating in the imperial cult.[12] Oakes also rejects the idea that here Paul intends to subvert the Roman Empire: "Paul does not seem to be wishing, as such, for Rome's overthrow. He is not writing anti-Roman polemic."[13]

However, Wright uses Oakes's thesis about a comparison between Christ and the emperor in Phil 2:9-11; 3:20-21 to support his interpretation of Phil 2 and 3 as anti-Roman polemic. With the statement that "[t]he fact that the poem, in its context in chapter 2, undergirds an ethical appeal should not blind us to the fact that Paul is here setting up themes he will later exploit,"[14] Wright seems to recognize that there is nothing anti-imperial in chapter 2. But in view of "such a clear challenge to imperial ideology and eschatology" in 3:20-21, he thinks we should understand the whole chapter 3 thus:

> Paul . . . has Judaism and paganism, particularly, in this case, the Caesar-cult, simultaneously in mind, and is here using warnings against the former as a code for warnings against the latter. Paul's main concern here is not to warn the Philippians against Judaism or an anti-Pauline Jewish-Christian mission. . . . His concern is to warn them against the Caesar-cult and the entire panoply of pagan empire. But his method of warning

8. Oakes, *Philippians*, 147.

9. Oakes, *Philippians*, 150.

10. Peter Oakes, "Re-mapping the Universe: Paul and the Emperor in 1 Thessalonians and Philippians," *JSNT* 27 (2005): 301-22 (quotation p. 320); in much greater detail, *Philippians*, 175-210.

11. G. D. Fee, *Paul's Letter to the Philippians*, NICNT (Grand Rapids: Eerdmans, 1995), 197.

12. Oakes, *Philippians*, 137, 169-70; "Re-mapping the Universe," 304, 313, 319.

13. Oakes, "Re-mapping the Universe," 321.

14. Wright, "Paul's Gospel and Caesar's Empire," 174.

them, and of encouraging them to take a stand for the counterempire of Jesus, is given for the most part in code. He tells them his own story, the story of how he had abandoned his status and privileges in order to find the true status and privilege of one in Christ, and he encourages them to imitate him.[15]

So, for Wright, the central point of chapter 3 is to argue: "as I, Paul, have re-thought my Jewish allegiance in the light of the crucified and risen Jesus, so you should rethink your Roman allegiance in the same light."[16] Philippians 3:17-21 issues the final appeal with "a coded warning" in vv. 18-19: "do not go along with the Caesar-cult. You have one Lord and Savior, and he will vindicate and glorify you, if you hold firm to him, just as the Father vindicated and glorified him after he had obeyed."[17]

Wright argues that this reading makes Phil 3 coherent and subtle. It ex-plains Paul's statement in 3:1, "To write the same things . . . is safe for you." Wright writes: "Why 'safe'? Because nobody reading verses 2-16 would at once deduce that the recipients of the letter were being encouraged to be disloyal to Caesar. This is the coded message of subversive intrigue."[18]

It is odd to think that Paul wields such harsh polemic against Judaism in 3:2-11, 18-19 only as a "code" for his criticism of the Roman Empire. But even more serious is the self-contradiction in Wright's interpretation. It begs the question: why, issuing such an explicit and direct challenge to the Caesar cult in 2:5-11 and 3:20-21, does Paul resort to "code" in the verses in between? Or, when he is so concerned about the "safety" of his readers be-fore the Roman authorities as to give his "message of subversive intrigue" in a coded form, why does he so carelessly repeat his emphatic statements in the two passages, assuring that Christ the true Lord will subjugate all, including Caesar, the parody? Having strongly stressed that in 2:5-11 and 3:20-21 the significance of the contrast between Christ and Caesar is to is-sue a "challenge to an alternative loyalty,"[19] why does Wright now say that in the rest of chapter 3 Paul codes the challenge so "subtly" that "nobody . . . would at once deduce" it? Did Paul code it so "subtly" that no Greek Christian reader or any reader at all has ever been able to decode Phil 3 in

---

15. Wright, "Paul's Gospel and Caesar's Empire," 174-75.
16. Wright, "Paul's Gospel and Caesar's Empire," 178.
17. Wright, "Paul's Gospel and Caesar's Empire," 178.
18. Wright, "Paul's Gospel and Caesar's Empire," 175.
19. Wright, "Paul's Gospel and Caesar's Empire," 174.

this way until Wright? Well, then, Paul's coding was quite self-stultifying! In any case, it would have been quite extraordinary if the Roman authorities had found the message of Phil 3:1-19, as decoded by Wright, more subversive than his interpretation of Phil 2:5-11 and 3:20-21. Thus, Wright's resorting to the device of "code" here for interpreting Phil 3 appears to be only an unwitting admission that with the normal exegesis he cannot obtain his desired anti-imperial interpretation of Phil 2–3 in spite of 2:5-11 and 3:20-21, as the apparent contrasts between Christ and Caesar in those passages are used for purposes other than calling the readers to change loyalty from Caesar to Christ or to resist the Roman rule or the imperial cult.

Like 1 Thess 4:13–5:11 with *parousia/apantēsis* and "peace and security," Phil 2:6-11 and 3:20-21, though evoking a comparison between Christ and the emperor and affirming the superiority of Christ and his salvation, are not meant to lead the Philippian Christians to counter the imperial claims politically. In a way, Phil 2:6-11 is analogous to 1 Thess 4:13-18, insofar as the language evoking the grandeur and majesty of Caesar is used to describe Christ in order to encourage the Philippian believers to work toward unity among themselves with humility and self-giving service, just as in 1 Thess 4:13-18 it is so used to assure the Thessalonian Christians of the salvation ("being with the Lord") of the dead and surviving believers. Likewise, Phil 3:20-21 is analogous to 1 Thess 5:1-11: both passages assure the believers with an eschatological salvation much greater than the *pax Romana,* yet both interpret that eschatological salvation not in terms of a political reality analogous to the *pax Romana,* but categorically differently, as deliverance from God's wrath and "living with the Lord Jesus Christ" (1 Thess 5:9-10) and transformation of our "body" to participate in divine glory (Phil 3:20-21).

Had Paul imagined Jesus' messianic reign in terms of a literal restoration of the Davidic kingship in Zion and a political subjugation of the nations, his Christology and eschatology would have been in the same category as the Roman imperial ideology and, as such, would mean a direct challenge to it.[20] But his Christology was rather in the category of, and derived from, the Jewish ascription of universal lordship to Yahweh. Certainly Jewish Yahwehism also had political implications, as did Paul's Christology. But, for that reason, were the Jews accused of subverting the Roman imperial rule by their belief in God as their king and lord? Appar-

20. Cf. Oakes, "Re-mapping the Universe," 315.

ently only certain kinds of Jews (e.g., the revolutionaries with "zeal") took their Yahwehism to mean active resistance to the Roman rule, while the majority contented themselves with recognizing the political lordship of Caesar. But neither in Phil 2–3 nor in 1 Thess 4–5 do we find Paul interpreting his belief in the universal lordship of the Messiah Jesus in the "Zealotic" sense and calling the believers to resist Caesar's authority and regime.[21]

## Romans

In Rom 1:3-5 and 15:12, N. T. Wright finds an *inclusio* on which he bases his political interpretation of Romans.[22] This *inclusio* is indeed remarkable for many reasons. In the opening verses of the well thought out epistle, Paul deploys a Christological conception of Jesus as the Seed of David, as he does nowhere else. He calls the enthronement of the Seed of David as the Son of God — i.e., to the position of the universal Lord — the "gospel." Then Paul concludes this introduction of the "gospel" by stressing that all the nations should render "the obedience of faith" to the name of the Lord Jesus Christ (1:5). In 15:12 Paul concludes the main body of the epistle by citing Isa 11:10, which speaks of the Son of David coming to rule the nations and the nations having hope in him. Thus, there is clearly an *inclusio* here; with it Paul emphasizes Jesus' Davidic Messiahship, apparently in the traditional sense of the Davidic Messiah reigning over the nations in peace. Therefore, Wright seems well justified in his attempt to read the whole epistle of Romans in terms of this sense suggested by the *inclusio*.

So, interpreting the concept of God's *dikaiosynē* (δικαιοσύνη) in the epistle in terms of the Roman imperial ideology of justice as well as the Old Testament/Jewish sense of covenant faithfulness, Wright says: "Paul's declaration that the gospel of King Jesus reveals God's *dikaiosynē* [1:16-17] must also be read as a deliberate laying down of a challenge to the imperial pretension. If justice is wanted, it will be found not in the *euangelion* that announces Caesar as Lord but in the *euangelion* of Jesus."[23] Wright goes on:

21. See below, ch. 4, "Philippians 1:19-26 and Paul's Attitude to the Roman Court," for further arguments supporting why Phil 1:12-14, 19-26; 4:22 make it impossible to see any anti-imperial intention in Philippians.

22. Wright, "Paul's Gospel and Caesar's Empire," 167-73.

23. Wright, "Paul's Gospel and Caesar's Empire," 172.

If Rom 3:21–4:25 concludes that God has been faithful to the covenant with Abraham, Rom 5–8 concludes that God has thereby been true to the implicit covenant with the whole of creation. It is in 8:18-27 that Paul finally shows how what God has done in Jesus the Messiah, in fulfillment of the covenant with Abraham, has addressed and in principle solved the problem of the whole world. God's covenant faithfulness has put the world to rights. Nothing Augustus or his successors could do, bringing their much-vaunted Pax Romana wherever they went, could compete with that; this is real justice, justice flowing from the throne of Jesus to the whole world.[24]

This is a rather interesting summary of the message of Rom 1–8. But it begs the question why, then, being concerned to present God's righteousness in Christ as a challenge to the Roman imperial propaganda, Paul says nothing about the fake "justice" of the Roman Empire or the parody character of the imperial *euangelion,* but concentrates his whole argument only on the sinfulness of all human beings (Gentiles and Jews) and their inability to achieve "justification" by the works of the law. Was Paul's criticism of Gentile depravity in Rom 1:18-32 intended as a polemic against the fake nature of Roman justice or the imperial order? Expressing skepticism about the suggestion that Paul meant his missionary conduct and his epistles to be "subversive" to the Roman Empire, S. R. F. Price, an authority on the Roman imperial cult, answers this question: it "was not necessarily intended by the author or perceived by the audience. The right context in which to set this argument of Paul's is the ongoing Greek and Roman polemic against the sexual passions."[25] Besides the absence of polemic against the Roman justice or "salvation" (σωτηρία, *sōtēria*) there is also no reference in this epistle to the Roman law. Why does Paul have only the Mosaic law in view and does not even allude to Roman law? For Wright's view, should Paul not rather argue for the inability of establishing justice in the world through the observance of the imperial (i.e., Roman) law? But in Romans we have none of that, only the argument that no human beings can be "justified" by the works of the Mosaic law. It is also strange that Paul polemicizes against the Jewish nationalistic hubris (2:1–3:20; 3:27-30) rather than the Roman imperialistic hubris.

24. Wright, "Paul's Gospel and Caesar's Empire," 172.
25. S. R. F. Price, "Response," in *Paul and the Roman Imperial Order,* ed. R. A. Horsley (Harrisburg, Pa.: Trinity Press International, 2004), 182-83.

Is this because countering the Roman imperial ideology was just one of a number of dimensions in Paul's presentation of the gospel in Romans? And was it less significant than countering Jewish nationalism, so that it did not come to the fore like the latter? It is not certain whether this sort of consideration stands behind Wright's talk of "integration of this political dimension with all the other themes of Paul's theology."[26] At any rate, Wright offers this "hint" to the integration in Romans:

> The result of the revelation of God's saving justice (chs. 1–4) is the creation of the worldwide family of faith promised to Abraham, the people whose sins have been forgiven and who have thereby been rescued from the world of paganism (ch. 1) in which problems the Jews share equally (ch. 2). As a result, this new people enjoy peace (ch. 5) and freedom (ch. 6), within the larger metanarrative which Paul outlines at this point, the retelling of the Exodus.[27]

But this feels rather unreal as an exposition of the message of Romans. For it is difficult to find any political dimension in the concepts of "righteousness/justice" in Rom 1–3, "peace" in Rom 5, and "freedom" in Rom 6. Or, to put the matter another way, in Romans Paul seems to make no effort to explain how restoration to right relationship with God and reconciliation to have peace with him also involve the kind of justice and peace of which Rome boasted, or how freedom from sin and death also involves the kind of freedom Rome promised. It is noteworthy that unlike Eph 2:11-22, in Rom 5 Paul propounds the doctrine of reconciliation exclusively with sinners' relationship to God in view, i.e., without reflecting on its social corollary of reconciliation between the Jews and the Gentiles in Christ, let alone universal reconciliation and peace.

How then are we to explain Paul's emphasis on Jesus' reign as the Davidic Messiah over the nations in the *inclusio* (Rom 1:3-5 and 15:12)? In view of Rom 13:1-7, the least we can affirm here is that Paul does not see it as a reason for resisting the rule of Caesar and his officials. It is indeed remarkable that even while proclaiming the risen Lord Jesus' present and future reign as the Davidic Messiah over the nations (1:3-5; 15:12), Paul enjoins Christians to be subject to the Roman authorities, to honor them as "ministers of God," and to pay taxes to them (13:1-7). Furthermore, in

26. Wright, *Paul: In Fresh Perspective*, 77.
27. Wright, *Paul: In Fresh Perspective*, 77.

Romans, in spite of Wright's *inclusio,* Paul does not at all speak of the Messiah's political reign, but rather emphatically presents Jesus' messianic work in terms of the eschatological act of redemption that consisted in his death of vicarious atonement for sins (3:24-26; 4:25; 5:6-11; 8:3-4, 32; etc.). Therefore, the *inclusio* in fact makes it all the more clear that Paul understands Jesus' Davidic Messiahship no longer in the traditional Jewish sense of political reign over the nations but in a transformed sense of the reign of redemption from the powers of sin and death (cf. 2 Cor 5:14-17, 21).[28] This new understanding *("interpretatio Christiana")*[29] of Jesus' Messiahship is then unfolded in the main body of Romans mainly in soteriological terms. If so, how is Paul's emphasis on Jesus' reign as the Davidic Messiah in the *inclusio* to be understood as "a deliberate laying down of a challenge to the imperial pretension"?[30] When Paul's conception of Christ's reign and salvation is categorically different from the Roman imperial rule and *sōtēria* (socio-political peace, freedom and justice, and economic prosperity), how can we say that Paul intended to subvert the Roman imperial rule by preaching the gospel of Christ? Paul certainly believes that in the *ekklēsia* of the people who confess and obey Jesus as their Lord there is (or should be) better socio-political justice, freedom, and peace, and greater material sharing than in the society under Caesar's rule, i.e., the *ekklēsia* of the people who confess and obey Caesar as their Lord (e.g., Rom 12:1-21; 14:17; 15:25-27; 2 Cor 8:14-15; Gal 3:28; 6:2; Phil 1:27; 2:1-5). But does Paul's gospel promise only this? If it does, it would indeed be regarded in the same category as, and issuing a challenge to, the imperial gospel. But his gospel promises redemption from sin, death, and God's wrath and entry into divine glory or inheritance ("eternal life" = divine life), and he conceives of this salvation as an eschatological and transcendental reality (resurrection or transformation into the "spiritual body" of glory; Rom 8:29-30; 1 Cor 15:42-54; Phil 3:20-21).

Certainly, Paul may have regarded the imperial *sōtēria* as a mere parody of this divine *sōtēria*. But apparently he did not think that one has to fight the former in order to obtain the latter, as Christians were not yet

28. Cf. S. Kim, "2 Corinthians 5:11-21 and the Origin of Paul's Concept of Reconciliation," in *Paul and the New Perspective: Second Thoughts on the Origin of Paul's Gospel* (Grand Rapids: Eerdmans/Tübingen: Mohr Siebeck, 2002), 226-36.

29. Cf. N. A. Dahl, "The Messiahship of Jesus in Paul," in *Jesus the Christ: The Historical Origins of Christological Doctrine,* ed. D. H. Juel (Minneapolis: Fortress, 1991), 15-25.

30. Wright, "Paul's Gospel and Caesar's Empire," 172.

forced into apostasy as a test for loyalty to the emperor (as happened in some places of the Empire from the time when the Revelation of John was written).[31] He would have thought that the imperial *sōtēria* ("peace and security" of 1 Thess 5:3), a mere human achievement, was totally inadequate and fading away as part of this age (1 Cor 7:31). Therefore, he would warn Christians not to rely on it and be complacent but to maintain the true faith and hope in the Lord Jesus Christ, but he would not encourage them to depreciate or even subvert the "peace and security" — albeit inadequate — that the imperial order was providing. Then, in Romans, is Paul trying to awaken the non-Christian Romans from their complacency about the imperial *sōtēria* by presenting to them the real divine *sōtēria* in Christ? Or is he trying to consolidate the Christian Romans' faith in the latter by preventing them from falling into complacency about the former? But unlike 1 Thess 5:1-11 and Phil 3:18-21, Romans has no argument about the inadequacy of the Roman *dikaiosynē, sōtēria, eirēne* (εἰρήνη, "peace"), or *eleutheria* (ἐλευθερία, "freedom"). On the contrary, Rom 13 contains positive statements about the Roman authorities as keepers of justice and order. So it is difficult to give an affirmative answer even to this question.

In view of this dearth of any recognizably anti-Roman political message in Romans in spite of the superficial parallelism of several key words in the epistle and in Roman imperial ideology, it is no surprise to find Dieter Georgi resorting to the notion that in Romans Paul gives his alleged counter-imperial gospel a "protective code."[32] So, in order to justify his political interpretation of Romans, which is similar to Wright's, Georgi does with Romans what Wright does with Philippians and Smith with 1 Thessalonians, and he is therefore subject to the same charge of self-contradiction. Since Georgi justified his anti-imperial political reading by highlighting the confession of Jesus' messianic kingship as Paul's gospel (Rom 1:3-4) as well as several parallel key words between the epistle and the Roman imperial ideology,[33] how can he now speak of a "protective code" in Romans? Georgi thinks that in the Roman court Paul was charged with *crimen (laesae) maiestatis,* or treason for an active political subversion, in contrast to the passive resistance of later Christians (refusal to sacrifice to

---

31. Cf. Oakes, "Re-mapping the Universe," 311.

32. D. Georgi, "God Turned Upside Down," in *Paul and Empire,* ed. R. A. Horsley (Harrisburg, Pa.: Trinity Press International, 1997), 157.

33. Georgi, "God Turned Upside Down," 148-52.

the emperor), and that "the argument employed by Paul in Romans, especially if its protective code is cracked, could easily lead to such a trial and justify a negative verdict."[34] It is amusing to think that Roman magistrates were able to crack the code that Christian exegetes could not for nearly two thousand years until Dieter Georgi. One has also to marvel that Paul was even more skillful in hiding (or expressing) his anti-imperial message in protective codes than the author of Revelation, who has carelessly left so many clues for cracking his codes. Or was Paul more afraid than the author of Revelation, so that he devised a more inscrutable code?

Thus the method that Wright and Georgi employ — first highlighting terms in Romans like *euangelion, sōtēria, dikaiosynē, pistis* (πίστις, "faith/loyalty"), *eirēnē, eleutheria,* and *elpis* (ἐλπίς, "hope"), which also appear in the Roman imperial ideology, and then forcing the passages in which they appear to yield the meanings that the terms bear in the imperial ideology — is not valid. Nor does their deductive logic from Jesus' Davidic Messiahship understood in the Jewish sense prove to be helpful in interpreting Romans. The text of the epistle is resistant to those methods. Regardless, any anti-imperial political interpretation of the epistle is destined to be shipwrecked at Rom 13:1-7 (see ch. 4 below).

## 1 Corinthians

In 1 Cor 2:6-8 and 15:24-28, however, is not Paul speaking about the Messiah Jesus' battle with and destruction of the "rulers of this age"? Political interpreters of Paul quite naturally tend to seize upon Paul's language in the two passages. So, for example, Richard A. Horsley takes them as the key texts for his political interpretation of 1 Corinthians.[35] The passages show that from his basic apocalyptic perspective Paul sees the crucifixion and resurrection of Christ as the turning point of the ages. In God's wisdom or in the course of God's implementation of his saving plan (the "mystery"), "the rulers of this age" crucified Christ, but Christ has been raised as the

34. Georgi, "God Turned Upside Down," 157. God forbid that a totalitarian regime ever "decode" Romans as Georgi does and charge Christians with treason!

35. R. A. Horsley, "1 Corinthians: A Case Study of Paul's Assembly as an Alternative Society," in *Paul and Empire,* ed. R. A. Horsley (Harrisburg, Pa.: Trinity Press International, 1997), 242-52; R. A. Horsley, "Rhetoric and Empire — and 1 Corinthians," in *Paul and Politics,* ed. R. A. Horsley (Harrisburg, Pa.: Trinity Press International, 2000), 90-102.

"Lord of glory," so that they have been doomed to destruction. Together with its "rulers," "this age" or "the scheme of this world" is destined to pass away imminently (2:6; 7:29-31). Apparently it is Christ who brings about their destruction, for in 15:24-28 Paul says that Christ "must reign until he has put all his enemies under his feet" and that at "the end" he will destroy "every rule and every authority and power" and deliver "the kingdom to God the Father." According to Horsley, "the rulers of this age" (2:6-8) and "every rule and every authority and power" (15:24) refer to the rulers of the Roman Empire.[36] Thus he takes the two passages as the most direct evidence for Paul's anti-imperial preaching of the gospel.

Neil Elliott does the same, but goes even beyond Horsley. Elliott starts by affirming the crucifixion of Jesus as an unequivocally political event, an instance of the imperial terror. Then, he contends: "If in his theologizing Paul muted or suppressed the politically engineered horror of the cross, then we would have to conclude that Paul himself mystified the death of Jesus, accommodating his 'word of the cross' to the interests of the very regime that had brought about that death."[37] But fortunately Elliott finds in 1 Cor 2:6-8 and 15:24-28 Paul's "insistence that this event [the crucifixion of Jesus] has begun the dissolution of the Roman order."[38] Then, after a long, not-so-transparent argument that "Paul's doctrine of the cross is . . . a doctrine of God's justice and God's partiality toward the oppressed," especially the nation Israel,[39] Elliott concludes:

> Paul has not obscured the nature of the cross as historical and political oppression; rather he focused it through the lens of Jewish apocalypticism. Only a gentile church unaccustomed to that perspective, and more familiar with the sacrificial logic of blood cults, could have transformed Paul's message into a cult of atonement in Christ's blood (the letter to the Hebrews) and a charter of Israel's disfranchisement (the *Letter of Barnabas*). Paul's own letters show that he recognized these tendencies within the gentile church of his own day, and opposed them.[40]

36. Horsley, "1 Corinthians: A Case Study of Paul's Assembly," 244.
37. N. Elliott, "The Anti-Imperial Message of the Cross," in *Paul and Empire*, ed. R. A. Horsley (Harrisburg, Pa.: Trinity Press International, 1997), 167.
38. Elliott, "Anti-Imperial Message of the Cross," 172-81 (quotation p. 181).
39. Elliott, "Anti-Imperial Message of the Cross," 181-83.
40. Elliott, "Anti-Imperial Message of the Cross," 183.

This incredible claim, being contrary to several obvious facts, hardly requires a detailed refutation. Such a claim can be made only by a person who, by his own dogmatic assumption about the alleged political meaning of the cross, is determined to bypass the numerous references to Christ's death "for our sins" in the Pauline Epistles in order to notice only the few instances, like 1 Cor 2:6-8, that he can enlist for his theory. However, if Elliott honestly faces the importance of the atoning significance of Christ's death for Paul, his assumption will have to lead him to affirm what he denies: "Paul himself mystified the death of Jesus, accommodating his 'word of the cross' to the interests of the very regime that had brought about that death."[41] But we do not have to think like this, if we appreciate that Paul did not regard the Roman imperial politics as the sole reality of evil, not even as the greatest manifestation of it; rather, he thought more fundamentally about the human predicaments — sin and death.

Let us return to Horsley's political interpretation of 1 Corinthians. He emphasizes how, with a fundamental apocalyptic understanding, Paul viewed the church in Corinth as "a new society alternative to the dominant imperial society," the society of this age. The church was composed mainly of the lowborn, weak, and despised believers in Christ, but through them as through the crucified Christ "God has shamed the pretentious elite questing after power, wealth, wisdom, noble birth, and honorific public office (1:21-23, 26-29; 4:8, 10)."[42] Paul urged the church to maintain group solidarity (chs. 1–4) and conduct its own affairs autonomously, in complete independence of "the world" (chs. 5–6). He exhorted the believers to maintain ethical purity and to handle their own disputes without resorting to the "unjust" civic courts (6:1).[43] According to Horsley, in chapters 8–10 Paul completely prohibited eating idol food, and he did so to ensure "the integrity and survival of [the church] as an exclusive alternative community to the dominant society and its social networks," which were constituted precisely in temple sacrifices and banquets.[44] For Horsley, Paul's refusal of material support from the Corinthian church (ch. 9) was motivated by his desire to repudiate the patronage system of the Roman society and to build up an alternative system of economic relations in the

---

41. Elliott, "Anti-Imperial Message of the Cross," 167.
42. Horsley, "1 Corinthians: A Case Study of Paul's Assembly," 244.
43. Horsley, "1 Corinthians: A Case Study of Paul's Assembly," 246.
44. Horsley, "1 Corinthians: A Case Study of Paul's Assembly," 248-49.

church under the controlling vision of the Kingdom of God.[45] Paul's grand collection scheme (1 Cor 16:1-4; 2 Cor 8–9) also had a similar intention, one of building up a network of "international economic solidarity and horizontal reciprocity" in his churches in opposition to "the tributary political economy of the empire."[46]

How are we to evaluate this interpretation? First of all, by "the rulers of this age" (1 Cor 2:6-8) or "every rule and every authority and power" (15:24), did Paul refer to the Roman rulers? Horsley castigates interpreting these phrases in terms of "cosmic forces" as a result of spiritualization influenced by the deutero-Pauline Colossians and Ephesians.[47] However, with his explicit reference to death as the last "enemy" (1 Cor 15:26) as well as his song of Christ's triumph over death, sin, and the law (15:54-57), Paul himself signals that those terms refer to evil forces broader than human rulers and enemies. In 2:8 surely Paul does not have in view only the handful of Roman officials who were involved in the crucifixion of Jesus and the extended circle of their direct superiors. It is difficult to imagine that Paul would have thought that only they constituted "the rulers of this age," since he speaks of Satan (5:5; 7:5) and demons (10:20-21) and even of "the god of *this age*" (2 Cor 4:4) as the forces that rule the world.

So, instead of exclusively identifying these forces with the Roman rulers, it is better to ask whether among the evil forces Paul has *also* the Roman rulers in view. It is possible that in his all-inclusive language *pas* (πᾶς), "every," in 1 Cor 15:24, and in his comprehensive designation "the rulers of this age" (2:6-8) he includes the Roman emperor and his officials along with other forces as instruments of the Satanic reign. Since he speaks of "the rulers of this age" crucifying Christ (2:8), this appears quite likely. So, then, there is a critique of the Roman Empire in 2:6-8 and probably also in 15:24. But what aspect is criticized here? In 1 Cor 1–4 Paul criticizes the humanistic wisdom that is ignorant of and opposed to God's wisdom

---

45. Horsley, "1 Corinthians: A Case Study of Paul's Assembly," 250-51. This thesis is developed by E. Agosto, "Patronage and Commendation, Imperial and Anti-Imperial," in *Paul and the Roman Imperial Order,* ed. R. A. Horsley (Harrisburg, Pa.: Trinity Press International, 2004), 103-23.

46. Horsley, "1 Corinthians: A Case Study of Paul's Assembly," 251. This thesis is developed by Sze-kar Wan, "Collection for the Saints as Anticolonial Act: Implications of Paul's Ethnic Reconstruction," in *Paul and Politics,* ed. R. A. Horsley (Harrisburg, Pa.: Trinity Press International, 2000), 191-215.

47. Horsley, "1 Corinthians: A Case Study of Paul's Assembly," 244.

embodied in the crucified Christ, and even "the pretentious elit[ism] questing after power, wealth, wisdom, noble birth, and honorific public office."[48] In 1 Cor 5–6 he criticizes their immorality and injustice. But are these criticisms applicable only to the Roman imperial system? And with them is Paul encouraging Christians to resist or even subvert it? Aren't they rather general criticisms of the state of this world and this age, applicable even to the Corinthian church? In 1 Cor 15, what of the Roman Empire is being criticized? Nothing particular or specific, beyond its being fundamentally implicated along with all other rules and authorities of this age in the kingdom of Satan, who inflicts death on human beings. In other words, in 1 Cor 15, Paul does not address any particular problems of the Roman Empire at all.

Certainly in 1 Corinthians as in his other epistles, Paul makes it clear that the *ekklēsia* of Christ, or of the people of God who believe in Christ, must be an alternative society to the world or the *ekklēsia* of non-Christian Corinthians, Philippians, Thessalonians, Galatians, or Romans. As the community of people of faith, love, and hope in Christ, it must embody a different spirit, represent a different value system, form a different relationship both inside and outside, and display a different lifestyle and behavioral pattern. But with this teaching, is Paul actively trying to undermine the Roman imperial system in order to turn the world into an alternative kingdom of Christ? Since Paul expects the Kingdom of God to come from divine transcendence at the imminent *parousia* of Christ, would he have the motivation to establish an alternative kingdom, beyond exhorting the believers to build up an *ekklēsia* that proleptically materializes the ideals of the coming Kingdom of God? (See below.) Shouldn't Horsley give a negative answer to this question, as he himself observes that "Paul did not come up with any vision of an alternative political economy for his alternative society"?[49]

At any rate, Horsley's interpretation of Paul's refusal to receive financial aid from the Corinthian church and of his collection scheme for the Jerusalem church grossly exaggerates, if not distorts, their meanings to support his view that Paul tries to subvert the Roman Empire and replace it with the church as the alternative society. In the face of the evidence in 1 Corinthians and elsewhere that Paul apparently enjoyed the patronage of

48. Cf. Horsley, "1 Corinthians: A Case Study of Paul's Assembly," 244.
49. Horsley, "1 Corinthians: A Case Study of Paul's Assembly," 250.

Crispus, Gaius, Stephanas, Phoebe, Prisca and Aquila, and others for his mission in and around Corinth (1 Cor 1:14-16; 16:15-18; Rom 16:1-2; cf. also 2 Cor 11:9; Phil 1:5-7; 4:10-20; 1 Thess 5:12-13; Phlm), it is difficult to know how Horsley can argue that Paul tried to repudiate the patronage system of the Roman Empire.[50] It is also difficult to accept Horsley's characterization of Paul's efforts to collect funds from his Gentile churches for the poor Jerusalem church as efforts to build up a network of "international economic solidarity and horizontal reciprocity" in opposition to the Roman imperial economic system. Quite apart from this exaggeration of the collection's economic significance and probable distortion of its eschatological meaning, Horsley's understanding of it as a "reciprocal" endeavor is contrary to fact. For Paul does not show anywhere that the Jerusalem church sent financial aid to Gentile churches. In fact, Roman imperial ideologists may take Paul's word in Rom 15:26-27 as his imitation of their tributary system which had the Roman provincials pay tributes to Rome for the blessings of the imperial rule, the *pax Romana*. For there Paul relates the Macedonian and Achaian Christians' financial contribution for the poor saints at Jerusalem to their spiritual indebtedness to the Jerusalem church, saying, "indeed they are in debt to them, for if the Gentiles have come to share in their spiritual blessings, they are under obligation also to be of service to them in material blessings." Horsley's interpretation of Paul's teaching about the idol meat in 1 Cor 8–10 must also be judged as a gross exaggeration. In those chapters it is obvious that Paul is mainly concerned about the religious dimension of idolatry and hardly discusses its socio-political dimension. It is also noteworthy that in that context Paul does not refer to the imperial cult at all.

This critical review of Horsley's interpretation of 1 Corinthians well illustrates the fundamental problem of employing a deductive argument with meanings drawn from outside, without paying sufficient attention to the intention of the text — a method usually employed in the anti-imperial reading of Paul (see below). So, from the language of 1 Cor 2:6-8; 7:29-31; 15:24-28, Horsley deduces that Paul is operating with an apocalyptic worldview and that he regards the crucifixion and resurrection of Jesus Christ as the turning point of the aeons, as the beginning of the passing of this age and the dawning of the new age. This deduction is proper as it is

---

50. In view of such evidence, Horsley apparently feels it challenging to maintain coherence in his argument ("1 Corinthians: A Case Study of Paul's Assembly," 250-51).

borne out by the texts themselves. Then, from this Horsley further deduces that in those passages Paul is talking about the destruction of the Roman Empire through Christ. But this further deduction is not supported by the texts, as throughout 1 Cor 1–7 there seems to be only a general criticism of the ethos, morality, and justice system of this world and this age, and in 1 Cor 15 only the destruction of death is immediately in view.

To Paul's teaching in 1 Cor 8–10 about eating idol meat Horsley applies the full socio-political implications of eating meat sacrificed to idols in the Greco-Roman world, even though Paul does not have them in view. Horsley deduces from Paul's apocalyptic worldview and cross theology that he was opposed to the Roman Empire. Then Horsley combines this conclusion with his appreciation of the great socio-political significance of patronage in the Roman imperial system. He next applies the result of this combination to Paul's refusal to accept the financial support of the Corinthian church: since Paul was opposed to the Roman Empire and the patronage system was a staying power of the imperial system, in rejecting the financial support of the Corinthian church, Paul must have been trying to subvert the Roman imperial system. But unfortunately this syllogistic deduction is contradicted by the epistle itself, which shows that he did not mind enjoying the patronage of some trusted people, and he probably had reasons for declining the Corinthian church's material offer other than the desire to subvert the imperial system.[51]

---

51. A prominent reason seems to be his desire to prevent his Corinthian (and Thessalonian) hearers from identifying him as one of the itinerant Sophistic and philosophic preachers and from misunderstanding his gospel as a variety of their philosophical wisdom teaching (cf. 1 Cor 1:18–2:16; 1 Thess 2:1-12). In order to differentiate his gospel from the messages of itinerant Sophists and philosophers who lived on fees and donations of their hearers, Paul sought to demonstrate the grace character of the gospel by preaching it *gratis*, earning his living by his own manual labor (cf. 1 Cor 9:14-18; 1 Thess 2:5-9). Cf. B. W. Winter, "The Entries and Ethics of the Orators and Paul (1 Thessalonians 2.1-12)," *TynB* 44 (1993): 57-72; S. Kim, "Paul's Entry (εἴσοδος) and the Thessalonians' Faith (1 Thessalonians 1–3)," *NTS* 51 (2005): 519-42.

# 3. The Problems of the Method

## "Parallelomania"

This review of the anti-imperial interpretations of 1 Thessalonians, Philippians, Romans, and 1 Corinthians reveals some fundamental problems in the methodology of the so-called political interpreters. These scholars build their anti-imperial reading first and foremost on the parallelism between some important terms from the Roman imperial ideology and propaganda and from Paul's preaching of Christ. But as our examination of the Pauline Epistles above demonstrates, if the passages in which those terms are employed show no clear anti-imperial intention, an anti-imperial interpretation based merely on the occurrence of the terms is a wrong exegesis driven by "parallelomania."[1]

1. N. T. Wright, "Paul's Gospel and Caesar's Empire," in *Paul and Politics,* ed. R. A. Horsley (Harrisburg, Pa.: Trinity Press International, 2000), 162, notes that some contributors to the volume edited by R. A. Horsley, *Paul and Empire* (Harrisburg, Penn.: Trinity Press International, 1997), are suffering from this disease previously warned about by S. Sandmel ("Parallelomania," *JBL* 81 [1962]: 1-13). But there is a question of how free from it is Wright himself. Cf. C. Bryan, *Render to Caesar: Jesus, the Early Church, and the Roman Superpower* (Oxford: Oxford University Press, 2005), 90; Peter Oakes, "Re-mapping the Universe: Paul and the Emperor in 1 Thessalonians and Philippians," *JSNT* 27 (2005): 315-18. It was A. Deissmann who, with his work *Light from the Ancient East: The New Testament Illustrated by Recently Discovered Texts of the Graeco-Roman World* (New York: George H. Doran, 1927; ET of the 4th German ed. [1923]), esp. 338-78, inaugurated the "anti-imperial" interpretation of Paul by observing the prevalent imperial cult in the Roman East and the parallel terms between the imperial cult and Pauline preaching. Yet Deissmann acknowledges that the Christian terms were derived "from the treasury of the Septuagint and the Gospels" and

Pointing this out, Christopher Bryan effectively argues:

> Thus . . . Romans spoke of living emperors as "son of God," "lord," and "savior." Paul and other Christians did the same for Jesus. Does it follow . . . that for Christians "to proclaim Jesus as Son of God was deliberately denying Caesar his highest title, and that to announce Jesus as Lord and Savior was calculated treason"?[2] No, it does not. Certainly Christians were using some of the same words about Jesus as pagans used about Caesar, but they were hardly using them in the same context, or meaning anything like the same thing by them.[3]

Then Bryan goes on to illustrate how differently the title "son of god" was used for Octavius (as son of the deified Julius) and for Jesus (with the meanings derived from the OT/Jewish tradition), and to point out the absurdity of the parallelomania that would make us see Paul countering Caesar with, for example, his talk of Jesus as "the son of God, who loved me and gave himself for me" (Gal 2:20) or of God having "sent the Spirit of his Son into our hearts, crying 'Abba! Father!'" (Gal 4:6). Bryan argues further for the politically innocuous nature of the Christian claim of Jesus as "lord," "son of God," or "savior," from the fact that Rome persecuted Christians not for such a belief about Jesus but for their refusal to honor the Roman gods.[4]

As we have seen above, in spite of some parallelism between the Roman imperial ideology and Paul's presentation of Christ in Phil 2:6-11; 3:20-21 (as with the terms *kyrios, politeuma,* and *sōtēr*) and the idea of the one who has been raised to universal lordship, coming as the *kyrios/sōtēr* to

---

"happen to coincide with solemn concepts of the imperial cult which sound the same or similar," and adds: "I am sure that in certain cases a polemical intention against the cult of the emperor cannot be proved; but mere chance coincidences might later awaken a powerful sense of contrast in the mind of the people" (342-43). See below n. 14.

2. Here Bryan cites J. D. Crossan and J. L. Reed, *In Search of Paul: How Jesus' Apostle Opposed Rome's Empire with God's Kingdom* (San Francisco: HarperSanFrancisco, 2004), 11.

3. Bryan, *Render to Caesar,* 90-91.

4. Bryan, *Render to Caesar,* 91-92. Apparently some Christians refused to address Caesar as "lord" in the belief that the title should be reserved only for God or Jesus, and from the time of Domitian's reign they were persecuted for that refusal, as the cases of the trials of Polycarp (A.D. 155; *Martyrdom of Polycarp* 8:2) and Speratus of Scillium (A.D. 180) show (see Deissmann, *Light from the Ancient East,* 356-57). They failed to make the distinction that Tertullian makes when he suggests that Christians can call the emperor "lord" "in the ordinary way," though "not in the sense of God" (*Apology* 35.1).

deliver his subjects, in Philippians there is neither an anti-imperial polemic nor any intent to subvert the Roman Empire. We have also seen that in spite of the abundant appearance in Romans of such terms as *euangelion, sōtēria, dikaiosynē, pistis, eirēnē, eleutheria, elpis,* and so forth, interpreters are not successful in demonstrating an anti-imperial or subversive aim in the epistle.

The same point can be made with the terms *parousia* and *apantēsis.* Since they were not prominent in Roman eschatology, or even in Roman ideology in general,[5] Paul's employment of them in his eschatological teaching in 1 Thess 4:13-18 does not in itself call for a comparison with the Roman eschatology. Surely Oakes's critical judgment is correct: "The language of παρουσία and ἀπάντησις does seem probably to be drawn from experience of Roman practice, but the passage does not seem to be a conscious challenge to Roman eschatology."[6] Even if we can see in his reference to "peace and security" in 1 Thess 5:3 Paul's attack on the Roman propaganda of *pax Romana,* the function of that attack within the overall message of 1 Thess 5:1-11 is not to call Christians to overthrow the imperial order but to exhort them not to fall into the complacency involved in the imperial propaganda.[7]

## Deduction from Assumptions

Along with parallelomania, deductive argument is also a characteristic of the method of the political interpreters. For their deductive argument, they start from various assumptions: (1) There was in the Roman East (Greek and Asian cities) an all-pervasive imperial cult in which religion and politics were thoroughly integrated: Caesar was worshipped as the savior and lord of the world. Therefore, proclamation and worship of Jesus as Lord and Savior necessarily were subversive to the imperial cult.[8] (2) Paul, as an heir to Jewish apocalypticism, thought in terms of the two ages. Therefore, he must have seen the Roman Empire as "the rulers of this

5. Oakes, "Re-mapping the Universe," 318.

6. Oakes, "Re-mapping the Universe," 317.

7. Cf. Oakes, "Re-mapping the Universe," 318.

8. E.g., R. A. Horsley, introduction to *Paul and Empire* (Harrisburg, Pa.: Trinity Press International, 1997), 1-4, 10-24; N. T. Wright, *Paul: In Fresh Perspective* (Minneapolis: Fortress, 2005), 62-65.

age" doomed to destruction (1 Cor 2:6), and himself and the church as engaged in struggle against it as the representatives of the new age of the Kingdom of God and the Lord Jesus Christ.[9] (3) Since Jesus was crucified by the Roman authorities, the gospel of the crucified Messiah as the Lord, Son of God, and the Savior of the world had an inherent anti-Roman character.[10] (4) Since *ekklēsia* was the designation for the assembly of citizens of a Greek *polis*, Paul's use of the term for the church had a political connotation, and by planting and networking churches *(ekklēsiai)* he intended to build them up as a worldwide organization of communities alternative to the Roman imperial system.[11] (5) Together with the imperial cult, the patronage system held the Roman imperial system together. So Paul's refusal to accept the patronage of the Corinthian church must have had an anti-imperial intention.[12] (6) Paul was often tried and imprisoned, and churches were also persecuted by the authorities. They must have been found in transgression of the imperial order, as Acts 17:1-9 testifies.[13] These assumptions appear quite impressive, and therefore it seems only natural to deduce from them that Paul's preaching could not help but have an anti-imperial character.

## Proof-Texting

With these assumptions the political interpreters go to the Pauline passages where they find the terms paralleling those in the imperial ideology, such as *kyrios*, Son of God, savior/salvation, *parousia*, *apantēsis*, *epipha-*

9. E.g., Horsley, "Introduction," 144-46; "1 Corinthians: A Case Study of Paul's Assembly as an Alternative Society," in Horsley, *Paul and Empire*, 242-52; also "Rhetoric and Empire — and 1 Corinthians," in *Paul and Politics*, ed. R. A. Horsley (Harrisburg, Pa.: Trinity Press International, 2000), 93-101; Wright, *Paul: In Fresh Perspective*, 40-58.

10. E.g., N. Elliott, "The Anti-Imperial Message of the Cross," in Horsley, *Paul and Empire*, 167-83.

11. E.g., Horsley, "1 Corinthians: A Case Study of Paul's Assembly," 242-52.

12. E.g., Horsley, *Paul and Empire*, 4-5, 88-95, 250-51; also "Rhetoric and Empire," 76-77; R. A. Horsley, ed., *Paul and the Roman Imperial Order* (Harrisburg, Pa.: Trinity Press International, 2004), 14-16; E. Agosto, "Patronage and Commendation, Imperial and Anti-Imperial," in Horsley, *Paul and the Roman Imperial Order*, 103-23.

13. E.g., D. Georgi, "God Turned Upside Down," in Horsley, *Paul and Empire*, 157; Wright, "Paul's Gospel and Caesar's Empire," 161-62; R. J. Cassidy, *Paul in Chains: Roman Imprisonment and the Letters of Paul* (New York: Crossroad, 2001), esp. 55-74, 167-70, 175-89.

*neia, euangelion, ekklēsia, dikaiosynē, pistis, eirēnē, elpis, eleutheria,* and *katallagē* (καταλλαγή, "reconciliation"). They first connect these terms with those assumptions, so that the terms take on counter-imperial meanings, regardless of the contexts in which they appear. Then they read the counter-imperial meanings out of the whole passage, regardless of the chief concerns and intentions of the passage itself. Really they impose anti-imperial meanings onto these terms and string those passages up, sometimes extrapolating the meaning of one passage to another, in order to claim that Paul preached the gospel in deliberate antithesis to the imperial ideology and cult.[14]

This looks like a new application of the old-fashioned proof-text method that dogmatists employed to construct doctrines, and dispensationalists used to construct elaborate eschatological scenarios. It is rather curious to see how some sophisticated exegetes as well as those who have an avowed interest in the so-called postcolonial hermeneutics use the method for their political interpretation, although they would loudly disapprove its use by dogmatists and dispensationalists.

## Appeal to Coding

When even the above three methods fail to elicit plainly counter-imperial messages from the Pauline Epistles, some anti-imperial interpreters appeal to the device of coding. They claim that Paul coded his counter-imperial messages in his attack on the Jews in 1 Thess 2:13-16 (Smith) and in Phil 3 (Wright) and in his debate mainly with Judaism in Romans (Georgi). But we have seen that this is a rather desperate attempt to obtain anti-imperial messages where there are none. Inevitably this method involves self-contradiction, as, having justified their anti-imperial reading by pointing to the prominence of the imperial terms and ideas applied to Christ in those epistles, such interpreters must then argue that Paul hid his counter-imperial message by coding it in his attack on the Jews or in politically innocuous language in order to protect himself and his readers from the charge of treason. Furthermore, these interpreters must explain why the

14. It is noteworthy that thus Deissmann's recent followers run free from the proper restraints that he showed (see p. 28, n. 1, above). Cf. D. G. Horrell, "Introduction," *JSNT* 27 (2005): 251 n. 2.

original recipients of the epistles and their successors in the early church were not able to decode Paul's counter-imperial messages even in the light of their actual life experience of imperial oppression,[15] something that the modern interpreters find so easy to do even with the distance of almost two thousand years. Thus, the anti-imperial interpreters' appeal to the device of coding amounts to an inadvertent admission of the failure of their whole interpretative scheme.

15. See below, pp. 60-64. In the case of the recipients of Philippians, 1 Thessalonians, and 1 Corinthians, we should also reckon with the light provided by Paul's original preaching and teaching in their cities. Had Paul really formulated his preaching and shaped his teaching in deliberate antithesis to the Roman imperial cult and ideology, his preaching and teaching must have clearly conveyed a counter-imperial sense to his converts in those cities during his founding mission. Then they would naturally have been led to detect any counter-imperial message hidden in those epistles. But is there any evidence that they or other early Christians under hostile Roman rule interpreted those epistles as calls for resistance to and subversion of the imperial system?

# 4. Factors That Make an Anti-Imperial Interpretation Difficult

## No Specific Critique of the Roman Empire

Our discussion so far has revealed that the Pauline Epistles contain no specific criticism of the Roman Empire beyond a few indications that the celebrated *pax Romana* is no real salvation (Phil 3:20-21; 1 Thess 5:1-11) and that the Roman imperial rule (as well as all other kinds of rule in this age), being immoral and unjust (1 Cor 6:1), will be abolished at the *parousia* of the Lord Jesus Christ (1 Cor 2:6-8; 15:24-28). Certainly these texts suggest Paul's detachment from, and critical attitude toward, the Roman Empire as the dominant reality of this world. However, in contrast to the Revelation of John, the Pauline Epistles make no specific criticism of the despotism of the imperial rule, the violence of its military, or the enslavement and economic exploitation of the nations. Above all, there is no criticism of the idolatry of the emperor.

## No Reference to the Imperial Cult

The political interpreters of Paul assume there was in the Roman East an all-pervasive imperial cult[1] and therefore Paul's proclamation and worship

---

1. See the famous words of Deissmann quoted in the introduction (p. xv); also, e.g., N. T. Wright, *Paul: In Fresh Perspective* (Minneapolis: Fortress, 2005), 63: "Freedom, justice, peace and salvation were the imperial themes that you could expect to meet in the mass media of the ancient world, that is, on statutes, on coins, in poetry and song and speeches. And

of Jesus as Lord and Savior necessarily had an anti-imperial intent. But we have seen that even in Phil 2:6-11; 3:20-21 and 1 Thess 4:13-18; 5:1-11, while using some vocabulary evoking imperial ideology and practices, Paul is concerned to deliver messages other than ones countering emperor worship. It is noteworthy that Paul does not seem to have emperor worship in view even while discussing the problem of pagan idolatry (1 Cor 8–10; Rom 1:18-32). The exception is 2 Thess 2:3-12 if it is interpreted as envisaging an emperor exalting himself as god in the temple of God (perhaps in the manner of Antiochus Epiphanes or Caligula) as the prelude to the *parousia* of Christ. But precisely because Paul says that the appearance of the self-deifying rebel is being restrained until the appointed time in the future, it would indirectly confirm that *at present* he is not concerned about the imperial cult as much as his political interpreters claim he is.

This lack of evidence about the conflicts with the imperial cult in the Pauline Epistles corresponds to what J. S. McLaren has found in the Jewish literature of the first century A.D. In the "synthesis" of his survey of this literature on the question of the Jews' relationship to the imperial cult, Mc-Laren stresses "the paucity of evidence," as there are "very few examples of interaction, whether hostile or peaceful."[2] He also notes that the Greek and Roman sources comment on such features of the Jewish life as circumcision, Sabbath observance, and avoidance of pork, but not on their failure to participate in the imperial cult.[3] From these facts, he draws the conclusion that "the [imperial] cult was only seldom an issue."[4] He thinks this was so because during this period, in spite of the aberrations of Gaius and Domitian, the imperial cult was no empire-wide requirement.[5] Citing D. Fishwick, Peter Oakes also stresses that during the New Testament period participation in the imperial cult was no general obligation.[6] Taking

---

the announcement of these themes, focused of course on the person of the emperor who accomplished and guaranteed them, could be spoken of as *euangelion*, 'good news,' 'gospel.'"

2. J. S. McLaren, "Jews and the Imperial Cult: From Augustus to Domitian," *JSNT* 27 (2005): 274-75.

3. McLaren, "Jews and the Imperial Cult," 275-76.

4. McLaren, "Jews and the Imperial Cult," 274.

5. McLaren, "Jews and the Imperial Cult," 275.

6. Peter Oakes, "Re-mapping the Universe: Paul and the Emperor in 1 Thessalonians and Philippians," *JSNT* 27 (2005): 312, citing D. Fishwick, *The Imperial Cult in the Latin West*, vol. 2: *Studies in the Ruler Cult in the Western Provinces of the Roman Empire*, part 1 (Leiden: Brill, 1991), 530-31.

Tertullian (*Apology* 35) as an example, he also shows how Christians could join in the festivals celebrating the birthday or accession of an emperor, affirming their loyalty to him, without compromising their faith.[7] So, Oakes concludes that "for most Christians, the imperial cult was probably a less pressing issue than other cults in which they had previously participated."[8] Some political interpreters[9] of the Pauline Epistles have based their anti-imperial readings on the work of H. L. Hendrix on Roman Thessalonica.[10] But it is noteworthy that Hendrix himself warns against the concept of "the imperial cult": "Sacrifices to Romans and emperors were not the norm in most places at most times. . . . [T]here is no direct evidence from the city [of Thessalonica] of any sacrificial ritual directed to Romans."[11]

Thus Paul was not yet facing the threat of the imperial cult that the author of Revelation was to face later, probably during the reign of Domitian (A.D. 81-96). Therefore, he did not yet see the need to shape his gospel proclamation in an anti-imperial way as the author of Revelation did. Romans 13:1-7 presents the best evidence for this argument.

## Romans 13:1-7

Certainly Rom 13:1-7 is the Achilles' heel for all anti-imperial readings of Paul, for there Paul exhorts the Roman Christians to "be subject to the governing authorities," since the authorities are instituted by God (v. 1). Paul stresses that rulers — so, most immediately the Roman rulers — are God's "servants" or "ministers" (vv. 4, 6), who have been appointed by God to work for the good of the people and to execute God's justice, or to administer his wrath on the wrongdoers on his behalf, with a God-given "sword" (v. 4). Therefore, since any resistance to rulers is an act of resistance to God and will naturally incur judgment (v. 2), Paul strongly enjoins genuine submission to rulers, "not only to avoid God's wrath but also for the sake of conscience" (v. 5). It is remarkable how Paul rounds up his exhortation with

---

7. Oakes, "Re-mapping the Universe," 312.

8. Oakes, "Re-mapping the Universe," 313.

9. See above, p. 4, n. 7.

10. H. L. Hendrix, "Thessalonicans Honor Romans," Th.D. diss. (Harvard University, 1984).

11. H. L. Hendrix, "Beyond 'The Imperial Cult' and 'Cults of Magistrates,'" in *SBL Seminar Papers, 1986*, ed. K. H. Richards, SBLSP 25 (Atlanta: Scholars Press, 1986), 304.

a stress on taxes: "For the same reason you also pay taxes, for the authorities are ministers of God, attending to this very thing. Pay all of them their dues, taxes to whom taxes are due, revenue to whom revenue is due, respect to whom respect is due, honor to whom honor is due" (vv. 6-7).

Recent commentators have realized that this passage must be read in connection with the specific situation at the time of Paul's writing (c. A.D. 57), rather than as a statement intended to lay down the fundamental principles concerning the relationship between church and state.[12] For that specific situation, they consider, first of all, the unrest unleashed during A.D. 57-58 with the complaints that the people brought to the Emperor Nero about publicans' avaricious and corrupt practices of collecting indirect taxes (Tacitus, *Annales* 13.50-51).[13] Probably Emperor Claudius's expulsion of the Jews (Christian Jews included) from Rome in A.D. 49 and their return to Rome after A.D. 54 had repercussions on both the relationship between the Jewish community and the Roman authorities and the relationship between the synagogue and the church.[14] Further, Paul may have been worried that the rising revolutionary fervor among the Jews in Palestine might affect the church as well as the Jewish community in Rome.[15] As commentators usually point out, in our passage (cf. Tit 3:1; 1 Pet 2:13-17) Paul generally follows the well-established OT/Jewish tradition that affirms the authority and power of pagan imperial rulers as given

---

12. Cf. e.g., P. Stuhlmacher, *Paul's Letter to the Romans: A Commentary*, trans. S. J. Hafemann (Louisville, Ky.: Westminster John Knox, 1994), 198-208; J. D. G. Dunn, *Romans 9–16*, WBC 38B (Dallas: Word, 1988), 768-69; J. A. Fitzmyer, *Romans*, AB 33 (New York: Doubleday, 1993), 662-63.

13. Stuhlmacher, *Romans*, 200-201; Dunn, *Romans 9–16*, 766, 768; Fitzmyer, *Romans*, 662.

14. Cf. E. Bammel, "Romans 13," in *Jesus and the Politics of His Day*, ed. E. Bammel and C. F. D. Moule (Cambridge: Cambridge University Press, 1984), 369-70; J. Moiser, "Rethinking Romans 12–15," *NTS* 36 (1990): 577.

15. Cf. Bammel, "Romans 13," 370-71; M. Borg, "A New Context for Romans XIII," *NTS* 19 (1972-73), 205-18; Fitzmyer, *Romans*, 662. Robert Jewett, *Romans: A Commentary*, Hermeneia (Minneapolis: Fortress, 2007), 780-803, presents a new suggestion: Paul makes pro-government statements and exhortations for submission to the governing authorities in Rom 13:1-7 in order to secure the support of the Roman Christians for his mission to Spain by correcting "[his] reputation as a subversive troublemaker" and presenting himself as "an advocate of good public order" in the eyes of the two Christian groups in Rome whose members were in the imperial bureaucratic service (see esp. 794, 796). Cf. also K. Wengst, *Pax Romana and the Peace of Jesus Christ*, trans. J. Bowden (Philadelphia: Fortress, 1987), 82-83. But see below, p. 40, n. 27.

by God (e.g., Gen 47:7-10; Isa 10:5-6; 44:24–45:7; Jer 25:9; 27:5-6; Dan 4:17-34; Wis Sol 6:3-4) and enjoins the Jews living under their rule to honor and obey them (e.g., Jer 29:7; Bar 1:11; 1 Macc 7:33).[16] As he is advising Roman Christians with their specific situation in view, Paul applies this general principle to their situation rather than giving a well-rounded instruction on the nature of political authority or the relationship between the church and the state. So here he does not entertain our usual question: what if rulers fail to be faithful to divine commission, become despotic, and commit injustice? Nor does Paul reflect the critical view of the rulers of this world that he expresses elsewhere (1 Cor 2:6-8; 6:1; 15:24-25; 1 Thess 2:18; etc.) and the unjust treatment that he himself has received from some of them (1 Cor 4:9-13; 2 Cor 1:8-10; 6:5; 11:23, 25a; 1 Thess 2:2, 18; etc.),[17] not to mention Pilate's trial and execution of Jesus. Instead, he simply, indeed naively, expresses a positive or optimistic view that they — again, most immediately the Roman rulers — "are not a terror to good conduct, but [only] to bad" (Rom 13:3).

However, even the recognition of the situation-bound nature of the passage does not help the anti-imperial interpreters of Paul with the stumbling block that it presents to them. So, some are stretched to employ all their ingenuity to explain it away. Neil Elliott best exemplifies this.[18] Curiously he starts by rejecting recent commentators' attempts to see the passage as bound to the particular situation of the Roman church. According to him, "these situational readings" cannot account for "the benign, even benevolent characterization of 'the governing authorities'" in the passage.[19] He sets Rom 13:1-7 in contrast to many passages within Romans (e.g., 1:18-32; 12:2, 19-20; 13:11-14) — quite unnecessarily and arbitrarily — in order to affirm that "Paul's generous characterization of 'the governing authorities' appears a 'monumental contradiction' of Paul's thought, at several levels."[20] This alleged "monumental contradiction" with the surrounding passages as well as with Paul's thought as a whole makes it all the

---

16. Cf. e.g., Dunn, *Romans 9–16*, 761, 770; Stuhlmacher, *Romans*, 199-200; Fitzmyer, *Romans*, 665. See C. Bryan, *Render to Caesar: Jesus, the Early Church, and the Roman Superpower* (Oxford: Oxford University Press, 2005), 11-37, 80, for the OT/Jewish tradition.

17. See below, p. 47, n. 40.

18. N. Elliott, "Romans 13:1-7 in the Context of Imperial Propaganda," in *Paul and Empire*, ed. R. A. Horsley (Harrisburg, Pa.: Trinity Press International, 1997), 184-204.

19. Elliott, "Romans 13:1-7," 185-86 (quotation p. 186).

20. Elliott, "Romans 13:1-7," 186.

more puzzling "why Paul should have allowed such glowing characterizations of the state to stand in this letter, *whatever* the situation that prompted it."[21] Quoting from his own previous work, Elliott answers thus:

> Paul's statements regarding authorities as servants of God "are mere rhetorical commonplaces, meant only to focus the audience's attention on the discernment of 'the good,'" and thereby "to keep members of the *ekklēsia* from making trouble in the streets."[22]

Then Elliott provides unconvincing, and at times arbitrary, arguments about the purpose of Romans, the historical situation and *Sitz im Leben* of Rom 13:1-7, and the alleged "correspondence of vocabulary, theme, and the rhetorical movement across chapters 8–11 and chapters 12–15 [of Romans],"[23] in order to conclude:

> The broad rhetorical movement across chapters 12–15, like that across chapters 8–11, is meant to quell gentile-Christian arrogance and to evoke sympathy and solidarity with Israel. That context suggests that Rom. 13:1-7 was intended to head off the sort of public unrest that could have further jeopardized the already vulnerable situation of the beleaguered Jewish population of Rome. Paul meant simply to deflect the Roman Christians from the trajectory of anti-Jewish attitudes and ideology along which they were already traveling, a trajectory that would implicate them ever more in the scapegoating of the Jews already visible in Roman culture — a scapegoating that would become a mainstay of Christian orthodoxy within a generation.[24]

Elliott repeats this in his final conclusion:

> Against the keen eschatological tenor of his letters elsewhere, Paul's positive characterization of "the governing authorities" here appears a foreign body. Within the rhetorical structure of Romans, however, these remarks have an important function: to encourage submission, for now, to the authorities, rather than desperate resistance; and thus to safe-

---

21. Elliott, "Romans 13:1-7," 187 (his italics).
22. Elliott, "Romans 13:1-7," 188, quoting N. Elliott, *Liberating Paul: The Justice of God and the Politics of the Apostle* (Maryknoll, N.Y.: Orbis, 1994), 223.
23. Elliott, "Romans 13:1-7," 188-95 (quotation p. 195).
24. Elliott, "Romans 13:1-7," 196.

guard the most vulnerable around and among the Roman Christians, those Jews struggling to rebuild their shattered community in the wake of imperial violence.[25]

There are many problems in this reading of Rom 13:1-7, but let it suffice to point out some self-contradictions.[26] Having started his argument by rejecting other commentators' "situational readings" of the passage, Elliott ends up doing the same thing. The "situational readings" by those who do not subscribe to an anti-imperial nature of Paul's gospel do not involve self-contradiction. But given his assumption of the radically anti-Roman nature of Paul's gospel, Elliott's reading clearly does contradict itself. His appeal to "mere rhetorical commonplaces" can hardly cover, in his own words, Paul's "benevolent characterization of the governing authorities, . . . such glowing characterizations of the state," or "absurdly positive comments about the purpose and function of the authorities"[27] in Rom 13:1-7.

In his essay, "Paul's Gospel and Caesar's Empire," N. T. Wright wrote:

Paul's main aim [in Rom 13:1-7] . . . is to point out that loyalty to Jesus does not mean anarchy in the state, and that however much the emperor

25. Elliott, "Romans 13:1-7," 203.

26. Cf. some strong words of Bruno Blumenfeld, *The Political Paul: Justice, Democracy and Kingship in a Hellenistic Framework*, JSNTSup 210 (Sheffield: Sheffield Academic Press, 2001), 396.

27. Elliott, "Romans 13:1-7," 196. It is also doubtful if Jewett's appeal to Paul's overriding concern for his Spain mission can cover all the one-sidedly positive statements about the governing authorities and all the insistence on Christians' submission to them (see p. 37, n. 15, above). Jewett's interpretation makes Paul akin to a bad politician who does not hesitate to reverse his beliefs and compromise his integrity to obtain his immediate political objective. So, according to Jewett, "for the sake of the proclamation of Christ crucified, who overturned the honor system and rendered Paul a debtor to 'Greeks as well as barbarians, educated as well as uneducated' ([Rom] 1:14), in Rome as well as Spain, Paul was willing to accept the system that demanded honor for the emperor and his officials whether they deserved it or not," and he did this in Rom 13:1-7 by "revert[ing] to the cultural stereotypes, and abandon[ing] the revolutionary approach to honor visible in the preceding chapters" (*Romans*, 803). So, like many other "anti-imperial" interpreters of Paul, Jewett also cannot avoid making Paul contradict himself or betray his own allegedly anti-imperial gospel in Rom 13:1-7 (see the following paragraphs). It is doubtful whether this self-contradiction, or what Jewett calls "irony" and "paradox," can be explained away by designating the pericope of Rom 13:1-7 as "an excruciating example of Paul's willingness to be in the world but not of the world, to reside between the ages, to be all things to all people, all for the sake of the gospel" (p. 803).

may proclaim himself to be sovereign, without rival in the divine as well as the human sphere, he remains answerable to the true God. Despite what has often been suggested, reminding the emperor's subjects that the emperor is responsible to the true God is a diminution of, not a subjection to, imperial arrogance.[28]

But this is hardly a fair presentation of the "main aim" of Paul in Rom 13:1-7. In fact, it just represents the usual attempt of some political interpreters to render Rom 13:1-7 harmless by passing quickly over the main point of the passage ("be subject to the governing authorities") and focusing rather on the subsidiary point (the governing authorities are appointed by God to be his ministers), which is stated only to support the main point.

However, in his new book, *Paul: In Fresh Perspective*, Wright produces a better exposition of the passage:

> [P]recisely because of all the counter-imperial hints Paul has given not only in this letter and elsewhere but indeed by his entire gospel, it is vital that he steer Christians away from the assumption that loyalty to Jesus would mean the kind of civil disobedience and revolution that merely reshuffles the political cards into a different order. The passage is closely integrated with the eschatological promise at the end of the chapter (13.11-14), which echoes the promise in the counter-imperial passage in 1 Thess 5: the night is nearly over, the day is at hand. The main thing Paul wants to emphasize is that, even though Christians are the servants of the Messiah, the true lord, this does not give them carte blanche to ignore the temporary subordinates whose appointed task, whether (like Cyrus) they know it or not, is to bring at least a measure of God's order and justice to the world. The church must live as a sign of the kingdom yet to come, but since that kingdom is characterized by justice, peace and joy in the Spirit (14.17), it cannot be inaugurated in the present by violence and hatred.[29]

Wright thinks that with this interpretation of Rom 13:1-7 he has properly located Paul "within the standard Jewish views of how to live within

---

28. N. T. Wright, "Paul's Gospel and Caesar's Empire," in *Paul and Politics*, ed. R. A. Horsley (Harrisburg, Pa.: Trinity Press International, 2000), 172.

29. Wright, *Paul: In Fresh Perspective*, 78-79.

pagan empire and within the new world inaugurated by the gospel of the crucified and risen Messiah."[30] But for his emphasis on the "counter-imperial" nature of Paul's teaching, this précis is an excellent summary of Paul's "political" teaching in Rom 13:1-7. However, "all the counter-imperial hints" that Wright sees Paul giving in Romans and elsewhere make this interpretation a serious self-contradiction. As we have seen above, Wright stresses that from the start (Rom 1:3-5) to the end (15:12) of Romans Paul highlights the real kingship and lordship of Jesus the Davidic Messiah over all the nations, and that by employing key terms of the imperial ideology, Paul counters the Roman imperial ideology with the true gospel of Jesus Christ and makes the Roman emperor and his "gospel" a mere parody of the Lord Jesus and his gospel. But then how can such a Paul highlight in Rom 13:1-7 God's institution of the governing authorities as his servants to maintain order and justice, and strongly urge Christians to respect, honor, and obey them? Isn't it Wright's basic thesis that in Romans Paul is deliberately throwing down a gauntlet to the Roman emperor as the source of justice and salvation on behalf of Christ?[31] And hasn't Wright stressed the "subversive" intent of Paul in all this?[32] But then, how can such a Paul now say so positively that the (Roman) rulers are the ministers of God appointed to execute God's justice for the common good, so that Christians must submit to them? It appears to defy elementary logic.

Thus, the examples of Elliott and Wright show that any anti-imperial reading of Romans or Paul's gospel is bound to stumble at Rom 13:1-7, exposing only its self-contradiction. For it cannot square with the genuinely positive comments on the function of rulers and authorities in this passage. Does the presence of such comments reflect Paul's appreciation of at least some aspects of the Roman Empire? He would certainly have included the Roman imperial system in his criticism of the idolatrous and immoral pagan world (Rom 1:18-32), of unjust pagan courts (1 Cor 6:1), of the "rulers of this age" often acting as agents of Satan (1 Cor 2:6-8; 1 Thess 2:18; cf. 2 Cor 4:4), of slavery (1 Cor 7:21; Phlm), and so forth. Yet he may have appreciated the *relative* order and justice of the Roman Empire. From Rom 13:1-7 it is clear that Paul preferred the Roman order and justice, in

---

30. Wright, *Paul: In Fresh Perspective*, 79.
31. E.g., Wright, "Paul's Gospel and Caesar's Empire," 172.
32. E.g., Wright, "Paul's Gospel and Caesar's Empire," 168, 175.

spite of all their imperfection, to chaos and anarchy.[33] May we not also infer from Paul's use of the Roman court system and from his apparently confining his mission to the Roman world (cf. Rom 15:19) that he appreciated the relatively better order and justice of the Roman Empire? He apparently was critical of the imperial propaganda of *pax et securitas* for its hubris and inadequacy (1 Thess 5:3), and yet he may well have taken the *pax Romana* as a precondition for his successful mission, the like of which he did not quite see present outside the Roman world.[34]

### Philippians 1:19-26 and Paul's Attitude to the Roman Court

In Phil 1:19-26 Paul cautiously expects his acquittal from a trial at a court (most probably in Rome). He says that he is imprisoned for the sake of Christ (1:13) and for the defense of the gospel (1:16). He shares with the Philippians his resolution that at the trial he shall "not be at all ashamed" (ἐν οὐδενὶ αἰσχυνθήσομαι) of Christ and his gospel but witness for Christ and his greatness with all boldness (ἐν πάσῃ παρρησίᾳ; 1:20). Then, implicitly claiming the promises of Jesus (Mark 8:38/Luke 9:26; Matt 10:32-33/Luke 12:8-9), Paul is confident that Christ will send the Holy Spirit to help with his defense, so that he may be acquitted and released from the prison (Phil 1:19-20).[35] He repeatedly expresses this conviction about his release and entertains the high hope of coming to the Philippians (Phil 1:25-26; 2:24).

---

33. Blumenfeld goes so far as to depict Paul as an admirer, lover, and supporter of the Roman Empire (*The Political Paul*, 282-84), and sees Rom 13:1-7 as an attempt to use the "political advantages of Christianity . . . to strengthen the Roman political system" (391). However, Blumenfeld's zeal to interpret Paul as a whole and especially his epistle to the Romans in terms of classical and Hellenistic political thought, especially Hellenistic Pythagoreanism, appears to lead him to neglect much of Paul's implicit criticism of the Roman imperial system.

34. Cf. Blumenfeld, *The Political Paul*, 290.

35. In the context it is more natural to take "deliverance" (σωτηρία) in 1:19 (NRSV: "this will turn out for my deliverance") in the sense of Paul's acquittal and release than his eschatological salvation. Cf. G. F. Hawthorne and R. P. Martin, *Philippians*, WBC 43, rev. ed. (Nashville: Nelson, 2004), 49-50. See S. Kim, *Paul and the New Perspective: Second Thoughts on the Origin of Paul's Gospel* (Grand Rapids: Eerdmans/Tübingen: Mohr Siebeck, 2002), 203-4, for an exegesis of this passage (Phil 1:19-20) with a more detailed demonstration of Paul's echoes of those sayings of Jesus.

This fascinating testimony has several important implications. First, it suggests that Paul probably was imprisoned and put on trial for preaching Jesus as "another king" (cf. Acts 17:7) and for his gospel being anti-imperial, as he was accused in Thessalonica, according to Luke, soon after his mission in Philippi (Acts 17:1-9). If he preached his gospel as he wrote in his epistles — we have no reason to doubt this — his gospel (euangelion) could have been so suspected by the Roman authorities or Roman loyalists. Even if he did not particularly stress the Davidic kingship of Jesus (Rom 1:3-4; 15:12), his proclamation of him as kyrios and Son of God, as the sōtēr who is to make a majestic visit (parousia) to earth (really, to Thessalonica [1 Thess 2:19; 3:13; 4:15; 5:23; 2 Thess 2:1, 8], Corinth [1 Cor 15:23], or Philippi [cf. Phil 3:20-21] — important Roman cities), bringing dikaiosynē, eirēnē, and eleutheria, and Paul's demand for his audience to show pistis could have sounded as proclaiming a rival emperor to Caesar and promising a rival sōtēria to the pax Romana, as the modern political interpreters of Paul insist. Then the Roman officials and the provincial rulers, like the Thessalonian politarchs who were eager to court the benefaction of Rome for their cities and provinces, could have charged Paul with violating the edicts of Augustus and Tiberius, the loyalty oaths, and so on, or even with committing treason.[36]

From this possibility or even probability, the modern political interpreters too hastily conclude that Paul formulated his gospel in imperial ideological terms, deliberately intending to present Christ as the real king and lord over against his parody, Caesar, and Paul's gospel as the real gospel over against its parody, the Roman imperial gospel. But Phil 1:19-26 clearly suggests that Paul did not intend this. This is the second important point that emerges from the passage. Had he intended this through preaching the gospel, how could he expect to be acquitted at his trial and released from prison? Clearly Paul was thinking that he could explain to the court that his gospel did not mean this, that it was not treasonous, in spite of some of its language. He would explain that the terms employed for his gospel, despite their superficial similarities, meant something quite different from those in the imperial ideology, as his terms were drawn mostly from the Jewish Scriptures. Thus, his expectation for his acquittal clearly suggests that in his mind his gospel was not anti-imperial.

36. See above, pp. 3-4. Cf. R. J. Cassidy, *Paul in Chains: Roman Imprisonment and the Letters of Paul* (New York: Crossroad, 2001), esp. 55-67, 154-206.

Third, Paul believed that the Roman court would be intelligent and fair enough to accept his explanation and *apologia.* Like any defendant, Paul also could not help but think of the worst case scenario, i.e., his failing to persuade the court and being condemned — to death. He seems to have considered this a real possibility (Phil 1:20b-23; 2:17). Since he basically viewed pagan courts as part of the unrighteous world (1 Cor 6:1),[37] it was only realistic for him to consider this. But ultimately faith and hope rise to the top, dispelling anxiety and despair: he "knows" (Phil 1:19, 25) that if he explains Christ with all the wisdom and boldness that the Holy Spirit supplies in response to the Philippians' fervent prayers, the court will see that his gospel is quite innocent of the anti-imperial charge (1:19-20, 25-26; 2:24). After all, the praetorian guard is treating him in a friendly way, knowing that he is imprisoned only for the sake of Christ (1:12-13), and some of them, or the members of "Caesar's household," have even accepted his gospel (4:22). Then they must have seen his gospel as politically quite harmless. So, surely the judges at the court would also be intelligent enough to see this and would acquit him. Thus, Paul's expectation for acquittal suggests his belief in the sufficient justice of the Roman court as well as in the politically innocuous nature of his gospel.

Thus, Paul's testimony in Phil 1:19-26 (cf. also 2:24) as well as 1:12-14; 4:22 deals a blow to those who would argue on the basis of Phil 2:6-11 and 3:20-21 that Paul preached his gospel in an anti-imperial sense in order to subvert the Roman Empire. It would be most strange if, hoping to be acquitted for preaching Christ's gospel, he wrote in the same epistle Phil 2:6-11 and 3:20-21 in order to extol Christ's triumph over Caesar! Clearly in those passages he so freely extolled Christ's universal lordship and his transcendental salvation because he did not consider them as posing any political threat to Caesar and his empire, or because he had no doubt that he could explain — and that any serious person could understand — the political innocuousness of such a belief in the Lord Jesus Christ. It boggles the mind to imagine that some members of Caesar's household accepted Paul's gospel even if it contained an anti-imperial intent, or that Paul was composing an anti-imperial letter in a prison guarded by the praetorian

---

37. Since in 1 Cor 6:1 Paul designated the pagan judges as τῶν ἀδίκων in contrast to Christians as τῶν ἁγίων, he was primarily interested in pointing out that they were part of the unredeemed world which had not yet been justified by faith in Christ, rather than that all the pagan judges had little care for justice.

guard while touting his friendly reception among those guardians of the empire (1:12-13; 4:22).

In fact, the very wording of Phil 1:12-13 dissociates any anti-imperial implication from Paul's gospel of Christ. By saying that the praetorian guard's knowledge that his imprisonment was for his connection with Christ (ἐν Χριστῷ γενέσθαι) amounts to an advancement of the gospel, Paul clearly implies that this "Christ" on whose account or in whose connection he is imprisoned has nothing to do with a most serious felony such as anti-imperial subversion. Otherwise, how could he say, "most of the brothers and sisters have been made confident in the Lord because of my imprisonment, so that they are much more bold to speak the word of God without fear" (1:14)? In view of all this, it is quite revealing that scholars who appeal to Phil 2:6-11 and 3:20-21 for their anti-imperial interpretation of Paul's gospel completely ignore Phil 1:19-26 and 1:12-14; 2:24; 4:22.[38]

Apart from Paul's faith backed up by Jesus' promise of the Holy Spirit's help, what else may have contributed to Paul's cautious optimism about the outcome of the impending trial? Paul speaks of his having suffered many imprisonments (2 Cor 6:5; 11:23). He also speaks about his experience of "shameful treatment" in Philippi during his pioneering mission in that city (1 Thess 2:2; cf. 2 Cor 1:8-10; 11:25a). Giving the details of that ill-treatment in Acts 16:20-24, Luke says that in Philippi Paul and Silas were accused before the magistrates for "disturbing" the city and advocating customs "which it is not lawful for us Romans to accept or practice," and that the magistrates had them beaten and thrown into prison. It is highly likely that this charge involved not just the religious or cultural evaluation of Paul's message but also a political evaluation. Quite apart from this Lucan account, it would be most strange if in his experiences of many imprisonments in Philippi and other cities Paul was charged only for advocating different religious and cultural customs. In view of the close integration of the religious, social, and political dimensions of various pagan cults, including the imperial cult, it is likely that his gospel was charged

---

38. Even Cassidy, *Paul in Chains*, 124-209, fails to deal with these passages in connection with Paul's cautious hope for his acquittal (the book does not even list Phil 1:19 in the index), while advancing the implausible thesis that Paul wrote Philippians in deliberate criticism of Nero while being held in Nero's praetorium and awaiting trial before Nero. J. D. Crossan and J. L. Reed, *In Search of Paul: How Jesus' Apostle Opposed Rome's Empire with God's Kingdom* (San Francisco: HarperSanFrancisco, 2004), 273-74, are an exception, but their treatment is partial and inadequate.

with being politically and socially "disturbing" (ἐκταράσσουσιν, Acts 16:20; cf. ἀναστατώσαντες, 17:6) or subversive, as well as religiously "disturbing."[39] Yet the point we must carefully note here is not just that Paul was probably imprisoned several times with his gospel politically suspected of an anti-imperial nature, but also that he apparently was released from all those imprisonments, rather than executed for treason. *Then, in each of these imprisonments, he must have succeeded in persuading the magistrates of the political innocence of his gospel.*

Luke gives the impression that in Corinth the Jews accused Paul at the court of Gallio, the proconsul of Achaia, only for advocating a theology that was not in accordance with the law of Moses. According to Luke, Gallio dismissed the case, even before hearing Paul's own defense, as he judged that it was not about a serious crime but only an internal Jewish dispute (Acts 18:12-17). If this report of Luke is a full and faithful account of Paul's trial before Gallio, it is noteworthy that Paul's gospel was charged not for any anti-imperial implications, but only for not being proper Judaism. It is possible that Luke omits the political charge here.[40] But if that is indeed the case, the point that we should really appreciate is not that Paul was so accused, but that he was acquitted by Gallio in spite of such an ac-

---

39. Cf. Wengst, *Pax Romana*, 73-79, who in reference to 1 Cor 4:8-9; 15:32; 2 Cor 1:8-10; 6:5; 11:23, 25-26, 32-33; Phil 1:13-26; 1 Thess 2:2, etc., argues that Paul suffered flogging and imprisonment from Roman authorities and vassal rulers who saw his preaching of the gospel as disloyal to the empire and disturbing the public order.

40. With the three divergent charges brought against Paul's gospel in Philippi (Acts 16:20-21), Thessalonica (Acts 17:6-7), and Corinth (Acts 18:13), respectively, is Luke trying to illustrate the range of charges it met in the cities of the Roman East? Crossan and Reed, *In Search of Paul*, 32-34, take Luke's accounts of Paul's repeated trials and acquittals by Roman officials to be motivated by his apologetic concern for "rapproachment between Christ and Caesar, between the Christian church and the Roman Empire." Therefore, they judge that with those accounts "Luke both reveals and conceals, admits and denies, that there were constant troubles between Paul and Rome," and that the Lucan account of Paul's trial before Gallio is "much more likely Lukan parable than Pauline history." Thus Crossan and Reed try to drive a wedge between Paul and Luke and minimize the historical reliability of Luke. But then how will they explain Paul's expectation of acquittal at the forthcoming trial in Phil 1:19-26 and his accounts of his imprisonment experiences which, as we have seen, also indicate or presuppose his repeated acquittals? Do Crossan and Reed think that Paul was tried by a Roman official (if not Gallio himself) in Corinth, the capital city of the Roman province of Achaia, or not? If he was not, then apparently his gospel did not provoke any anti-imperial charge. If he was, then he must have been acquitted. Otherwise, why was he let go from that city and able to pay it multiple visits?

cusation. Subsequently, Paul apparently had no trouble with the authorities in Corinth during his multiple visits to the city; nobody there, not even his opponents, took him to court for preaching the gospel as he did in 1 Cor 2:6-8; 6:1; 15:24-28; etc.

Thus, these experiences of trials before the magistrates in Philippi and before Gallio in Corinth, and other trials before provincial and Roman officials elsewhere, may well have given Paul some confidence in his ability to defend his gospel against any anti-imperial charge, as well as in the relative justice of the Roman courts.

If the traditional Roman provenance and dating of Philippians is upheld, which still appears the best option available, in Phil 1:19-26 Paul is probably sharing his thoughts preceding the impending trial before Caesar Nero in ca. A.D. 62. In his commentary on Acts, C. K. Barrett affirms the historicity of the Lucan narrative of Paul's appeal to Caesar (Acts 25:1-12), repudiating the contrary arguments of Ernst Haenchen and others.[41] Barrett also upholds the traditional view that Paul's epistle to the Philippians was written in this context.[42] According to Luke, during his last journey to Jerusalem Paul fell into the hands of the Jews in the Jerusalem temple, and he was arrested by the Roman soldiers and sent to prison in Caesarea (Acts 21:27-36; 23:12-35). So he was tried before Felix, the Roman procurator of Judea. But the trial dragged on for two years during Felix's governorship, and his successor, Festus, also failed to give Paul confidence in a fair trial as he was eager to please the Jews. In such a difficult situation, Paul knew it was futile to insist before Festus that "I have offended neither against the law of the Jews, nor against the temple, nor against Caesar" (Acts 25:8). Therefore, taking advantage of his Roman citizenship, he appealed to Caesar (Acts 25:10-12). So Paul was sent to Rome to stand trial before Caesar.

Why did Paul appeal to Caesar? Or what did he hope to get out of it? According to Barrett, Paul reckoned that he would not be safe with the Jews even if he were to be released by Festus, and so with the appeal he aimed at

41. C. K. Barrett, *A Critical and Exegetical Commentary on the Acts of the Apostles*, 2 vols., ICC (Edinburgh: T&T Clark, 1994, 1998), 2:1121-23; contra E. Haenchen, *The Acts of the Apostles: A Commentary*, trans. B. Noble et al. (Oxford: Blackwell/Philadelphia: Westminster, 1971), 668-70 (in spite of his skepticism about the historicity of the Lucan narrative of Paul's trial before Festus, Haenchen does accept the historicity of Paul's appeal to Caesar itself; see pp. 669-70).

42. Barrett, *Acts*, 2:1123.

safe passage to Rome under the escort of the Roman troops.[43] This may indeed have been a motive for his appeal to Caesar. But would it have been the only motive? In view of his clear statements that the trial was for the sake of Christ and "for the defense of the gospel" (Phil 1:13, 16), a weightier motive seems to have been that through the trial Paul hoped to explain the gospel of Jesus Christ to Caesar himself and obtain his verdict that it was no offense "against the law of the Jews, or against the temple, or against Caesar" (cf. Acts 25:8). Paul hoped to obtain an official recognition from the highest authority in the Roman Empire that the gospel of Jesus Christ was the fulfillment of Judaism and that the Christian faith posed no offense to the empire.

Paul's trial at the court of Gallio in the fall of A.D. 51 (Acts 18:12-17) probably set a precedent with its verdict that Paul's gospel or Christianity as part of Judaism was free of any illegality, so that for several years thereafter Paul could go on preaching the gospel freely without harassment by the Roman or provincial authorities.[44] However, about a decade later, as he could not expect in Caesarea a similarly fair trial from the Roman procurator of Judea, Paul appealed to Caesar. Therefore, it seems he hoped for at least a confirmation of Gallio's verdict from the emperor himself. Should this happen, it would mean that the Roman emperor recognized Christianity as a continuation of Judaism and as constituting no threat to the imperial order. Then Christians would not be persecuted by the Roman authorities, but instead enjoy those privileges that the Roman emperors since Julius Caesar had granted to the Jews. Thus the Christian mission could be furthered in freedom and peace. Through the trial before Caesar, Paul seems to have aimed, at least, at securing this freedom.[45]

---

43. Barrett, *Acts*, 2:1121.

44. So F. F. Bruce, *Paul: Apostle of the Heart Set Free* (Grand Rapids: Eerdmans, 1977), 254-55.

45. Cf. F. F. Bruce, *The Acts of the Apostles: The Greek Text with Introduction and Commentary*, 3rd rev. and enl. ed. (Grand Rapids: Eerdmans/Leicester: Apollos, 1990), 490. In my article, "To Win Caesar: A Lesson from the Missionary Strategy of the Apostle Paul," in *Theology and Higher Education in a Global Era: Festschrift for Professor Doctor Sang Chang*, ed. S. J. Kim and K. S. Lee (Seoul: Theological Study Institute, 2005), 218-29, I have considered whether Paul's hope went further than this, i.e., whether he also hoped to bring Caesar personally to the obedience of faith to the name of the Lord Jesus Christ (Rom 1:5) and dedicate him to God as the "firstfruits" of the whole world, since Paul saw he could no longer implement his plan to travel through the whole empire, preaching the gospel and gathering the "firstfruits" of the nations (cf. Rom 15:14-33). In other words, Paul's ultimate hope for the trial before Caesar might have been to convert Caesar Nero for Christ (cf. Acts 26:28-29) and

Some critical scholars may reject this line of consideration as mere conjecture, in spite of the rather good comport between Luke's account of Paul's appeal to Caesar and Paul's testimony about his impending trial in Phil 1:19-26. But even if Acts 25:10-12 and Phil 1:19-26 refer to two different trials, they still suggest at least that Paul hoped to persuade a Roman court and Caesar himself about the political innocence of his gospel and obtain from them freedom to preach it. A man with such a hope could hardly have preached his gospel in an anti-imperial sense.

## Maintaining the Status Quo before the Imminent End

Paul's expectation of an imminent end of this world/age with the *parousia* of the Lord Jesus Christ is also a factor that makes an anti-imperial interpretation of his gospel difficult. It is well known that Paul expected in the near future the coming of Jesus for the consummation of salvation (e.g., 1 Thess 4:13-18; 1 Cor 15:51-52; Rom 13:11-12; Phil 3:20-21; 4:5), although he discouraged anxious speculations about its date (1 Thess 5:1-11). He wrote to the Corinthians: "the appointed time has grown very short" (1 Cor 7:29), and "the scheme of this world is passing away" (1 Cor 7:31). Some political interpreters of Paul take such words together with those in 1 Cor 2:6-8; 15:24-28; Phil 3:20-21, and so on, as supporting their anti-imperial reading of Paul, as we have seen above. But in fact Paul wrote those words in the context of 1 Cor 7:17-40 in order to exhort the believers in Corinth not to bother altering their status quo in this transitory world at this time of "distress": "Only, let each of you lead the life that the Lord has assigned, to which God has called you. This is my rule in all the churches" (v. 17). "Each of you should remain in the calling in which you were called" (v. 20). "So, brothers and sisters, in whatever state you were called, there remain with God" (v. 24). "I think that in view of the present (or impending) distress it is well for you to remain as you are" (v. 26). "I say this, brothers and sisters, the appointed time has grown very short" (v. 29). "For the scheme of this world is passing away" (v. 31).

It is wrong to designate this stance simply as "conservatism." For Paul rejected the scheme of this world/age as crooked and perverse (e.g., Phil

---

thus trigger what the conversion of Caesar Constantine eventually triggered about 250 years later, namely, the dedication of the whole empire to the Lord Jesus Christ.

2:15; Rom 1:18–3:20; 1 Cor 7:29-31), and therefore he exhorted the *ekklēsia* of Christ not to conform to this world (Rom 12:2) but to be an alternative society that embodied the proleptic realization of the Kingdom of God in the present (Rom 14:17): a society of holiness and righteousness (e.g., 1 Cor 6:11; 1 Thess 4:1-12; Phil 2:14-15; Rom 12:14-21) in which the inequalities of race, gender, and social status were done away with (Gal 3:28; 1 Cor 12:13), characterized by self-giving service of one for another (Phil 2:1-11). He exhorted the believers to form such an alternative society by doing the duties of the citizens (πολιτεύεσθε) of the Kingdom of God in conformity to the gospel of the Lord Jesus Christ (Phil 1:27; cf. 3:20), that is, by living in obedience to Christ or "walking by the Holy Spirit" (Gal 5:13-25), which in a practical sense means maintaining purity, faithfulness, and humility and, above all, loving and serving one another (Gal 5:22-25; Phil 1:27–2:16).

However, nowhere in his epistles does Paul suggest that doing the duties of the citizens (πολιτεύεσθε) of God's Kingdom involves fighting a human kingdom. Paul never exhorts the believers to subvert the political system of the Roman Empire or change the social structure of their city or province. Instead, he gives the opposite advice: "Let every person be subject to the governing authorities. . . . Pay all of [the authorities] dues, taxes to whom taxes are due, revenue to whom revenue is due, respect to whom respect is due, honor to whom honor is due" (Rom 13:1, 7); and "We exhort you, brothers and sisters, . . . to aspire to live quietly, to mind your own affairs, and to work with your own hands, as we have charged you; so that you may command the respect of outsiders" (1 Thess 4:10-12).[46] We find him also disavowing his or the church's role as a judge over the nonbelievers: "For what have I to do with judging outsiders? Is it not with those inside [the church] whom you are to judge? God judges those outside" (1 Cor 5:12-13).

In view of these apparently conflicting data, J. Christiaan Beker char-

---

46. On the probable political implications of this exhortation, see C. S. de Vos, *Church and Community Conflicts: The Relationships of the Thessalonian, Corinthian, and Philippian Churches with Their Wider Civic Communities*, SBLDS 168 (Atlanta: Scholars Press, 1999), 162-70, who takes this verse together with Paul's warning against ἄτακτοι/ἀτάκτως in 1 Thess 5:14 and 2 Thess 3:6-13 and interprets it as exhorting the Thessalonian Christians not to retaliate against their non-Christian neighbors' persecution with some form of civic disturbance or political agitation. See further 1 Cor 10:32 for Paul's concern that Christians should "give no offense to Jews or to Greeks or to the church of God." Cf. also Rom 13:13; 1 Cor 7:35; 14:40 for Paul's concern for the orderliness and decency of the church. Cf. Bammel, "Romans 13," 381-82.

acterizes Paul's stance in terms of "ecclesial revolution" and "social conservatism."[47] Why did Paul fall short of turning his radical criticism of this world and his radically new vision for the *ekklēsia* of Christ as an alternative society into a motivation for a revolutionary transformation of the crooked and perverse world, the Roman Empire? Did he learn lessons from the recent Spartacus revolt (73-71 B.C.) and the like that it was futile and counterproductive (cf. Rev 13:4b)? Or was he alarmed by the rising "Zealotic" or revolutionary fervor in Judea (cf. Rom 13:1-7)? Beker considers Paul's possible concern for the survival of the tiny church at that time which would be wiped out by any such revolutionary movement. Beker also appreciates that "the revolution within the church carried within itself important seeds of revolution for the structures of society." But in the end he accounts for the apparent discrepancy with the standard view (at least before the movement of anti-imperial interpretation of Paul gathered strength), namely, "that the church's apocalyptic expectation — the expectation of the imminent coming of the kingdom of God — allowed Christians to diffuse their revolutionary impulses and to wait patiently (and socially passively?) for God's ultimate establishment of his kingdom."[48] Indeed, for the twofold reason that *God* (through Christ his Son) would judge the world and bring in the new age of salvation (e.g., 1 Cor 5:12-13; 12:14-23; 15:24-28; Phil 3:20-21), and that he would do this *very soon*, Paul, it appears, neither projected a politico-socio-economic vision[49] of the transhistorical and transcendental new world in any concrete detail, nor actively sought to subvert the existing system of this world. He just concentrated

---

47. J. C. Beker, *Paul the Apostle: The Triumph of God in Life and Thought* (Philadelphia: Fortress, 1980), 325.

48. Beker, *Paul the Apostle*, 326. C. J. Roetzel, "Response: How Anti-Imperial Was the Collection and How Emancipatory Was Paul's Project?" in *Paul and Politics*, ed. R. A. Horsley (Harrisburg, Pa.: Trinity Press International, 2000), 227-30, expresses the same view in response to some recent anti-imperial interpreters: "given Paul's imminent expectation of the end, . . . what incentive would there be for Paul to develop an anti-imperialistic program? The kingdom of God would soon replace the Roman hegemony" (p. 228). To be sure, Beker is not happy to stay with Paul's "social conservatism." So he suggests that to be faithful to Paul's vision that "God's coming reign will establish an order of righteousness that encompasses the created order (Rom. 8:19-21), . . . the church as the blueprint and beachhead of the kingdom of God" must "strain itself in all its activities to prepare the world for its coming destiny in the kingdom of God" (*Paul the Apostle*, 326).

49. This is acknowledged even by R. A. Horsley, "1 Corinthians: A Case Study of Paul's Assembly as an Alternative Society," in Horsley, *Paul and Empire*, 250.

on winning believers in Christ and forming alternative communities in preparation for the eschatological consummation.

In this respect, the Revelation of John presents a sharp contrast. For, in his call for the church to resist the imperial ideology and cult and bear witness to the Kingdom of God unto martyrdom, the author appeals precisely to the apocalyptic expectation of God's imminent judgment of this world (the Roman Empire) and his imminent inauguration of his Kingdom. This contrast reflects the different circumstances of Paul and the author of Revelation. Paul was not yet facing the situation in which Christians were forced to submit to the imperial cult and their belief in the Lord Jesus Christ was looked upon as disloyal to the emperor. His situation was still flexible enough that when his gospel was suspected of disloyalty he could try to prove it otherwise at Roman courts. Therefore, unlike the author of Revelation, Paul did not contrast obedience to the *kyrios* Jesus Christ with that to the *kyrios* Caesar as an either-or matter, and he did not have to call Christians to resist Caesar in order to follow Jesus Christ as Lord.

## Preaching the Gospel to Hasten the *Parousia*

One more factor is associated with Paul's expectation of an imminent *parousia* of the Lord Jesus Christ, namely, his apostolic consciousness (Gal 1:15-16). Apparently convinced that as a leading (if not *the*) apostle to the Gentiles he must proclaim the gospel to all nations (Rom 1:5, 13-14; 11:13; Gal 2:7-9) and bring "the full number of the Gentiles" into the Kingdom of God to trigger the conversion of "all Israel" — and, in turn, the *parousia* of the Lord and the consummation of universal redemption (Rom 11:25-26; cf. vv. 11-16)[50] — Paul concentrated on preaching the gospel in the whole *oikoumenē* (οἰκουμένη, "inhabited world"). Understanding himself as a pioneer missionary (Rom 15:20-24; 1 Cor 3:6, 10), he rapidly moved from one city to the next, usually content just to plant a church and offer his first converts to God as the "firstfruits" of the city or province (Rom 15:16; 16:5; 1 Cor 16:15). Thus, at the time of writing Romans, he was happy to have completed his missionary work from Jerusalem to Illyricum, i.e., in the

---

50. For Paul's understanding of God's plan of salvation ("the mystery" of Rom 11:25-26) and his Gentile apostleship in connection with it, cf. Kim, *Paul and the New Perspective*, 113-14, 123-25, 239-57.

eastern half of the Roman Empire, and was looking forward to going to Rome to start a new phase of his mission in the west as far as Spain (Rom 15:17-24). It is not certain whether he thought of Spain as the end of the earth or he planned a further mission beyond Spain, to go around North Africa in order to make a full circle of the *oikoumenē* back to Jerusalem via Alexandria.[51] But it seems quite probable that he hurried to preach the gospel to as many nations as possible in order to hasten the conversion of Israel and the *parousia* of Christ.[52] Such a missionary mindset would have allowed him little room for thinking about and working toward revolutionary changes to the Roman imperial order. On the contrary, it would have made him cautious to avoid entanglement with the Roman authorities. Moreover, he would have appreciated the political unity of the Roman Empire and its relative peace, order, and justice as a foundation for his all-important mission in the whole *oikoumenē*.[53]

## The Ethic of Perseverance, Nonretaliation, Enemy Love, and Peace

It is noteworthy that whenever Paul refers to persecution by the authorities and/or local communities he admonishes his readers to persevere with suffering by firm faith and hope. So he exhorts the Philippian Christians, building up an alternative community as a colony of the heavenly Kingdom of God (Phil 1:27; 3:20), that they must stand firm, united together, in their faith with the hope of salvation from God, and bear the persecution by their opponents (the citizens of this worldly kingdom, the Roman Empire) as a constituting element of their faith (Phil 1:27-30; 3:20-

51. R. Riesner, *Paul's Early Period: Chronology, Mission Strategy, Theology*, trans. D. Stott (Grand Rapids: Eerdmans, 1998), 305, opts for the former possibility, while J. Knox, "Rom 15:14-33 and Paul's Conception of His Apostolic Mission," *JBL* 83 (1964): 10-11, argues for the latter, and Knox is followed by A. J. Hultgren, *Paul's Gospel and Mission: The Outlook from His Letter to the Romans* (Philadelphia: Fortress, 1985), 132-33.

52. Cf. J. Munck, *Paul and the Salvation of Mankind*, trans. F. Clarke (London: SCM Press/Richmond, Va.: John Knox, 1959), 36-55; Stuhlmacher, *Romans*, 238.

53. Cf. Origen, *Against Celsus* 2.30: "It is quite clear that Jesus was born during the reign of Augustus, the one who reduced to uniformity, so to speak, the many kingdoms on earth so that he had a single empire. Accordingly, how could this teaching, which preaches peace and does not even allow men to take vengeance upon their enemies, have had any success unless the international situation everywhere had been changed and a milder spirit prevailed at the advent of Jesus?" (cited in Wengst, *Pax Romana*, 172). See below, pp. 177-79.

21). During his pioneering mission in Thessalonica, Paul taught the believers that it was the lot of Christians to suffer afflictions (1 Thess 3:3b-4a). With a good understanding of the nature of the gospel and the Christian faith, they have suffered persecution from their compatriots (1 Thess 1:6; 2:14; 3:4b), but are not shaken as they "stand fast in the Lord" (1 Thess 3:6-8). Therefore, breathing a sigh of relief, he exhorts them to go on living a life of holiness and love that pleases God and earns the respect of outsiders (1 Thess 4:1-12) and to persevere with the unshakable hope for the consummation of salvation at the *parousia* of Jesus Christ (1 Thess 4:13–5:11). It is highly significant that in this context Paul exhorts the Thessalonian Christians not only to build up a community of love and peace but also to shun retribution (1 Thess 5:12-21). When he says, "See that none of you repays evil for evil, but always seek to do good to one another and *to all*" (1 Thess 5:15), he clearly includes the Thessalonian "compatriots" who have persecuted the believers (1 Thess 2:14) and prohibits the believers from retaliating against them. Rather, they are to do good even to their persecutors.

The exhortation to bear with persecution and to repay persecutors not evil but good is more fully expounded in Rom 12:14-21:

> Bless those who persecute you; bless and do not curse them. . . . Live in harmony with one another. . . . Repay no one evil for evil, but take thought for what is noble in the sight of all. If possible, so far as it depends upon you, live at peace with all. Beloved, never avenge yourselves, but leave it to the wrath of God; for it is written, "Vengeance is mine, I will repay, says the Lord." No, "if your enemy is hungry, feed him; if he is thirsty, give him drink; for by so doing you will heap burning coals upon his head." Do not be overcome by evil, but overcome evil with good.

Thus, echoing several sayings of Jesus in the Sermon on the Mount/Plain (Luke 6:28/Matt 5:44; Luke 6:29/Matt 5:39b-41; Mark 9:50; Matt 5:9),[54] Paul

---

54. This is recognized even by N. Walter, who takes up the "minimalist" position on the question of how many allusions to and echoes of the Jesus tradition are recognizable in Pauline Epistles ("Paul and the Early Christian Jesus-Tradition," in *Paul and Jesus: Collected Essays,* ed. A. J. M. Wedderburn, JSNTSup 37 [Sheffield: JSOT Press, 1989], 56). Cf. S. Kim, "Jesus, Sayings of," in *Dictionary of Paul and His Letters,* ed. G. F. Hawthorne, R. P. Martin, and D. G. Reid (Downers Grove, Ill.: InterVarsity Press, 1993), 474-92 (reprinted as "The Jesus Tradition in Paul," in *Paul and the New Perspective,* 259-92).

emphatically forbids vengeance, insists on active love for persecutors and enemies, and commends a life of peace and harmony with all people. The wording of v. 18 ("If possible, so far as it depends upon you, live at peace with all") hints at the reality that the peace of the Christian believers of the first-century Roman Empire was often disturbed through persecution by hostile neighbors and authorities. Even in such a situation, the believers are to abandon any thought of avenging themselves but try to develop a peaceful relationship with the persecutors by actively loving them. Then, it is clear that the believers should not do anything that may disturb the peace of the community. Really, they should "aspire to live quietly, to mind [their] own affairs, and to work with [their] hands . . . so that [they] may command the respect of outsiders" (1 Thess 4:11-12).

These exhortations are not merely theoretical, but really what Paul himself practiced in the face of persecution:

> Already you are filled! Already you have become rich! Without us you have become kings! And would that you did reign, so that we might share the rule with you! For I think that God has exhibited us apostles as last of all, like men sentenced to death; because we have become a spectacle to the world, to angels and to humans. We are fools for Christ's sake. . . . We are weak. . . . We are in disrepute. To the present we hunger and thirst, we are poorly clothed and beaten and homeless, and we labor, working with our own hands. When reviled, we bless; when persecuted, we endure; when slandered, we try to conciliate; we have become, and are now, as the scum of the world, the refuse of all things. (1 Cor 4:8-13; cf. also 2 Cor 6:4-10)

Using the vivid and tragic picture of conquered slaves led to death in the triumphal procession of a victorious Roman general (cf. 2 Cor 2:14), Paul speaks of his experiences of suffering as an apostle. Here he is not thinking only of suffering from the want of elemental physical needs or from general disdain and scorn. Together with the brutal imagery of the triumphal procession, the rest of his language clearly points to public persecution: "beaten," "reviled," "persecuted," "slandered." When he is persecuted in such a way, he indeed perseveres, repaying evil not with evil but with good, and seeking reconciliation and peace with persecutors. Thus, the exhortations that he imparts to the Roman Christians on how to meet with persecution (Rom 12:14-21) are exactly what he himself has practiced. It is noteworthy that 1 Cor 4:8-13 also contains echoes of several sayings of Jesus in the Sermon on the Mount/Plain (Luke 6:21/Matt 5:6; 10:9-10; 11:19; Luke 6:22-23/Matt 5:11-12; Luke 6:27-28/Matt 5:44)[55] similar to those contained in Rom 12:14-21. It clearly suggests that in his ethic of persevering with persecution, repaying persecutors with love rather than with vengeance, and pursuing reconciliation and peace Paul consciously follows his Master Jesus (cf. 1 Cor 11:1).

It is curious why in Romans Paul so emphatically exhorts perseverance during persecution, nonretaliation and active love for persecutors, and the pursuit of peace. As seen above, in 1 and 2 Corinthians he himself adopts that stance (cf. also 2 Cor 1:3-11; 4:7-12; 6:4-10), but he stops short of exhorting the Corinthian Christians to do the same (cf. 2 Cor 1:6-7). In Philippians, he emphasizes for the believers there to be united in humility and self-giving love for one another as they face persecution (Phil 1:27–2:30; 4:1-9). But as for dealing with persecutors, he does no more than advise the believers to persevere under persecution, standing firm in their faith in Christ and their hope for his glorious salvation (Phil 1:27-30; 3:18-21). Besides Romans, only in 1 Thessalonians does Paul exhort nonretaliation and active love for persecutors as well as perseverance under persecution (1 Thess 5:15). But there he does it in a single sentence. Why is he expanding the exhortations to much greater length and emphasis in Rom 12:14-21 as part of the new lifestyle of the justified people of God that is not conformed to the world but to the will of God (Rom 12:1-2)?

May this expansion be related to Paul's exhortations immediately following that passage, encouraging Christians to be subject to the governing authorities, to pay taxes, and so forth (Rom 13:1-7)? Do these two facts together suggest that Paul emphatically issues both sets of exhortations for proper stance toward persecutors and the governing authorities in Romans, as he is conscious that he is addressing the believers in the capital city of the Roman Empire, as well as being concerned about their vulnerability before Roman authorities? If so, we may be confident here even more than in 1 Cor 4:8-13; 2 Cor 6:4-10; Phil 1:27-30; and 1 Thess 2:14 that in dealing with persecutors Paul has in view not only communal ostracism and lynching but also the persecution of a more official character, that is, persecution by the imperial and local authorities. However, even if the latter is not immediately in view, it cannot be doubted that Paul would have ap-

---

55. See the preceding note.

plied these principles of perseverance, nonretaliation, active love, and the pursuit of peace to state persecutors as much as to private assailants. For, his echoing Jesus' words in the Sermon on the Mount/Plain (Rom 12:14-21; 1 Cor 4:8-13), as well as his autobiographical statements in 1 Cor 4:8-13 that are part of his apostolic self-understanding as a preacher and representative of "Jesus Christ and him crucified" (1 Cor 2:2; cf. 1:18–4:21), suggest that Paul clearly thought those principles were part of the way of his Lord Jesus Christ, the crucified one (cf. 1 Pet 2:21-25), and that propagating those principles was the essence of his apostolic task.

In any case, a man who propounds this ethic of perseverance with suffering, nonretaliation and love for persecutors, and the pursuit of peace even with enemies, as well as commending a life of quietude (1 Thess 4:11-12), could hardly have intended to provoke imperial officials himself or encourage his readers to do so.

Many activist Christians today, not to mention the determined anti-imperial interpreters, may find most dissatisfactory this ethic and this stance to the powers that be. But would it be a proper exegesis and honest historical study to present Paul as having taught a contrary ethic and encouraged a contrary stance, in order to remove the stumbling block or "offense" of his way of preaching the gospel of Christ crucified?

## The Transcendental Conception of Salvation

Certainly Paul made efforts to provide pastoral care to his churches by sending his associates and letters to them and sometimes even by his revisits, and he was happy to see other Christian leaders nurturing them further (1 Cor 3:5-15). Even so, it is doubtful whether his church planting can be compared with modern revolutionaries' planting their "cells" in communities in preparation for a revolutionary uprising.[56] Not only Paul's imminent eschatology and his hurried missionary movement, but also his transcendental soteriology is not conducive to that idea. For the ultimate form of salvation that Paul expects with the *parousia* of Christ is not the peace, justice, and prosperity of the messianic kingdom on Zion that would supersede *pax Romana,* but something categorically different, namely, obtaining individually a "spiritual body" of glory like that of the resurrected

---

56. Cf. Wright, "Paul's Gospel and Caesar's Empire," 161.

and glorified Christ, which is completely free from the forces of sin and death (Rom 8:29-30; 1 Cor 15:42-57; 2 Cor 5:1-10; Phil 3:20-21; etc.), and cosmically gaining redemption of the whole creation from the power of corruption and death (Rom 8:18-22). What revolution in or against the Roman Empire would be able to contribute to obtaining such a "spiritual body" and such redemption of the whole creation? How would Paul have thought that with this gospel he could subvert the Roman imperial order? Or what subversive motives would the imperial authorities have found in this gospel?

This conception of salvation, of course, is the corollary of the understanding that the fundamental predicament of human beings and the creation is their captivity to the Satanic forces of sin and death — sin that alienates human beings and the world from God, their Creator (Rom 3:23), and death that results from this alienation from the Creator and Sustainer of life (Rom 5:12; 6:23a; 8:20-22; 1 Cor 15:21-22, 56). This biblical understanding of the human and cosmic predicament leads Paul naturally to conceive of salvation as restoration to God, the Creator. Hence he sees the atoning sacrifice of Christ Jesus on the cross as the fundamental saving event (Rom 3:24-26) and formulates the gospel or good news of salvation through imagery that connotes restoration to God: justification (for righteousness or the right relationship with God), reconciliation (for peace with God), adoption (for inheritance of the Creator's infinite wealth), and new creation (for overcoming the Adamic destiny of alienation, condemnation, and death). The outcome of this salvation is participating in divine glory or obtaining divine likeness (the image of God) — i.e., becoming like God (Rom 8:29-30; 1 Cor 15:49; 2 Cor 3:18; Phil 3:21) and obtaining his immortal or "eternal life" (Rom 1:17; 5:15-21; 6:23b; 1 Cor 15:51-57), instead of condemnation and death (Rom 5:9, 15-21; 8:1; etc.).[57] The creation that has been implicated in the human fall is to share also in human redemption: "the creation itself will be set free from its bondage to decay and obtain the glorious liberty of the children of God" (Rom 8:21).[58] It goes without say-

57. Of course, Paul does not neglect the ethical requirements involved in justification, reconciliation, adoption, and new creation for our relationship with fellow human beings, but there is no question that with these images he has our relationship with God primarily in view.

58. It is a question whether in Wright's emphasis on the "transhistorical" character of the salvation of the Lord Jesus Christ (*Paul: In Fresh Perspective,* 12) he takes an adequate account of this transcendental character of salvation as well.

ing that a most striking feature of Pauline soteriology is its strong emphasis on the divine nature of salvation: it is God who has wrought salvation
in Christ Jesus and will bring about its consummation with his *parousia.*
Hence salvation is by God's grace alone *(sola gratia).*

When Paul is expecting such individual and cosmic salvation from
God, and very shortly at that, how interested would he be in changing the
present "scheme of the world" that "is passing away" (1 Cor 7:31), in order
to make life in it a little fuller during the short interim period (v. 29) before
such total salvation?

## The Absence of Anti-Imperial Interpretation in the Early Church

Finally, the reception history of the Pauline Epistles in the early church
runs decidedly against an attempt to read a counter-imperial message out
of them. Hardly any evidence can be found for an early Christian inter-
preter of Paul drawing such a message from his epistles. To be sure, it is
safe to presume that the martyrs of Scillium near Carthage (A.D. 180) were
not the only ones who were inspired by Paul's writings to worship only the
one invisible God (1 Tim 6:16) in heaven and so to choose martyrdom
rather than submitting to the imperial cult.[59] But the significance of such
passive resistance specifically to the requirement of worshipping the emperor should not be exaggerated as an act of subversion to the imperial order. For, as Adolf von Harnack emphasizes, from the earliest days of the
early church, in spite of their rejection of the imperial cult, Christians tried
to show their loyalty to the Roman Empire by instituting prayer for the
emperor and the state as a firm element in their worship service, as well as
by obeying the governing authorities and paying taxes punctually.[60] Ap-

59. Cf. K. L. Gaca and L. L. Welborn, "Introduction: Romans in Light of Early Patristic
Reception," in *Early Patristic Readings of Romans,* ed. K. L. Gaca and L. L. Welborn (New
York and London: T&T Clark, 2005), ii-iii, who refer to T. D. Barnes, *Tertullian: A Historical
and Literary Study* (Oxford: Clarendon, 1971), 60-62, for a reprint of an apparent transcript
of the trial of the Scillitan martyrs (from the *Acts of the Scillitan Martyrs*). The transcript
shows that the martyrs appeared for trial before the proconsul Saturninus, carrying with
them Paul's writings in a satchel.

60. A. von Harnack, *The Expansion of Christianity in the First Three Centuries,* trans.
and ed. J. Moffatt, 2 vols., Theological Translation Library 19-20 (London: Williams &
Norgate/New York: Putnam's Sons, 1904-5), 1:372-74. Cf. also R. M. Grant, *Augustus to*

parently Paul's teaching in Rom 13:1-7 (cf. also 1 Tim 2:1-2; Tit 3:1) contributed as much to forming this attitude as did Jesus' saying, "Render to Caesar the things that are Caesar's, and unto God the things that are God's" (Mark 12:17 pars.).[61]

This attitude is best exemplified in the prayer of Clement of Rome, contained in his epistle to the Corinthians (ca. A.D. 95):

> "direct our steps to walk in holiness and righteousness and purity of heart," and "to do what is good and pleasing in your sight" and in the sight of our rulers. Yes, Lord, "let your face shine upon us" in peace "for our good," that we may be sheltered "by your mighty hand" and delivered from every sin "by your uplifted arm"; deliver us as well from those who hate us unjustly. Give harmony and peace to us and to all who dwell on the earth, just as you did to our fathers when they reverently "called upon you in faith and truth," that we may be saved, while we render obedience to your almighty and most excellent name, and to our rulers and governors on earth. You, Master, have given them the power of sovereignty through your majestic and inexpressible might, so that we, acknowledging the glory and honor which you have given them, may be subject to them, resisting your will in nothing. Grant to them, Lord, health, peace, harmony, and stability, that they may blamelessly administer the government which you have given them. For you, heavenly Master, King of the ages, give to the sons of men glory and honor and authority over those upon the earth. Lord, direct their plans according to what is good and pleasing in your sight, so that by devoutly administering in peace and gentleness the authority which you have given them they may experience your mercy. (1 Clement 60:2–61:2)[62]

---

*Constantine: The Thrust of the Christian Movement into the Roman World* (New York: Harper & Row, 1970; repr. Louisville, Ky.: Westminster John Knox, 2004), 77-119, who shows how the apologists such as Justin Martyr, Apollinaris, Melito, Athenagoras, Theophilus, Apollonius, Irenaeus, Tertullian, etc. expressed their loyalty to the Roman state, while rejecting the imperial cult.

61. Cf. C. N. Jefford, *The Apostolic Fathers and the New Testament* (Peabody, Mass.: Hendrickson, 2006), 196, who says that Paul's teaching in Rom 13:1-7 "seems to have become popular with the Roman church." Cf. also U. Wilckens, *Der Brief an die Römer,* 3 vols., EKKNT 6 (Neukirchen: Benziger and Neukirchener, 1978-82), 3:44-45, for the *Wirkungsgeschichte* of Rom 13:1-7 in the early church.

62. The translation is taken from M. W. Holmes, *The Apostolic Fathers: Greek Texts and English Translations,* updated ed. (Grand Rapids: Baker Books, 1999), 97-98.

It is quite obvious that this prayer for Christians' holy and righteous living and the rulers' good and successful administration is strongly permeated with the language and spirit of Rom 13:1-7 and its related passages in the New Testament (1 Tim 2:1-2; Tit 3:1; 1 Pet 2:13-17). It is striking to note how many times Clement repeats here the idea that God has given the earthly rulers ("our rulers and governors" — i.e., the Roman rulers) the sovereign power, glory, and honor. Since God has so established them to rule over all things on the earth, Christians must submit to them. So obedience to God and to the rulers is spoken of in the same breath, and failure to obey the rulers is understood as resistance to God's will. Therefore, Clement relates Christians' holy and righteous living to obedience to the rulers as well as to God. Certainly Clement would not recognize the emperor as a god or a son of god, because the rulers are merely "the sons of men" who received their sovereign power and glory and honor from God (cf. 59:4: "Let all the nations know that you are the only God, and Jesus Christ is your child/servant [παῖς]"). However, Clement's emphasis is on God's endowment of them with power, glory, and honor as well as Christians' submission to them. Clement fervently prays for God to help the rulers not only with good health but also with good counsel for successful administration, an administration in accordance with God's will. It is also striking how repeatedly Clement prays for peace, harmony, and stability, the typical slogans of the imperial ideology. In this prayer, he clearly reveals his understanding that through the rulers' wise administration and the Christian and other subjects' obedience to them *pax Romana* should be promoted.[63]

We may also take Tertullian (ca. A.D. 160-220) as a good example of loyalty to the Roman emperor and his empire even while refusing to submit to the imperial cult. Tertullian makes it plain that Christians worship only the one eternal, true, and living God and therefore cannot worship Caesar as a god, but insists that on that account they are not to be judged as disloyal or treasonous to Caesar (*Apology* 28-37). For, according to Tertullian, they honor Caesar as the second highest being after God, the being "before and over all gods" (*Apology* 30; "a second majesty," 35), and

---

63. For a full exposition of Clement's thorough commitment to *pax Romana* and his Roman imperial perspective in 1 Clement, see Wengst, *Pax Romana*, 105-18. See below, pp. 183-84, for the deeper reason for the prayer for the rulers' wise administration and Christians' blameless life in submission to the rulers.

as "the chosen of our Lord" and therefore "more ours" than the pagans' "because he has been appointed by our God" (*Apology* 33), and they pray for him "long life, a secure rule, a safe home, brave armies, a faithful senate, and honest people, a quiet world" (*Apology* 30). For such praying, Tertullian specifically refers to the exhortation in 1 Tim 2:1-2, clearly expressing the fear that if the empire is shaken, Christians would also be caught up in the disaster (*Apology* 31). Then, alluding to 2 Thess 2:6-8, he suggests that Christians need to pray "for the emperors, and for the whole estate of the Empire and the interests of Rome," because the Roman Empire is the force that delays the onset of "the great force which threatens the whole world, the end of the age itself with its menace of hideous suffering" (*Apology* 32). Finally, echoing Jesus' teaching in the Sermon on the Mount/Plain and Paul's teaching in Rom 12:14-21; 1 Cor 4:8-13, Tertullian argues that Christians should not be treated as enemies of Rome, as they are benevolent people who are forbidden to wish anybody evil or practice retaliation, but instead taught to love their enemies, so that they persevere even with the most savage persecutions without engaging in rebellion, passive or active (*Apology* 36-37).[64]

When loyalty to the empire, obedience to her authorities (except the requirement of emperor worship), and perseverance under persecution in the spirit of loving one's enemy marked the usual attitude of early Christians, it is clear that they did not draw any counter-imperial inspiration from the Pauline Epistles and other New Testament books. They were adamant against the imperial cult because it was so obviously contrary to the most fundamental tenet of their faith in the one true God revealed in Christ. But apparently they did not feel that on account of it they had to fight the imperial order as a whole. We cannot here engage in a more detailed study of the early church's attitude to the Roman Empire, so we will merely report here that, from some of the recent studies of the Apostolic Fathers and the Apologists,[65] it is not noticeable that any of them inter-

---

64. Cf. *Epistle of Diognetus* 5.9-17 for extensive and clear echoes of Paul's teachings of law-abiding life, perseverance with persecution, nonretaliation, and enemy love in 1 Cor 4:10-12; 2 Cor 4:7-12; 6:4-10; etc.

65. Cf. A. Lindemann, *Paulus im ältesten Christentum: Das Bild des Apostels und die Rezeption der paulinischen Theologie in der frühchristlichen Literatur bis Marcion*, BHT 58 (Tübingen: Mohr Siebeck, 1979); M. F. Wiles, *The Divine Apostle: The Interpretation of St Paul's Epistles in the Early Church* (Cambridge: Cambridge University Press, 1967); R. M. Grant, *Greek Apologists of the Second Century* (Philadelphia: Westminster, 1988); Jefford,

preted the Pauline Epistles as containing calls to resist and subvert the imperial order. It must be significant that even Tertullian, the jurist and most uncompromising critic of paganism including the Roman religion and imperial cult, seems to be more influenced by some Pauline texts that are taken as "pro-imperial" than those interpreted as anti-imperial. The same point can be made also of Paul's immediate pupils who tried to preserve, interpret, and apply his theological legacy to their situations in the Pastoral Epistles (1 and 2 Timothy, and Titus). In Part Two we shall see that, writing only a couple of decades after Paul's death, Luke also does not present his favorite apostle, Paul, as preaching a counter-imperial gospel and including subversion of the imperial order as part of his mission.

If the early Christian interpreters did not find any counter-imperial message in the Pauline Epistles in spite of all the facility that they had with the Greek speech and all the light shed by their experiences of the imperial order, should we not conclude that they did not find it because there was none to find?

All these considerations make an anti-imperial reading of Paul quite difficult.

---

*Apostolic Fathers and the New Testament;* H. Rathke, *Ignatius von Antiochien und die Paulusbriefe,* TUGAL 99 (Berlin: Akademie-Verlag, 1967); R. Noormann, *Irenäus als Paulusinterpret: Zur Rezeption und Wirkung der paulinischen und deuteropaulinischen Briefe im Werk des Irenäus von Lyon,* WUNT 2.66 (Tübingen: Mohr Siebeck, 1994); Gaca and Welborn, *Early Patristic Readings of Romans;* M. Edwards, M. Goodman, and S. Price, eds., *Apologetics in the Roman Empire: Pagans, Jews, and Christians* (Oxford: Oxford University Press, 1999). Note the summary statement of Robert Grant (*Augustus to Constantine,* 119): "The political views of the apologists, which we have already discussed [pp. 77-119], are almost uniformly expressions of loyalty to the Roman state."

# 5. Summary and Conclusion

The various assumptions about the pervasive imperial cult in the Roman East, Paul's apocalyptic thinking, and his gospel of the crucified Jesus as the Lord and Savior, as well as the parallelism of important terms (e.g., *kyrios, sōtēr/sōtēria, euangelion, dikaiosynē, pistis, eirēnē, eleutheria, elpis, parousia, apantēsis*) between the Roman imperial ideology and Paul's preaching of the gospel of Jesus Christ, all seem to invite an anti-imperial reading of the Pauline Epistles. It appears natural to suppose that in the Roman world Paul's proclamation of Jesus as the messianic king, Lord *(kyrios)*, and Son of God, and as the Savior *(sōtēr)* who would come *(parousia)* to destroy the rulers of this age/world and establish the Kingdom of God, could have been understood as proclaiming a rival king to Caesar and subverting the Roman imperial order. At least some of Paul's several imprisonments (2 Cor 11:23) must have been due to this political charge.

Yet Paul's epistles lead us to assume that he was repeatedly released to continue his mission of preaching the gospel of the Lord Jesus Christ. So he went on preaching messages like those in Rom 1:3-5; 15:12; 1 Cor 2:6-8; 15:24-28; Phil 2:6-11; 3:20-21 without any reservation. It is most remarkable that he had no hesitation in writing Phil 2:6-11; 3:20-21 even while waiting for his trial, most probably before Caesar. Rather, he vowed to bear witness to the Lord Jesus Christ or to "magnify" him without flinching at the imperial court (perhaps by presenting him as in Phil 2:6-11 and 3:20-21), and yet still expressed his confidence about his eventual acquittal and release (Phil 1:19-26). He must have done this only because he did not see preaching the Lord Jesus Christ — as in Rom 1:3-5; 15:12; 1 Cor 2:6-8; 15:24-28; Phil

2:6-11; 3:20-21; 1 Thess 1:9-10; 4:13–5:11 — as containing any anti-imperial meaning, or because he was confident of explaining at the Roman court that his message does not contain any subversive element to the imperial order. The combination of the *inclusio* of Rom 1:3-5/15:12 with Rom 13:1-7 suggests at least one line of his *apologia*.

Our examinations of 1 Thessalonians, Philippians, Romans, and 1 Corinthians in interaction with some representative "anti-imperial" interpreters have confirmed that in those epistles there is no warning about the imperial cult and no message subversive to the Roman Empire. Certainly Paul's epistles present a clear vision of the Kingdom of God (Rom 14:17; 1 Cor 4:20; 6:9-10; 15:24-28, 50; Gal 5:21; 1 Thess 2:12) and the universal Lordship of Jesus Christ (Rom 1:3-5; 15:12; 1 Cor 2:6-8; 15:24-28; Phil 2:6-11; 3:20-21; 1 Thess 1:9-10; 4:13–5:11, etc.). There is also criticism of "the rulers of this age" as agents of Satan that are doomed to destruction at the *parousia* of the Lord Jesus Christ (1 Cor 2:6-8; 15:24-28; 1 Thess 2:18, etc.; cf. 2 Cor 4:4), and it is quite probable that Paul includes Roman rulers also among "the rulers of this age." Yet, while there is a general criticism of the pagan world under their rule as idolatrous, immoral, unrighteous, perverse, and hopeless (Rom 1:18-31; 12:2; 1 Cor 1:18-25; 6:1; Phil 2:15; 1 Thess 4:13; etc.), there is no specific criticism of the Roman imperial order for the imperial cult, political despotism, military violence, imperialistic subjugation of nations, economic exploitation, and so forth.

At most Paul points to the total inadequacy of the much-celebrated *pax Romana* (1 Thess 5:3) and of the Roman commonwealth and its *sōtēria* (Phil 3:20-21). But apparently he understands this inadequacy as due to the fact that the Roman imperial order is part of "the scheme of this world" which is ruled by Satan (2 Cor 4:4) and "is passing away" (1 Cor 7:31). Paul does not suggest that it is because the Roman Empire is particularly evil and therefore needs to be subverted to create a state of more adequate peace and welfare in this world. In fact, he does not entertain any idea of creating such a state. So, although he has a clear conception of the church as an alternative *ekklēsia* of the people of the Kingdom of God over against the *ekklēsia* of the citizens of this world — even as the "colonial outpost" of the heavenly (i.e., transcendental) Kingdom of God in this world (Phil 3:20) that materializes the ethos, value system, relationships, and behavioral pattern of the Kingdom (Phil 1:27) and therefore embodies the real "justice, peace, and joy" (Rom 14:17) — Paul does not consider the church eventually replacing the Roman Empire in this world. Nor does he project any political, social, and economic program with which the King and Lord Jesus Christ will rule this world for more adequate justice, peace, freedom, and well-being than those of the Roman Empire.

Apparently his apocalyptic thinking of "the scheme of this world" as doomed to "pass away" imminently (1 Cor 7:29-31) and his conception of salvation as a transhistorical and transcendental reality prevent Paul from developing such conceptions. For him, the salvation that the Lord Jesus Christ is bringing is not a material order of justice, peace, freedom, and prosperity in this world, but rather, negatively, human beings' and the whole creation's freedom from the forces of sin and death and, positively, their restoration to God, the Creator, and participation in his life and glory. It is a new creation. It is God who has wrought this salvation, and not by letting his Son Jesus Christ wage a politico-socio-economic revolution against any human rulers but by letting him fight with the cosmic forces of sin and death, that is, through his atoning death and resurrection. This salvation will be consummated by the imminent *parousia* of the Lord Jesus Christ, the Son of God. This divine salvation, this participation in divine life and glory, may be imagined as containing in it perfect justice, peace, freedom, and well-being (Rom 14:17; Phil 4:7), compared to which those of the Roman Empire will prove only to be a parody. But such a comparison runs the risk of reducing salvation to this worldly order. There may be an analogy between the divine salvation and the aspired politico-socio-economic values of this world, but it is only an analogy and no more. Therefore, one should not stick only to their comparability and therefore lose sight of the categorical difference between them. At any rate, Paul concentrates on proclaiming the good news *(euangelion)* of the categorically different salvation of God in Christ, without dwelling on comparing the perfect justice, peace, freedom, and well-being of the Kingdom of God with the imperfect ones of the Empire of Caesar.[1] When he rarely makes such a comparison (e.g., Phil 3:20-21; 1 Thess 5:3), he merely warns Christians of the latter's inadequacy or assures them of the bliss of the former,[2]

---

1. Even while expounding the gospel of Jesus Christ in terms of such key concepts like "righteousness/justice," "peace," and "freedom" in Rom 1–8, Paul does not make any efforts to compare the righteousness/justice, peace, and freedom of Jesus Christ with those of the Roman Empire (see above, pp. 16-21).

2. Thereby, of course, Paul seeks to encourage his churches to hold fast to their faith with hope, not giving in to the threats of the representatives of the imperial gospel (the enemies of the cross). Can we understand this as a form of "passive resistance"?

but does not call them to fight the Roman Empire to expose her fakery or parody and replace it with the real justice and peace of the Kingdom of God. With such a gospel, then, it is no wonder that Paul is not afraid of standing trial at the Roman court.

Thus, there is no anti-imperial intent to be ascertained in the Pauline Epistles. All attempts to interpret them as containing such an intent, as shown above, are imposing an anti-imperial reading on the epistles based merely on superficial parallelism of terms between Paul's gospel preaching and the Roman imperial ideology, while the texts themselves clearly use those terms to express other concerns. Several attempts have turned out to suffer from grave self-contradiction. Some have betrayed their arbitrariness or desperation by appealing to the device of "coding," that Paul coded his real anti-imperial message in politically innocuous language or in anti-Jewish polemic.

Therefore, our survey has found that the fundamental problem of the anti-imperial interpreters of the Pauline Epistles is their methodology. Their fundamental basis is twofold: First are some assumptions about the allegedly pervasive and compulsory imperial cult in the Roman East, the apocalyptic thinking of Paul, the Pauline gospel of the crucified Jesus as the Lord and Savior, and Paul's frequent imprisonment. The other basis is the parallelism between terms in Paul's gospel preaching and in the Roman imperial ideology (such as *kyrios,* Son of God, *sōtēr/sōtēria, parousia, apantēsis, epiphaneia, euangelion, ekklēsia, dikaiosynē, pistis, eirēnē, elpis, eleutheria, katallagē,* and so on). Their tools are deductive argument and proof-texting: from the assumptions and the terminological parallelism they deduce an anti-imperial intent of Paul, then impose it on the texts that contain those terms, regardless of the explicit concerns of the texts themselves, and then string such texts together to declare that Paul proclaims his gospel in deliberate antithesis to the imperial ideology and cult. In our view, it is hard for this methodology to escape the charges of parallelomania and the old-fashioned practice of proof-texting.

It is assumed though not elaborated here that Paul's use of those terms is largely dictated by the Old Testament and Jewish tradition (especially in its LXX and Hellenistic version). It naturally happens that there is a large overlap between the OT/Jewish tradition and the Greco-Roman tradition (as there is also, to some extent, between it and my own Far Eastern tradition) in honorific titles for king-savior and the soteriological terms, although there often is a wide variance in their meanings and nuances. At times Paul uses some of the terms (e.g., *parousia, epiphaneia, apantēsis,* etc.) with no greater motive than to present the Lord Jesus Christ in a majestic and glorious way, as these terms have been well established for royal ceremonies in the Hellenistic world. Therefore, it is simply wrong to impose the Greco-Roman political meanings on the honorific titles of Christ and the soteriological terms, and then the anti-imperial meanings on the texts that contain them, without carefully discerning distinctive Pauline meanings of those terms and the intentions of those texts.[3]

Besides his transcendental conception of God's salvation through Christ, we have ascertained several other factors that have restrained Paul from developing his gospel in an anti-imperial way. First and foremost is his expectation of the imminent *parousia* of the Lord Jesus Christ and the consummation of his salvation. Paul's beliefs that Christ's death and resurrection have inaugurated the age of salvation (see Rom 5:1; 8:1-2; 2 Cor 6:2) and that the risen and exalted Jesus Christ presently exercises his saving Lordship through his Spirit (e.g., Rom 15:18-19; 1 Cor 15:24-28; 2 Cor 2:14-17; 3:17-18; 12:9; Gal 3:5; Phil 1:11, 19; 1 Thess 3:11-13; and many instances of the "in the Lord" formula) provide a theological foundation for him to reflect positively on the present benefits of Christ's saving Lordship in the politico-socio-economic spheres and present them over against the politico-socio-economic ills of the Roman Empire. But apparently his imminent eschatology provides him with little impetus for such thinking. So, we see how such a belief leads Paul, on the one hand, to advise the Corinthians not to change the status quo (1 Cor 7:17-31), and, on the other hand, to encourage the Philippians to wait for the glorious transcendent salvation (transformation into the glorious body like that of the risen Christ), even while implicitly pointing to the parody character of the Roman Empire and its *sōtēria,* with no thought of encouraging them to fight the latter for a better commonwealth and *sōtēria* (Phil 3:20-21).

Paul's imminent eschatology also spurred on his universal mission. His understanding of God's plan of salvation (Rom 11:25-26) and of the decisive role of his Gentile apostleship in it apparently drove him to concentrate on preaching the gospel to all the Gentiles and bringing "the full number of the Gentiles" into the Kingdom of God so as to trigger the conversion of "all Israel" and, in turn, the *parousia* of the Lord Jesus Christ and the consummation of universal redemption. It also made him

3. See above, pp. 28-30.

hurry with his missionary journey through the whole *oikoumenē*, leaving him little room to think about and work toward revolutionary changes to the Roman imperial order.

From the perspective of such a missionary mindset, we have come to presume that Paul could well have appreciated the *pax Romana* (in spite of his awareness of its fundamental inadequacy — 1 Thess 5:3), since the political unity, peace, order, and justice that the Roman Empire secured through the rule of law as well as her military might provided him with a necessary presupposition for his all-important mission in the whole *oikoumenē*. His positive view of the (Roman) authorities as the divinely appointed guardians of justice and order (Rom 13:1-7) seems to confirm this. In light of this positive view in Rom 13:1-7 and the negative view in 1 Cor 2:6-8 and 15:24-28 (cf. also 1 Thess 2:18), we may say that Paul had a dialectical notion of the rulers of the world. Yet, in spite of many experiences of the diabolic side of the imperial and provincial authorities (his many imprisonments), he may well have judged that the Roman imperial system was, on the whole, more conducive than detrimental to his universal mission, and that it certainly was to be preferred over anarchy and chaos. His later interpreters, the Apostolic Fathers and the Apologists, tried to show their loyalty to the Roman Empire, following Paul's explicit exhortations in Rom 13:1-7 and elsewhere, rather than trying to subvert it and interpreting politically such texts as 1 Cor 2:6-8; 15:24-28; Phil 2:9-11; 3:20-21, as some modern interpreters do. At any rate, Rom 13:1-7 is the Achilles' heel of any anti-imperial interpretation of Paul. Moreover, the reception history of the Pauline Epistles in the early church also presents a serious hindrance to such interpretation.

With its assessment of the Roman authorities that is diametrically opposed to that of Rev 13, Rom 13:1-7, together with the rest of the Pauline writings, suggests that the situation of the Roman Empire in which Paul worked was quite different from that of the time of Revelation. In Paul's day, even in Asia apparently the imperial cult was not forced upon Christians and they were not persecuted for resisting it. The gospel was sometimes suspected of an anti-imperial ethos and Christians were charged with political or civic crimes by the local authorities, but the possibility was still open for Paul and other Christians to explain themselves as innocent of such intentions. Apparently Paul was quite successful with this *apologia*, as his repeated release from imprisonment indicates. Hence he was not yet inspired to see the Roman Empire as the author of Revelation was to view it later, and to issue a call to resist her as the latter did.[4] Therefore instead, with the teaching and example of Jesus in mind, he exhorted Christians to persevere under persecution in firm faith and hope, to repay persecutors with love rather than retaliation, to pursue reconciliation and peace with them, and to live a life of quietude, earning the respect of the non-Christian community.

4. See below, pp. 180-90.

# 6. The Gospel Charged as Anti-Imperial

In the first of the "we" sections of Acts (16:6-40), Luke reports Paul's mission in Philippi, the Roman colony with the privilege of *ius italicum* (Italian law). There Paul and Silas are said to have been accused before the city's magistrates for "disturbing [ἐκταράσσουσιν] our city" by "proclaiming customs [ἔθη] which it is not lawful for us Romans to accept or practice." The magistrates had them stripped and beaten with rods and threw them into the inner prison (16:20-24). Here Luke does not explain what characteristics or aspects of Paul's gospel about the Most High God's "way of salvation" (16:17) were perceived as unlawful for the Romans to accept or practice. Paul's preaching of the gospel of the Kingdom of "the Most High God" and the Lord Jesus Christ may have been seen as an attempt to convert Roman citizens away "from the worship of the colony's gods, especially Roma and Augustus."[1]

Luke immediately follows up this account of Paul's mission in Philippi with a report of his mission in Thessalonica, whose citizens were also eager, like the Philippians, to show their loyalty to Rome for her benefaction (Acts 17:1-9). In that city, Luke says, some Jews took offense at the proclamation of Paul and Silas that Jesus was the Christ, and accused Paul and Silas before the *politarchs* of the city as those "who have led the whole world into revolt"[2] (ἀναστατώσαντες, 17:6; cf. 21:38) and for "acting

---

1. H. W. Tajra, *The Trial of St. Paul: A Juridical Exegesis of the Second Half of the Acts of the Apostles*, WUNT 2.35 (Tübingen: Mohr Siebeck, 1989), 13.

2. So renders C. K. Barrett, *A Critical and Exegetical Commentary on the Acts of the Apostles*, 2 vols., ICC (Edinburgh: T&T Clark, 1994, 1998), 2:806, 815.

against the decrees of Caesar, saying that there is another king, Jesus" (17:7). Then, later on, Luke shows Paul having to defend himself before the Roman procurator of Judea that he had not committed any crime "against Caesar" and against the Jewish law (25:8).

These accounts suggest that Luke is well aware that sometimes in the Greco-Roman cities Paul's gospel was perceived as anti-imperial and was even susceptible to the charge of treason. Having reported in his Gospel that Jesus, the messianic preacher of the Kingdom of God, was accused before the Roman procurator Pilate for claiming to be the King of the Jews and was condemned to crucifixion for that treason (Luke 23:2-3, 35-38), Luke naturally is aware of this political perception that Paul's proclamation of Jesus as the Messiah/Christ was bound to arouse in the Greco-Roman cities. But in his Gospel, the first of his two-volume work, Luke emphasizes that the political interpretation of Jesus' Messiahship was mistaken and the Roman procurator Pilate actually knew that Jesus had committed no crime against the empire (23:13-25). Likewise, in his Acts of the Apostles, the second volume, Luke makes clear that the political interpretation of Paul's gospel was mistaken and the Roman procurators Felix and Festus actually knew that it had no anti-Roman or treasonous character (Acts 24:22-27; 25:18, 25; 26:30-32). Just as in his first volume Luke shows that Pilate nevertheless yielded to the pressure of the Jewish leaders and wrongly condemned Jesus to crucifixion, so in his second volume he shows that Felix and Festus yielded likewise to the pressure of the Jewish leaders and failed to administer justice in their trials of Paul.

## 7. Jesus the Davidic Messiah and Universal Lord, and His Liberation of Israel

While seeking to demonstrate the politically innocuous nature of both the gospel of Jesus and the gospel of Paul, why does Luke stress Jesus' Davidic Messiahship and his liberation of Israel? Why does he even present Jesus' Messiahship or kingship/lordship in deliberate contrast to the kingship/lordship of Caesar? Why does he do that in a book explicitly addressed to a member of the Roman nobility, "Theophilus"?[1]

### The Annunciation Stories (Luke 1:26-80)

In the annunciation stories Luke has the angel Gabriel announce to Mary that she will bear a son named "Jesus" ("Yeshua" — "Yahweh, help" or popularly "savior" — cf. Matt 1:21),[2] and that

> He will be great, and will be called the Son of the Most High; and the Lord God will give to him the throne of his father David, and he will reign over the house of Jacob for ever; and of his kingdom there will be no end. (Luke 1:32-33)

Clearly this announcement echoes God's promise that the prophet Nathan delivered to David (2 Sam 7:12-14), which was one of the most important

---

1. The seriousness of this question is not reduced even if "Theophilus" in Luke 1:3 and Acts 1:1 was not a real individual but only a symbol for a certain group of readers whom Luke had in mind.

2. Cf. J. A. Fitzmyer, *The Gospel according to Luke I–XI: A New Translation with Introduction and Commentary*, AB 28 (New York: Doubleday, 1981), 347.

texts to shape the Jewish messianic expectations (e.g., 4QFlor; 4Q246). Thus, the announcement by Gabriel makes it clear that Jesus was to be the messianic king, the Son of David and the Son of God, and that he was to restore the Davidic throne and kingdom.

Then, Luke has Mary sing of the Lord's redemption that the birth of her child will bring in terms of a socio-political revolution and Israel's deliverance (Luke 1:46-55):

> He has shown strength with his arm;
>> he has scattered the proud in the imagination of their hearts;
> he has put down the mighty from their thrones,
>> and exalted those of low degree;
> he has filled the hungry with good things,
>> and the rich he has sent empty away.
> He has helped his servant Israel,
>> in remembrance of his mercy,
> as he spoke to our fathers,
>> to Abraham and to his posterity for ever.          (1:51-55)

Then, finally, Luke has Zechariah, the father of John the Baptist, prophesy in the fullness of the Holy Spirit concerning God's redemption of Israel through Jesus, the child to be born as the Son of David (Luke 1:67-79):

> Blessed be the Lord God of Israel,
>> for he has visited and redeemed his people,
> and has raised up a horn of salvation for us
>> in the house of his servant David,
> as he spoke by the mouth of his holy prophets from of old,
> that we should be saved from our enemies. . . .
>> when the dayspring shall visit us from on high
> to give light to those who sit in darkness and in the shadow of death,
>> to guide our feet into the way of peace.          (1:68-71, 78-79)

## The *Inclusio* of the Birth Narrative (Luke 2:1-14) and Paul's Proclamation in Rome (Acts 28:30-31)

Having thus strongly emphasized that Jesus was to be born as the messianic Son of David and Son of God for Israel's liberation, in fulfillment of

God's promises to Israel, Luke then narrates the event of Jesus' birth, highlighting it against the oppressive backdrop of Caesar Augustus's imperial reign (Luke 2:1-20). The stark contrast that Luke draws between Caesar Augustus, the emperor of Rome, who decreed a universal census for collection of taxes from the subjugated peoples, and Jesus, the son born into the family of David which had to obey the decree, is unmistakable.[3] In those days of Caesar Augustus, who was hailed as "son of God," "the *sōtēr* [savior] of the whole world,"[4] and bringer of the universal peace *(pax Augusta/Romana)*,[5] and whose birthday was celebrated as the *euangelion* of the new beginning of the world,[6] this baby Jesus was born in the humblest manger in Bethlehem, "the city of David," in colonial Judea. But an angel declares the *euangelion* that as the Son of David he *is* the Messiah, the true *sōtēr* and *kyrios* (and Son of God — cf. 1:32, 35), and the heavenly host celebrates him as the bearer of the true *pax* on earth among human beings (2:10-14).

In the world where the Roman rulers were so sensitive to any suggestion of the rise of a new ruler as to issue the edicts of Augustus (A.D. 11) and Tiberius (A.D. 16), banning even rumors about the health of the emperor and prediction of his death,[7] how would this announcement of the

3. As we are primarily concerned about Lucan presentation of Jesus, we need not attend to the notorious historical problem about the census.

4. V. Ehrenberg and A. H. M. Jones, *Documents Illustrating the Reigns of Augustus and Tiberius*, 2nd ed. (Oxford: Clarendon, 1976), no. 72 (ET in D. C. Braund, *Augustus to Nero: A Sourcebook on Roman History, 31 BC–AD 68* [Totowa, N.J.: Barnes and Noble, 1985], no. 66).

5. See Augustus's own boast in *Res Gestae Divi Augusti* (in Ehrenberg and Jones, *Documents Illustrating the Reigns of Augustus and Tiberius*, 1:12-13; ET in Braund, *Augustus to Nero*, no. 1.12-13); also the Halicarnassus inscription in Ehrenberg and Jones, *Documents Illustrating the Reigns of Augustus and Tiberius*, no. 98a (ET in Braund, *Augustus to Nero*, no. 123); see further, Braund, *Augustus to Nero*, nos. 38-39.

6. See the letter of Paulus Fabius Maximus, the proconsul of Asia (9 B.C.), and the calendar inscription of Priene, in Ehrenberg and Jones, *Documents Illustrating the Reigns of Augustus and Tiberius*, no. 98 (ET in Braund, *Augustus to Nero*, no. 122). On the letter and inscription, see G. N. Stanton, *Jesus and Gospel* (Cambridge: Cambridge University Press, 2004), 30-32: "There is an unmistakable whiff of eschatology and soteriology here. The coming of the divine Augustus as 'good news' had been eagerly expected. He came as saviour and benefactor, bringing benefits for all. He has brought peace and will continue to do so. He was himself 'the good news'" (p. 32).

7. Cassius Dio, *Roman History* 56.25.5-6: "the seers were forbidden to prophesy to any person alone or to prophesy regarding death even if others should be present. Yet so far was Augustus from caring about such matters in his own case that he set forth to all in an edict

birth of a new king (Christ/Messiah), *kyrios, sōtēr,* and Son of God, the bearer of "peace on earth," have been heard? Would it not be perceived as a direct violation of those edicts and a direct challenge to the emperor?

In the main body of his Gospel, Luke will show how this Jesus was duly inaugurated by God as the messianic king and Son of God with the anointment of the Holy Spirit during the reign of Tiberius Caesar (3:1-22); how Jesus proclaimed the Kingdom of God, bringing its salvation to those who were variously oppressed; how he entered Jerusalem with people hailing him as "the King who comes in the name of the Lord" and as the bringer of "peace in heaven and glory in the highest" (19:38); and how he was crucified by the representative of Caesar for claiming to be the Messiah, the King of the Jews (23:1-38). Luke will show further how God vindicated Jesus by raising him from the dead and enthroned him as the *kyrios* and Messiah at his right hand in fulfillment of Ps 110:1 (Luke 24:51; cf. Acts 1:9-11; 2:34-36; 5:30-31). Then, in his second volume Luke will show how Jesus' apostles proclaimed to Israel and the Gentiles that Jesus was the Messiah and the Lord. Luke will climax his story of Jesus by having Paul the apostolic representative of Jesus reach his long-pursued, God-appointed goal (Acts 19:21; 23:11; 27:24; 28:14), namely Rome, the very heart of the Empire of Caesar, the *kyrios,* and "preach the *Kingdom of God* and teach about the *kyrios Jesus Christ* with all boldness [μετὰ πάσης παρρησίας] and without hindrance [ἀκωλύτως]" (28:31).[8]

Thus, by constructing a sort of *inclusio* between Luke 2:1-14 and Acts 28:30-31, Luke deliberately contrasts Jesus the Messianic king/lord to Caesar Augustus,[9] and implicitly claims that Jesus is the true *kyrios* and

---

the aspect of the stars at the time of his own birth. Nevertheless, he forbade this practice. *He also issued a proclamation to the subject nations forbidding them to bestow any honours upon a person assigned to govern them* either during his term of office or within sixty days after his departure . . ." (see also 57.15.8). Cf. E. A. Judge, "The Decrees of Caesar at Thessalonica," *RTR* 30 (1971): 3-4, who cites F. H. Cramer, *Astrology in Roman Law and Politics,* MAPS 37 (Philadelphia: American Philosophical Society, 1954), 248-81, and R. MacMullen, *Enemies of the Roman Order: Treason, Unrest, and Alienation in the Empire* (Cambridge, Mass.: Harvard University Press, 1966), 128-62.

8. Mindful of the legal connotations of the two Greek adverbial phrases (cf. Phil 1:20), F. F. Bruce, *The Acts of the Apostles: The Greek Text with Introduction and Commentary,* 3rd rev. and enl. ed. (Grand Rapids: Eerdmans/Leicester: Apollos, 1990), 543, renders them "with all freedom of speech" and "without let or hindrance" respectively.

9. Even without noting the *inclusio,* R. E. Brown, *The Birth of the Messiah: A Commentary on the Infancy Narratives in the Gospels of Matthew and Luke,* new updated ed., ABRL

*sōtēr*, the true bearer of the kingship of God, and that he will bring the true *pax* on earth, replacing the false *pax* brought about by the military conquests of Caesar, a false *kyrios* and *sōtēr*.[10]

## Peter's Sermon to the Roman Officer Cornelius (Acts 10:34-43)

Here and there in between Luke 2:1-14 and Acts 28:30-31 Luke tries to help his readers ("Theophilus" et al.) see Jesus as the true Lord by presenting him implicitly in contrast to Caesar and other Gentile rulers. This inten-

(New York: Doubleday, 1993), 415-16, sees this contrast in Luke 2:1-14. Luke's intention of contrasting Jesus and Caesar with each other is further indicated in his explicit dating of Jesus' baptism and messianic inauguration in reference to the reign of Tiberius Caesar (Luke 3:1-22), which is parallel to his dating of Jesus' birth in reference to the reign of Augustus Caesar (Luke 2:1-14). See below, pp. 84-87. Since Luke 3:1-22 does not suggest any positive role of Tiberius Caesar, Pontius Pilate, Herod, Philip, Annas, and Caiaphas in the ministry of John the Baptist and the messianic inauguration of Jesus, the passage weakens the attempt to see the reference to the regime of Augustus Caesar in 2:1-14 in the positive sense of it helping realize God's plan for the Messiah to be born in Bethlehem (see the next note).

10. Contra P. W. Walaskay, *'And So We Came to Rome': The Political Perspective of St Luke*, SNTSMS 49 (Cambridge: Cambridge University Press, 1983), 27-28, who interprets the reference to Augustus in Luke 2:1-14 as a positive appreciation of his role in God's plan of salvation. It is quite astonishing to see how Walaskay speaks of the "willing" obedience of Joseph and Mary to the Roman decree and so "testifying to the legitimacy and authority of that government," and interprets the angelic song in v. 14 as meaning "the *pax Augustus* was completed (complemented) by the *pax Christi*." C. Bryan, *Render to Caesar: Jesus, the Early Church, and the Roman Superpower* (Oxford: Oxford University Press, 2005), 98-99, also stresses that in Luke 2:1-14 "Luke shows Mary and Joseph loyally obeying Caesar Augustus' decree, and in so doing, *identifying* themselves with the Roman Empire," and so sees Mary and Joseph as examples of faithful Jews who "find no difficulty in giving to Caesar what is Caesar's while at the same time giving to God what is God's" (his italics). Cf. also P. F. Esler, *Community and Gospel in Luke-Acts: The Social and Political Motivations of Lucan Theology*, SNTSMS 57 (Cambridge: Cambridge University Press, 1987), 201-2. But this view is based on an unrealistic assumption as if Mary and Joseph had an option or means to resist the decree. In his reaction against the recent movement to see Jesus and the NT writers as anti-Roman campaigners, Bryan does not appreciate sufficiently their critical attitude to the Roman Empire. So, in Luke's narrative of Jesus' birth, Bryan is able to see at most a "relativizing" of Caesar's power and his "political peace." But this is quite inadequate. In fact, it is difficult to imagine that Luke makes the elaborate reference to the regime and decree of Augustus in 2:1-2 as well as to the regime of Tiberius in 3:1-2 only to say that God made even the Roman emperor serve his purpose of having his Messiah born in Bethlehem in accordance with the prophecy (Mic 5:2).

tion perhaps is clearest in Luke's account of Peter's sermon to the Roman centurion Cornelius, his relatives, and friends in Acts 10:34-43:

> [You know] the word which he sent to the children of Israel, *proclaiming the good news of peace* [εὐαγγελιζόμενος εἰρήνην] *through Jesus Christ* — *this one is the Lord of all* [οὗτός ἐστιν πάντων κύριος]. You know the word that was proclaimed throughout the whole of Judea, beginning from Galilee after the baptism which John preached, [the word concerning] Jesus of Nazareth, how God anointed him with the Holy Spirit and power, who went about doing good and healing all who were oppressed by the devil, for God was with him. And we are witnesses to all that he did in the country of the Jews and in Jerusalem. They killed him by hanging him on a tree, but God raised this one on the third day and granted to him that he should be revealed, not to all people but to the witnesses who had been appointed beforehand by God, namely to us, who ate and drank with him after he had risen from the dead. And he commanded us to preach to the people and to testify that he is the one ordained by God to be judge of the living and the dead. To this one all the prophets bear witness that everyone who believes in him receives forgiveness of sins through his name. (10:36-43)

This is clearly Luke's summary of his own gospel, i.e., what he wrote in his first volume.[11] Recently Kavin Rowe has stressed that the sentence οὗτός ἐστιν πάντων κύριος (10:36) is not a mere passing remark in parenthesis, but an emphatic statement with the full directive force of the demonstrative pronoun οὗτος: "Jesus Christ, *this one* is the Lord of all." Rowe argues that with the emphatic formulation Luke seeks to affirm Jesus Christ's universal lordship, denying the Roman emperor's rival claim.[12] Rowe supports this view by observing the narrative context of Acts 10 in which the statement is made.

> The context of this claim is remarkable. The narrative has turned a corner, explicitly rejected pagan reverence/worship [10:25-26] and now looks out upon an active mission to the Gentiles. Consider the scene:

11. This is recognized by R. C. Tannehill, *The Narrative Unity of Luke-Acts: A Literary Interpretation*, 2 vols., FF (Minneapolis: Fortress, 1986, 1990), 2:140-41.

12. C. K. Rowe, "Luke-Acts and the Imperial Cult: A Way Through the Conundrum?" *JSNT* 27 (2005): 289-94. Tannehill has also made essentially the same point in his *Narrative Unity of Luke-Acts*, 2:139-40.

the leading Gentile character, [Cornelius], a ranking member of the Roman military; the city, founded in honor of Augustus; the audience, a group of Gentiles [10:27]; the sermon, the inaugural for the mission. These elements taken *in toto* create an ethos in which the presence of the Roman Empire is keenly felt. And it is into this setting that Peter introduces the crucified Jesus — οὗτος — as the κύριος πάντων.[13]

Rowe rightly comments that in view of this context the Roman audience of this text "would have heard the stress of this claim in connection with the Roman emperor and his cult."[14]

This is a fine observation. But it needs to be strengthened by noting the importance of the phrase εὐαγγελιζόμενος εἰρήνην διὰ 'Ιησοῦ Χριστοῦ ("proclaiming the good news of peace through Jesus Christ") directly preceding the emphatic declaration here and by discussing this text of Acts 10:36 in connection with the *inclusio* of Luke 2:1-14 and Acts 28:30-31. Since the phrase appears in a context that clearly evokes an ethos of the Roman Empire, as Rowe has well described, and since it appears together with the emphatic declaration οὗτός ἐστιν πάντων κύριος, "this one is the Lord of all," a Roman officer like Cornelius and other Roman hearers would have understood the phrase εὐαγγελιζόμενος εἰρήνην in terms of the εὐαγγέλιον and εἰρήνη of the imperial propaganda. So, by making the declaration "this one [namely, Jesus Christ] is the Lord of all" immediately after speaking about the "gospel" (εὐαγγέλιον) of "peace" (εἰρήνη) brought by Jesus Christ, Luke clearly intends to make Cornelius and his Roman colleagues (or Theophilus and his colleagues) understand that Jesus Christ, not Augustus or his successor, is "the Lord of all" who has brought the gospel (εὐαγγέλιον) of peace (εἰρήνη). If the phrase διὰ 'Ιησοῦ Χριστοῦ is construed with the immediately foregoing word, εἰρήνην, the contrast between Jesus Christ and Augustus may be clearer:

---

13. Rowe, "Luke-Acts and the Imperial Cult," 292. We may further point out the significance of the location of Caesarea (10:24): the city not only bore the name of Caesar, as it was founded by Herod the Great in honor of Augustus, but also had a grand and beautiful temple of Caesar prominently placed, with a colossal statue of Augustus and a statue of Roma, which were modeled after Zeus on Mt. Olympus and Hera at Argos respectively (Josephus, *Jewish War* 1.414). If the "we" sections in Acts are somehow related to Luke's personal experiences, Acts 25:5-15 and 27:1 would suggest his firsthand knowledge of Caesarea and the Roman military set-up in the city. If so, it is quite probable that in composing Acts 10:34-43 he was conscious of the city's imperial cult.

14. Rowe, "Luke-Acts and the Imperial Cult," 292.

Jesus Christ and not Augustus is the *author* of peace. But even if the phrase is taken as referring to Jesus Christ's role of bringing God's word (λόγος), i.e., the gospel of peace, that contrast is still unmistakable: Jesus Christ and not Augustus is the *bringer* of God's gospel of peace. Anyway, with the whole statement εὐαγγελιζόμενος εἰρήνην διὰ 'Ιησοῦ Χριστοῦ — οὗτός ἐστιν πάντων κύριος, Luke seeks to make his Roman audience understand that Jesus Christ and not Caesar is the universal Lord who has brought the gospel of peace. Thus, with that opening sentence of his own summary of what he wrote in his Gospel, Luke clearly harks back to the beginning of the main body of his Gospel, Luke 2:1-14.[15] Therefore, if we see Acts 10:36 within the framework of the *inclusio* of Luke 2:1-14 and Acts 28:30-31, this intention becomes all the more clear. Luke is in effect saying at Acts 10:36 that Peter preached to Cornelius and his colleagues at Caesarea the gospel of peace of the universal Lord Jesus Christ which the angels proclaimed at Christ's birth (Luke 2:1-14), and at Acts 28:31 that Paul brought to the city of Caesar the gospel of the universal Lord Jesus Christ which Peter preached to Cornelius and his colleagues at Caesarea (Acts 10:36).

### Jesus' Baptism by John the Baptist (Luke 3:21-22)

There are also other places where Luke presents Jesus as the messianic liberator of Israel, implicitly drawing a contrast between Jesus and Caesar. So, after depicting Jesus' auspicious birth under the angelic proclamations (Luke 2:1-14), Luke narrates how the baby Jesus was celebrated at his presentation in the temple by the Spirit-filled Simeon, the genuine Israelite, and Anna, the faithful prophetess, as the Lord's Messiah, who would bring about the redemption of Israel as well as the light of revelation to the Gentiles (2:22-38). Then, Luke gives an account of Jesus' messianic inauguration: at his baptism, the heavens were opened, Jesus was anointed with the Holy Spirit descending, and the heavenly voice declared: "You are my beloved Son; with you I am well pleased" (3:21-22).

15. So Tannehill, *Narrative Unity of Luke-Acts*, 2:138-39, citing C. Burchard, "A Note on 'PHMA in JosAs 17:1f.; Luke 2:15, 17; Acts 10:37," *NovT* 27 (1985): 290-94. Cf. also B. Witherington III, *The Acts of the Apostles: A Socio-Rhetorical Commentary* (Grand Rapids: Eerdmans/Carlisle: Paternoster, 1998), 357.

Thus, what the angel Gabriel had announced at Jesus' conception (Luke 1:35) and another angel at his birth (2:11), which is also what the Spirit-directed Simeon had prophesied at his presentation, is confirmed or realized at Jesus' baptism.

Although unlike Matthew and Mark, Luke does not explicitly state that Jesus was baptized by John the Baptist, he suggests it implicitly. Like Matthew and Mark, Luke also shows John the Baptist announcing the coming of the Lord and demanding preparation in the words of Isa 40:3: "The voice of one crying in the wilderness: Prepare the way of the Lord, make his paths straight" (Luke 3:4). By doing so, Luke evokes the whole narrative of God's redemption of Israel from the Babylonian captivity and arouses a hope for its eschatological reenactment through the Messiah whom John was announcing. Unlike Matthew and Mark, Luke does not stop citing from Isa 40 at verse 3 but goes on with verses 4 and 5:

> Every valley shall be filled,
> and every mountain and hill shall be brought low,
> and the crooked shall be made straight,
> and the rough ways shall be made smooth;
> and all flesh shall see the salvation of God.  (Luke 3:5-6)

With this additional citation, Luke seems to be underlining the revolutionary nature of the Messiah's redemption, as he thereby lets his audience hear the words along with or in the spirit of the foregoing Song of Mary (Luke 1:46-55; note the parallelism in vocabulary [πληρωθήσεται, ταπεινωθήσεται, σωτηρία] as well as in the general spirit). This is made quite clear, as Luke follows this additional citation with a description of John's demand for people's repentance specifically in terms of correction in the realm of socio-economic relationships (Luke 3:7-14). Matthew 3:7-10 has only John's general demand for people to bear fruit befitting repentance in order to escape from God's impending judgment. But Luke not only has this Q material (Luke 3:7-9/Matt 3:7-10) but goes on to add John's specific instructions for "bearing fruits that befit repentance":

> [To the crowds:] He who has two coats, let him share with him who
> has none; and he who has food, let him do likewise. . . .
> [To tax collectors:] Collect no more than is appointed to you. . . .
> [To soldiers:] Rob no one by violence or by false accusation, and
> be content with your wages.  (Luke 3:10-14)

These words make clear how acutely Luke was conscious of politico-military oppression and socio-economic injustice and exploitation. By mentioning here specifically tax collectors and soldiers, the imperial agents, Luke plainly suggests his view that the Roman imperial system was at least partly the root cause of these problems.

In Luke 19:41-44; 21:20-24, Luke presents Jesus as lamenting over Israel's rejection of his teachings on the Kingdom of God ("the things that make for peace," 19:42) and prophesying the fall of Jerusalem:

> your enemies will cast up a bank about you and surround you, and hem you in on every side, and dash you to the ground, you and your children within you, and they will not leave one stone upon another in you. . . . (19:43-44)

> But when you see Jerusalem surrounded by armies, then know that its desolation has come near. . . . these are days of vengeance, to fulfill all that is written. Alas for those who are with child and for those who give suck in those days! For great distress shall be upon the earth and wrath upon this people; they will fall by the edge of the sword, and be led captive among all nations; and Jerusalem will be trodden down by the Gentiles, until the times of the Gentiles are fulfilled. (21:20-24)

Luke 19:41-44 is Lucan special material, and Luke 21:23b-24 is mostly made up of Lucan additions to Mark 13:14-20 (//Matt 24:15-22). As many critics recognize, it is probable that these prophecies reflect Luke's knowledge of the Roman troops' siege and destruction of Jerusalem during the Jewish War of A.D. 66-70. Here it is noteworthy that going beyond his Marcan *Vorlage* and Matthean parallel, Luke highlights the brutality of the Roman troops and the terrible nature of the Jewish suffering. It is consistent with this that again Luke alone among the Evangelists contains an episode about the brutality of Pilate (Luke 13:1-5). Clearly Luke is quite conscious of the military violence of Roman imperialism and the suffering of the subjugated peoples.

This negative view of the Roman Empire seems to be reflected in his introduction of the world in which or the time at which John the Baptist's ministry took place: it was during the reign of Tiberius Caesar, when Judea was under Pilate's governorship and Galilee under the rule of Herod, the Roman client king, and when the Roman collaborators Annas and Caiaphas were the high priests (Luke 3:1-2). Against the stark background of the politico-socio-economic malaise in the Roman imperial system, says Luke, the prophet John the Baptist arose to announce the coming of the Lord who would bring about God's salvation, a revolution of political liberation and socio-economic justice, and indeed Jesus the Son of God inaugurated his God-anointed messianic mission. Thus, by dating the ministry of John the Baptist and the inauguration of Jesus' mission by reference to the reign of Caesar Tiberius and the rules of Pilate and Herod, Luke achieves the same effect as by dating the birth of Jesus with reference to the reign of Caesar Augustus and the governorship of Quirinius in Luke 2:1-14: the contrast between the messianic work of Jesus and the reign of the Roman emperor. Thus Luke seems to repeat this way of dating twice in order to make the contrast unmistakably clear: Jesus, born to be the messianic King and Lord (2:11) during the reign of Augustus Caesar, was inaugurated as such with the anointment of the Holy Spirit during the reign of Tiberius Caesar (3:4, 15-16, 22-23).

## Jesus' Inaugural Sermon (Luke 4:18-19)

It is no wonder, then, that in his inaugural sermon at the synagogue of Nazareth the Lucan Jesus declares his messianic program in the words of Isa 61:1-2 and 58:6:

> The Spirit of the Lord is upon me,
>> because he has anointed me to preach good news to the poor.
> He has sent me to proclaim release to the captives
>> and recovery of sight to the blind,
>> to set at liberty those who are oppressed,
> to proclaim the acceptable year of the Lord. (Luke 4:18-19)

With this declaration, Luke lets his audience understand that Jesus, the messianic Servant of the Lord (Isa 61:1-2), set out to deliver Israel as the eschatological fulfillment of its typological antecedents: God's redemption of his people from the Babylonian captivity and from Egyptian slavery. The first-century audience could not help but understand this declaration as Jesus' promise to liberate Israel from their Roman slavery and oppression. By adding to this Jesus' claim, "Today this scripture has been fulfilled in your hearing" (Luke 4:21), Luke indicates that in his view Jesus did indeed fulfill this promise. So we will have to study his Gospel and Acts closely to see how he thinks Jesus fulfilled it, or brought about Israel's redemption and socio-economic justice, which this declaration and all the prophecies of the angels, Mary, Zechariah, Simeon, Anna, and John the Baptist promised.[16]

## Jesus' Temptations by Satan (Luke 4:1-13)

According to Luke as well as Mark and Matthew, Jesus launched this messianic mission after overcoming Satan's temptations to be the kind of Messiah that would correspond to Satan's will and character. Recently Richard B. Hays has observed that one of the two differences in the Lucan version of Jesus' temptations (Luke 4:1-13) from its Matthean parallel (Matt 4:1-11) has the effect of making the Roman emperor diabolic. One difference is Matthew and Luke's reverse arrangement of Satan's challenge for Jesus to jump down from the pinnacle of the temple and Satan's offer of kingship over all the kingdoms of the world. The other difference concerns the offer Satan makes after he has shown Jesus all the kingdoms: while Matthew has Satan say only "I will give you all these" (Matt 4:9), Luke has him add two more clauses: "To you I will give all this authority and their glory, *for it has been delivered to me, and I give it to whom I will*" (Luke 4:6). According to Hays, "in the first century Mediterranean world," these additional clauses "can mean only one thing": the Roman emperor and all the kings within the Roman Empire received their authority from Satan.[17] If so, Luke is here intending to draw a contrast between the Roman emperor who received his authority from Satan and Jesus who repu-

16. The Lucan version of the Beatitudes (Luke 6:20-26) with woes pronounced upon the rich and arrogant as well as blessings upon the poor and oppressed is also in line with Jesus' inaugural sermon and all the prophecies of these people, and it underlines the revolutionary character of Jesus' gospel more strongly than the Matthean version (Matt 5:2-12) without these woes accompanying the blessings.

17. R. B. Hays, "The Liberation of Israel in Luke-Acts: Intertextual Readings as Resistance," paper presented at Fuller Theological Seminary, Pasadena, Calif., Jan. 26, 2006, p. 9. This point was already observed by R. Maddox, *The Purpose of Luke-Acts*, FRLANT 126 (Göttingen: Vandenhoeck & Ruprecht, 1982), 95. Cf. also J. Jervell, *The Theology of the Acts of the Apostles*, NTT (Cambridge: Cambridge University Press, 1996), 106; S. Walton, "The State They Were In: Luke's View of the Roman Empire," in *Rome in the Bible and the Early Church*, ed. P. Oakes (Carlisle: Paternoster/Grand Rapids: Baker, 2002), 27-28.

diated Satan's offer of kingship but affirmed his worship and service only of God so as to maintain his authority received from God, his divine sonship to represent the Kingdom of God (Luke 3:22; cf. 22:29). This interpretation is supported by the contrast between the messianic kingship of Jesus and the reign of Tiberius Caesar, Pontius Pilate, Herod, and Philip, which Luke presents, as we have seen, by dating Jesus' messianic inauguration to the reign of these rulers (3:1-22), immediately before this account of his temptation by Satan. While these and other rulers of the Roman imperial system received their authority from Satan, Jesus received his messianic kingship and divine sonship from God and rejected Satan's temptation to replace the latter with the former.

## Jesus' Contrast with Pagan Kings (Luke 22:24-27)

This interpretation is further supported by Luke's account of the contrast Jesus drew between the pagan kings and himself:

> A dispute also arose among them [the twelve disciples] as to which one of them was to be regarded as the greatest. But he said to them, "The kings of the Gentiles lord it over them; and those in authority over them are called benefactors. But not so with you; rather the greatest among you must become like the youngest, and the leader like one who serves. For who is greater, the one who is at the table or the one who serves? Is it not the one at the table? But I am among you as one who serves. (Luke 22:24-27; cf. Matt 20:24-28; Mark 10:41-45)

This common Synoptic tradition clearly indicates that Jesus was troubled by the evil nature of the pagan conception of authority and that he was critical of "the kings of the Gentiles." Mark and Matthew may also see Jesus including the Roman emperor among "the kings of the Gentiles," if not in fact pointing to him as the chief of the despotic pagan kings. But since Luke explicitly contrasts Jesus with Caesar (Luke 2:1-14; 3:1-22), reports Jesus' referring to Herod Antipas as "that fox" (Luke 13:32), and refers to the brutality of Pilate (Luke 13:1-5), we may be certain that at least Luke perceives the inclusion of the emperor in Jesus' criticism.[18] In view

18. Bryan, *Render to Caesar*, 101, thinks that this passage (Luke 22:24-27) makes only a general critique of pagan kings' abuse of power and is therefore not specifically anti-Roman,

of the fact that the first temptation by the devil ("If you are the Son of God, command this stone to become bread," Luke 4:3) was trying to make Jesus exercise his power for his own benefits rather than in obedience to God,[19] and also that the devil's second temptation contrasts worshipping Satan and worshipping/serving God (4:6-8), the pagan kings' "lording it over" (κυριεύουσιν) their subjects (22:25) must be seen as them exercising their authority in conformity to the devil's direction or in service of the devil's intention. So Jesus saw Caesar and other pagan rulers exercising their political authority in the Satanic way and for the Satanic purpose, i.e., for the kingdom of Satan. But having rejected at his temptation by Satan the exercise of his authority for his own good as a diabolic temptation and having resolved to follow only God's word, Jesus embodies "as one who serves" the conception of lordship befitting the Kingdom of God (cf. also Luke 12:37).[20] So, the new people of God whom Jesus has gathered into God's Kingdom should embody this divine conception of leadership and authority.

---

and that, while calling for the disciples to build up an alternative society like the one described in Acts 4:32-37, it does not call for an overthrow of the abusive power structures. But this appears to be an under-interpretation of this passage. If it is seen not in isolation but in connection with all the passages of Luke-Acts that have so far been surveyed here, and especially if it is borne in mind that Luke represents it as a teaching of Jesus, the bearer of the Kingdom of God, the implication of an anti-Roman criticism cannot be underestimated. Cf. S. Freyne, *Jesus, a Jewish Galilean: A New Reading of the Jesus-Story* (London and New York: T&T Clark International, 2004), 144-47, who sees Jesus' criticism of Gentile rulers (Mark 10:41-45/Luke 22:24-27/Matt 20:24-28) as having especially Herod Antipas in view, and takes it together with Jesus' criticism of the luxurious lifestyle of Herod Antipas and his elitist circle — the "Herodians" — in the Q account of Jesus' praise for John the Baptist in the wake of his reply to the envoys of John (Luke 7:24-28/Matt 11:7-11). But when the passage specifically speaks of "the kings of the Gentiles," why should it be seen as referring only to Herod Antipas? Cf. K. Wengst, *Pax Romana and the Peace of Jesus Christ*, trans. J. Bowden (Philadelphia: Fortress, 1987), 55-57. Bryan is right to suggest that the passage should not be overinterpreted as though Luke were calling for the church to overthrow the Roman Empire. But it should not be under-interpreted, either, as if Luke did not have in mind the necessity for the kingdoms of the world to be replaced by Jesus' Kingdom of God.

19. So I. H. Marshall, *The Gospel of Luke: A Commentary on the Greek Text*, NIGTC (Grand Rapids: Eerdmans, 1978), 170-71; Fitzmyer, *Luke I–IX*, 511.

20. Cf. Rowe, "Luke-Acts and the Imperial Cult," 298-99.

## Jesus' Politics through Symbolic Acts

While stressing Jesus' rejection of "the politics of physical force," Gerd Theissen highlights Jesus' "political strategy of symbols."[21] Characterizing "the historical period of Jesus" as one "full of conflict expressed in political symbols,"[22] Theissen notes the following symbolic acts of Jesus as part of his political strategy: (1) his exorcism, through which he demonstrates "a breakthrough of the kingdom of God," or God's victory over demons;[23] (2) his appointment of the twelve to govern Israel (Mark 3:13-19/Luke 6:12-16/Matt 10:1-4; Luke 22:28-30/Matt 19:28): by appointing common people to rule over restored Israel, Jesus is expressing his stance against both the Judean high-priestly government and its colonial master, the Roman Empire; (3) his entry into Jerusalem as "king" or representative of the "kingdom of our father David," "in antithesis to the entry of the prefect at all great temple feasts";[24] and (4) his temple action, which, as an act of his prophetic announcement of its destruction in protest to the high-priestly rule, led to his trial before the Sanhedrin. Theissen stresses that especially Jesus' entry into Jerusalem and his temple action were the symbolic acts that negated both the political and the religious system of power of their legitimacy. Then Theissen concludes: Even if Jesus rejected the way of violent revolution, he masterfully used symbolic actions with clear political purposes, so that his followers and adversaries were not mistaken to assume "that Jesus envisaged political goals."[25]

Theissen notes that even if some elements of the above symbolic acts of

---

21. G. Theissen, "The Political Dimension of Jesus' Activities," in *The Social Setting of Jesus and the Gospels,* ed. W. Stegemann, B. J. Malina, and G. Theissen (Minneapolis: Fortress, 2002), 237-39.

22. Theissen, "Political Dimension of Jesus' Activities," 237. He illustrates this with Herod Antipas's naming his capital Tiberias, Pilate's introducing shields with emblems of Caesar into Jerusalem and minting coins with symbols of Roman cults, John's baptismal movement, and the Samaritan prophetic pretender promising to recover the temple vessels hidden by Moses on Mount Gerizim (Josephus, *Jewish Antiquities* 18.85). See further Josephus, *Jewish Antiquities* 20.97-98, 169-70, for Theudas and an Egyptian prophetic pretender who tried to reenact the Exodus liberation symbolically.

23. Theissen, "Political Dimension of Jesus' Activities," 238. However, in reference to the "Legion" in the story of the exorcism of the Gerasene demoniac (Mark 5:9 pars.), Theissen suggests that foreign powers may be latent in the demons. But on this, see below, pp. 117-21.

24. Theissen, "Political Dimension of Jesus' Activities," 238.

25. Theissen, "Political Dimension of Jesus' Activities," 239.

Jesus should be seen as ahistorical they are still valid for the transmitters of Jesus traditions.[26] For our purpose here, we need only to affirm that what Theissen has delineated as Jesus' "political strategy of symbols" is quite an accurate representation of an aspect of Luke's view of Jesus' politics.

## Jesus' Exaltation to the Throne of David

Finally, we must consider Luke's emphasis on Jesus' Davidic kingship. Having repeatedly stressed in the annunciation and birth narratives that Jesus was born as the Son of David/Son of God in fulfillment of Nathan's oracle (2 Sam 7:12-14), Luke shows how Jesus' apostles proclaimed God's exaltation of Jesus as Lord and Messiah upon the throne of David through his resurrection (Acts 2:30-36; 13:23, 32-41) in fulfillment of the divine pledge. They proclaimed that God brought this about, overcoming the resistance of "the kings and the rulers of the earth" represented by Herod and Pontius Pilate against the Davidic Messiah in fulfillment of Ps 2 (Acts 4:24-31). Through the mouth of James, Luke makes it known that this enthronement of Jesus on David's throne represented the restoration of "David's fallen tent" (Acts 15:16; see Amos 9:11-12), and that "the remnant" of the Jews who "seek the Lord" and "all the Gentiles who bear [Christ's] name" are the eschatological people of God, the restored kingdom of David or Israel, over which Jesus the Davidic Messiah reigns (Acts 15:17). Jesus bequeathed the Twelve with the kingdom as God had bequeathed it to him, so that as his representatives they might rule and judge the twelve tribes of Israel (Luke 22:28-30).

Is it possible to imagine that Luke narrates this account of Jesus' fulfillment of the Jewish messianic expectation for the restoration of the Davidic kingdom of Israel (cf. Acts 1:6; also Luke 24:21) without considering its implications for the Roman Empire? If nothing else, then, at least Luke's reference to the hostile resistance of "the kings and the rulers of the earth" of Ps 2 and his specification of them in terms of "Herod and Pontius Pilate" seem to make it impossible (Acts 4:25-28). For Luke, Jesus is the King, indeed the Davidic King. He was born as such (Luke 2:1-14), and he entered Jerusalem, the City of David, as such (Luke 19:28-40).[27] He was

---

26. Theissen, "Political Dimension of Jesus' Activities," 238.

27. With the explicit designation "king" in Luke 19:38, this is emphasized more in the

crucified as such, namely as "the King of the Jews," by Pilate and Herod (Luke 23:2, 38). But God raised him and vindicated him, exalting him to his right hand or to the throne of David (Acts 2:29-36). He is the Lord of all because he is the Messiah, the Davidic King (Acts 2:25-36; 10:36).[28] But then, how does Luke think of Jesus' Davidic kingship vis-à-vis Caesar?

---

Lucan account of the triumphal entry into Jerusalem than in the Marcan and Matthean parallels (Mark 11:9-10/Matt 21:9).

28. Cf. N. T. Wright, *Paul: In Fresh Perspective* (Minneapolis: Fortress, 2005), 69-79, for the stress on this NT understanding of Jesus' Messiahship within the framework of the OT/Jewish theology of creation and election/covenant.

## 8. Jesus' Redemption: It Is Not a Deliverance from the Roman Empire

We noted earlier Luke's emphasis that the political interpretation of Jesus' Messiahship was mistaken as the Roman procurator Pilate knew that Jesus committed no crime against the empire (Luke 23:13-25), and that likewise the political interpretation of Paul's gospel (Acts 17:1-9) was mistaken as the Roman procurators Felix and Festus knew that it had no anti-Roman or treasonous character (Acts 24:22-27; 25:18, 25; 26:30-32). Here, then, Luke presents what appears a self-contradiction: having emphatically presented Jesus as the Messiah, the Davidic King, who came to redeem Israel or restore the Davidic kingdom of Israel — indeed as the true "Lord of all" who brought the *euangelion* of the true universal *pax,* liberty, and justice — and having presented such a Jesus in deliberate contrast to Caesar, Luke says that preaching Jesus as Christ and Lord in this way is no treason "against Caesar," no political act of presenting "another king" (Acts 25:8; cf. 17:1-9). How are we to understand this logic?

Did Luke make a distinction between the religious (or spiritual) sense and the political sense of Messiahship and affirm Jesus' kingship/lordship only in the former sense, as many later Christians were to do in the course of church history? In view of Luke's vital concern for the poor and oppressed as well as all the points that have been observed in the foregoing chapter, this question cannot seriously be entertained.[1]

---

1. Cf. N. T. Wright, *Jesus and the Victory of God,* vol. 2 of *Christian Origins and the Question of God* (Minneapolis: Fortress, 1996), 295-97, against the split between "political" concerns and "spiritual" or "theological" concerns and presentation of the Jesus movement as an apolitical movement, and for his insistence on the political implications of Jesus' King-

In order to understand Luke's logic, we first have to examine what in his understanding are the redemption, revolution, and peace that Jesus the Messiah and Lord has brought, and what is the Davidic kingdom of Israel that Jesus has restored.

## No Promise or Call for an Overthrow of the Roman Imperial Rule

Evidently Luke does not think that the redemption that Jesus has brought has to do with overthrowing the Roman imperial system or replacing it with a politically independent government of Israel. For in his report there is no promise, call, or action by Jesus for an overthrow of the Roman imperial rule.[2] As Christopher Bryan stresses, unlike Mahatma Gandhi, Jesus does not advocate even nonviolent passive resistance to it, and does not even challenge Pilate's right to try him.[3] Furthermore, as Richard J. Cassidy recognizes, Jesus does not "support any of the other forms of government (including that probably advocated by the Zealots) that might have been considered as replacements for Roman rule."[4] While including his special material about Jesus hearing that Pilate mixed the blood of some Galilean pilgrims with their sacrifices, Luke has Jesus use the incident to warn his hearers of the need to repent, but not to condemn Pilate's brutality or the oppressiveness of the Roman rule, let alone call for a fight against it (Luke 13:1-5). Again, in his special account of Herod's attempt to kill Jesus, Luke has Jesus respond to the news not by calling his followers to fight the harm-

---

dom ministry and on the political nature of even his opposition to the armed resistance of his contemporary revolutionaries.

2. Cf. C. Bryan, *Render to Caesar: Jesus, the Early Church, and the Roman Superpower* (Oxford: Oxford University Press, 2005), 46: "Indeed, if independence from Rome were Jesus' agenda, it is strange overall that there is not a single saying attributed to him in any gospel that unambiguously states that agenda."

3. Bryan, *Render to Caesar*, 99.

4. R. J. Cassidy, *Jesus, Politics, and Society: A Study of Luke's Gospel* (Maryknoll, N.Y.: Orbis, 1978), 79. Cf. also R. T. France, "Liberation in the New Testament," *EvQ* 58 (1986): 8: "The gospels do not support the view that [Jesus] advocated or even countenanced any specific programme to change the existing socio-economic system" — a conclusion of France's study, "God and Mammon," *EvQ* 51 (1979): 3-21. In R. J. Cassidy's subsequent book, *Society and Politics in the Acts of the Apostles* (Maryknoll, N.Y.: Orbis, 1987), 17, he also acknowledges that Luke does not present Jesus as ever "challeng[ing] the Roman presence in Judea and the overall character of Roman rule there."

ful ruler ("that fox"), but rather by pointing to his determination to carry on his messianic mission of exorcism and healing and ultimately of his death, and by lamenting over the impending judgment of God on Jerusalem for her failure to respond to his saving mission (Luke 13:31-35). While availing his healing power for the slave of a centurion at Capernaum (Luke 7:1-10), Jesus does not demand the centurion to stop serving the Roman government. We have seen that in Acts 10:36-43 Luke seeks to make Cornelius and his Roman colleagues understand that Jesus Christ, not Augustus or his successor, is "the Lord of all" who has brought the gospel (εὐαγγέλιον) of peace (εἰρήνη). In that episode, while stressing this point, Luke does not let Peter demand the Roman officer Cornelius and his colleagues to stop, therefore, serving Caesar's empire in order to serve the true Lord Jesus Christ.[5] Jesus does not make such a demand of Zacchaeus, the rich chief tax collector, either, even while rejoicing in his personal change and generous sharing of his wealth with the poor (Luke 19:1-10).[6] The same point can be made of Jesus' attitude to "the large company of tax collectors" with whom he enjoyed a banquet at the home of Levi, the tax collector whom he called to be his disciple (Luke 5:27-29; cf. also 7:29).

When Jesus is directly challenged to declare his position about Caesar and his imperial rule with the trap question of whether it is lawful for the Jews to pay tribute to Caesar, Jesus answers: "Render to Caesar the things that are Caesar's, and to God the things that are God's" (Luke 20:20-26/ Mark 12:13-17/Matt 22:15-22). Interpretation of this riddle is disputed. Jesus may be affirming the OT/Jewish teaching of submission even to a heathen ruler's authority, grounding this submission in obedience to God, as even the heathen ruler is viewed as commissioned by God.[7] Or Jesus may be

---

5. Just as in Paul, so also in Luke-Acts, the imperial cult is never explicitly mentioned. Acts 10:36 may be regarded as an exception, and there we may see an indirect allusion to it. But then it is significant that Luke does not follow up his affirmation of Jesus as the only Lord of all with a demand for the Roman officer Cornelius and his friends to stop participating in the imperial cult. See p. 181, n. 49, below.

6. R. S. Sugirtharajah, *Postcolonial Criticism and Biblical Interpretation* (Oxford and New York: Oxford University Press, 2002), 90; Bryan, *Render to Caesar*, 42-43. Note also how Luke points to the problems of the Roman imperial rule by representing John the Baptist as saying to tax collectors and soldiers, respectively, "Collect no more than is appointed to you" and "Rob no one by violence or by false accusation, and be content with your wages" (Luke 3:12-14), but does not represent him as demanding that they stop working for the Roman imperial system.

7. So I. H. Marshall, *The Gospel of Luke: A Commentary on the Greek Text*, NIGTC

pointing out here that those who are willing to carry the coins bearing Caesar's image and so be engaged with them in the trade system maintained by the Caesarean order have already made their decision to honor the order; and he may mean that they should then have no problem with paying tax to Caesar for the benefits they are drawing from the system with the coin that belongs to Caesar, but that even they as bearers of God's image (Gen 1:26-28) ought to regard themselves as God's and so render their whole being to God.[8] If the former is the right interpretation, Jesus encourages an understanding of Caesar's authority as delegated by God and enjoins submission to it. If the latter interpretation is right, Jesus does no more than point out the logical consequences of the questioners' commitment to the system of Caesar, while making it clear that submission to God is the absolute demand laid on all human beings. So, this interpretation would imply a critical attitude of Jesus toward the Roman Empire. However, this critical attitude still falls short of advocating resistance to Caesar's authority or overthrow of the Roman Empire. Later, Luke reports that the Sanhedrin accused Jesus before Pilate of "perverting our nation, and forbidding us to give tribute to Caesar, and saying that he himself is Christ a king" (Luke 23:2). But Luke represents Pilate as having told the Jewish accusers that he "did not find [Jesus] guilty of any of [their] charges against him" (23:14). Thus, it is clear that Luke did not understand Jesus' answer on the question of paying tax to Caesar as an unequivocal prohibition.

In his book *Jesus and Empire*, Richard A. Horsley devotes considerable space to Jesus' temple action and ensuing controversies. He sees the temple action (Mark 11:15-17) as Jesus' "forcible if not violent" protest against the high priestly oppression and exploitation of the people and his "symbolic prophetic demonstration" of God's judgment and destruction of the temple system.[9] Then Horsley examines the Marcan accounts of ensuing controversies with the high priests, scribes, and elders (Mark 11:27–12:44), especially the parable of the vineyard tenants (12:1-12), noting how Jesus

---

(Grand Rapids: Eerdmans, 1978), 736; cf. Bryan, *Render to Caesar*, 11-37, who also elaborates on the OT and Jewish teachings of submission to heathen political authority.

8. Cf. G. Bornkamm, *Jesus of Nazareth*, trans. I. and F. McLuskey and J. M. Robinson (New York: Harper & Row, 1960), 121-23; K. Wengst, *Pax Romana and the Peace of Jesus Christ*, trans. J. Bowden (Philadelphia: Fortress, 1987), 58-61.

9. R. A. Horsley, *Jesus and Empire: The Kingdom of God and the New World Disorder* (Minneapolis: Fortress, 2003), 92-93.

condemns the high priests, Sadducees, and scribes. Horsley stresses that we must appreciate Mark's placing Jesus' prophecy of destruction of the temple (13:1-2) at the conclusion of these confrontations of Jesus with those ruling groups in Jerusalem: "After acting out or pronouncing God's condemnation of Temple, high priests, Sadducees, and scribes, Jesus announces that the Temple (or Jerusalem as a whole), the basis of their power, is to be destroyed."[10] These confrontations lead to Jesus' trial before the Sanhedrin with the charge of having threatened to destroy the temple and build another temple "not made with hands" (14:58; cf. 15:29). Horsley sees the "another (temple) not made with hands" as meaning the renewed people of Israel. So, he highlights the way, in Jesus' prophecy, the destruction of the temple or a temple-state, "an imperial institution," "is juxtaposed with the building or renewal of the people, now free of the oppressive ruling institutions."[11] Then, saying that this Marcan account forms a striking parallel to Q 13:28-29, 34-35 and is supported by other Jesus traditions such as *Gospel of Thomas* 71 and John 2:14-22, Horsley appreciates the broadly historical foundation of the Marcan and Q accounts.[12]

However, there is a question about how relevant Jesus' temple action and words are to the subject of "Jesus and Empire." Although Horsley is eager to point to the fact that the priestly rulers of Jerusalem had imperial connections,[13] the accounts of Jesus' temple action and words in the Gospels do not indicate their imperial connections.[14] In the parable of the vineyard tenants (Mark 12:1-12 pars.) — which should be seen as an integral part of the pericope of the controversy with the Sanhedrin delegation, the high priests, the scribes, and the elders (Mark 11:27-33 pars.), indeed as

10. Horsley, *Jesus and Empire*, 95.

11. Horsley, *Jesus and Empire*, 97.

12. Horsley, *Jesus and Empire*, 97-98.

13. Horsley, *Jesus and Empire*, 86-87, 91.

14. Cf. W. H. Kelber, "Roman Imperialism and Early Christian Scribality," in *Orality, Literacy, and Colonialism in Antiquity*, ed. J. A. Draper, SemeiaSt 47 (Atlanta: Society of Biblical Literature, 2004), 139-40; Kelber also notes the absence of reflection on political concerns. It is interesting to note that N. T. Wright, who has lately made a common cause with Horsley in interpreting Paul's teaching as a conscious effort to counter the imperial ideology and cult of Rome, emphatically opposes Horsley's attempt to interpret Jesus as an anti-Roman revolutionary (see below). So, regarding Jesus' temple action, Wright presents an opposite view to Horsley's. See Wright, *Jesus and the Victory of God*, 420: one reason why Jesus prophesied and symbolically acted out the destruction of the temple was that it had become "the focal point of the hope of national liberation" and "the talisman of nationalist violence."

Jesus' concluding pronouncement at the end of that controversy[15] — it is suggested that the Jerusalem rulers are condemned for not rendering as tenant farmers "fruits" of the "vineyard" to its owner, that is, for not leading God's people Israel (cf. Isa 5:1-2; Ps 80:8-9) in such a way as for her to realize her divinely appointed ideals, in spite of God's repeated calls through his prophets and even his "beloved son" whom he has sent. The same point is made by the story of the cursing of the fig tree, which is narrated together with the episode of Jesus' temple action in Mark and Matthew (Mark 11:12-14, 20-25/Matt 21:18-22). But in all these there is no suggestion that the Jerusalem rulers are condemned because of their collusion with the Romans.

It is quite likely that with the new temple "not made with hands" Jesus designated the renewed people of God that he was creating or gathering. That people would be represented by the Twelve whom Jesus has appointed. The Twelve would rule over them (Luke 22:28-30/Matt 19:28), but they would do so through service rather than by lording it over them (Mark 10:42-45/Matt 20:25-28/Luke 22:25-27). So it is possible that one of the things Jesus had in mind in his prophecy of the destruction of the Jerusalem temple and the building of a new temple was abolishment of the present oppressive high priestly rule and its replacement by a new kind of rule by service. But still it is noteworthy that in the pericope of Mark 10:42-

---

15. For this view of the unity of Mark 11:27-33 and 12:1-12, see S. Kim, "Die Vollmacht Jesu und der Tempel — Der Sinn der 'Tempelreinigung' und der geschichtliche und theologische Kontext des Prozesses Jesu," an article accepted for *ANRW* in the Spring of 1985. While its publication was being delayed, it was translated into Korean and printed in my Korean volume of essays (S. Kim, *Jesus and Paul* [Seoul: Chammal, 1993], 119-65). Its content was also summarized in the beginning of its sequel article, S. Kim, "Jesus — The Son of God, the Stone, the Son of Man, and the Servant: The Role of Zechariah in the Self-Identification of Jesus," in *Tradition and Interpretation in the New Testament: Essays in Honor of E. Earle Ellis*, ed. G. F. Hawthorne and O. Betz (Grand Rapids: Eerdmans/Tübingen: Mohr Siebeck, 1987), 134-48. In the first article, I argued also for the view that the Synoptists have properly placed this episode of the controversy with the Sanhedrin delegation (Mark 11:27-33 + 12:1-12/Luke 20:1-8 + 9-19/Matt 21:23-27 + 33-46) in the context of Jesus' temple action (Mark 11:15-17/Matt 21:12-13/Luke 19:45-46). I interpreted that in the preliminary questioning by a Sanhedrin delegation in the wake of the temple demonstration Jesus reveals discreetly that he performed the sign act as the Son of God sent by God for the last call to Israel (Mark 12:6 pars.) and installed as such at the baptism of John the Baptist (Mark 11:29-30 pars.; cf. Mark 1:9-11 pars.), and that his sign act signified God would destroy the temple and he would build a new temple (the eschatological people of God) as the Son of God in fulfillment of Nathan's oracle (2 Sam 7:12-14), through his death and resurrection (Mark 12:6-8, 10 pars.).

45/Matt 20:25-28/Luke 22:25-27 Jesus contrasts the ideal of service among the new people of God with the oppressive rule of *Gentile* rulers, and not with that of the existing Jerusalem temple establishment. Therefore, it seems that one cannot be as confident as Horsley in asserting that in Jesus' temple demonstration and temple words Jesus targeted the *oppressive rule* of the priestly establishment in Jerusalem.

## No Call to Establish a Davidic Kingdom of Israel

Luke-Acts presents no call or effort to establish a literal Davidic kingdom of Israel either. In the Gospel, Luke does not depict Jesus as working to restore the Davidic dynasty as a political entity. Instead, he records the disappointment of the two disciples on the road to Emmaus that Jesus was crucified without accomplishing the redemption of Israel: "But we had hoped that he was the one to redeem Israel" (Luke 24:21). The disappointment must have been especially great with the Twelve, as their election gave them not only a general hope for national redemption but also a special, individual hope for their own ruling positions within the coming kingdom of Israel, a real hope that had led them to dispute about their rank within it (Luke 22:24-30/Mark 10:41-45/Matt 20:24-28). Therefore, according to Luke, when the resurrected Jesus appeared to them and taught them further about the Kingdom of God, they eagerly asked him, "Lord, will you at this time restore the kingdom to Israel?" (Acts 1:6). But Luke has Jesus brush the question aside and instead commission them for a worldwide mission with the promise of the Holy Spirit (Acts 1:7-8). Then, Luke has Jesus' Spirit-filled apostles themselves declare that God's exaltation of the crucified Jesus to his right hand to be both Lord and Christ *was* Jesus' enthronement on the throne of David in fulfillment of God's promise to David (Acts 2:29-40; 13:23, 32-34; cf. 2 Sam 7:12-14; Ps 2:7), and it represented the restoration of "David's fallen tent" (Acts 15:16). The Lord Jesus Christ is exalted to the right hand of God, but nowhere is he said to sit on a physical throne at Zion. And he reigns over and through his people, but nowhere is he shown to reign like an earthly king with his bureaucracy and military forces.

## Redefinition of God's People, Israel

According to Luke, after Jesus declared in his inaugural sermon his mission to preach the good news to the poor, redeem the captives, heal the blind, and so forth, Jesus suggested making the believing Gentiles such as the widow at Zarephath in Sidon (1 Kings 17:1-24) and Naaman the Syrian (2 Kings 5:1-14) also benefit from his redemption, while hinting at exclusion of the faithless Jews (Luke 4:16-30). A similar thought is expressed in Luke 13:22-30, in which Jesus warns his faithless Jewish hearers of their exclusion from the company of "Abraham and Isaac and Jacob and all the prophets" in the Kingdom of God while prophesying of Gentiles' participation in its banquet. This idea is further reinforced in the Parable of the Great Banquet (Luke 14:15-24). In the parable, Jesus warns the Jews like the lawyers and the Pharisees (cf. 14:3) who are unresponsive to his preaching that they will be excluded from the banquet in the Kingdom of God and that their places will be taken by Gentiles as well as the outcasts of the Jews. The Matthean version of the parable has in view only the outcasts of the Jews participating in the banquet (Matt 22:1-10). But in the Lucan version not only they, "the poor and maimed and blind and lame" who are brought in from "the streets and lanes of the city" (Luke 14:21), but also Gentiles who are gathered from "the highways and hedges" (14:23) are envisaged as taking part in the banquet of God's Kingdom.

It is well known that in his second volume, Acts, Luke describes this warning against the Jews and this promise for the Gentiles becoming reality in the course of the apostles' mission: many Jews accept the apostles' gospel of the Kingdom of God and the Lord Jesus Christ, but still the greater portion of Israel reject it and persecute the apostles, while ever more Gentiles come to accept the gospel and obtain salvation. According to Luke, faced with this situation, Paul and Barnabas declare to the Jews at Antioch of Pisidia: "Since you thrust [the word of God] from you, and judge yourselves unworthy of eternal life, behold, we turn to the Gentiles" (Acts 13:46), and Paul repeats such a declaration twice (18:5-6; 28:23-28). It is especially significant that in the book in which Luke describes the progress of the gospel from Jerusalem to the end of the earth (Acts 1:8) he makes it part of his climax (28:23-28) to affirm with the lengthy citation of Isa 6:9-10 the hardening of the hearts of the Jews against the gospel and to declare: "Let it be known to you then that this salvation of God has been sent to the Gentiles; they will listen" (Acts 28:28).

However, in Acts 15:13-21 Luke seems to explain the mission to the Gentiles and their inclusion in the people of God differently. There Luke has James declare at the apostolic council his support for Gentile mission and the inclusion of Gentiles in God's people by quoting Amos 9:11-12 (LXX), where God promises to return to "rebuild the fallen tent of David . . . , so that the rest of humankind may seek the Lord, and all the Gentiles upon whom my name has been called" (Acts 15:16-18). Here, through the mouth of James, Luke seems to suggest that now that the "rebuilding of the fallen tent of David" has been progressing with the resurrection and enthronement of the Davidic Messiah Jesus (cf. Acts 2:29-40; 13:23, 32-34), as well as the election of the Twelve as the representatives of the eschatological Israel and gathering of believing Jews into this body, "the rest of humankind [i.e., the Gentiles] may seek the Lord" and be incorporated into the eschatological people of God, being marked out as God's possession like the Jews (cf. Exod 19:5-6; Deut 14:2) when God's name is called upon them at baptism (cf. Jas 2:7).

The traditional view that Luke presents the scheme of the Jews' rejection of the gospel and self-exclusion from God's Kingdom issuing in the mission to the Gentiles usually results in affirming that Luke redefines God's people, Israel, in terms of the believing Jews and the believing Gentiles. However, on the basis of Acts 15:13-21 and some other related passages in Acts (e.g., 3:11-26), Jacob Jervell has strongly argued that Luke views the mission to the Gentiles and their inclusion in God's people as issuing from the successful "rebuilding of the fallen tent of David," the successfully completed mission to the Jews and restoration of the people of Israel, rather than the Jews' rejection of the gospel and their self-exclusion from God's eschatological people.[16] According to Jervell, Luke is thus faithful to the Jewish expectation that at the eschaton the promise to Israel would be fulfilled and consequently the Gentiles would be included in "the restored Israel."[17] This thesis entails the view that for Luke "the repentant, believing Jews [i.e., the Christian Jews] are the true Israel,"[18] "into which the Gentiles have now been incorporated,"[19] while the unrepentant Jews have "forfeited their right to belong to the people of God"[20] and so

16. J. Jervell, *Luke and the People of God: A New Look at Luke-Acts* (Minneapolis: Augsburg, 1972), 41-74.

17. Jervell, *Luke and the People of God,* 53.

18. Jervell, *Luke and the People of God,* 53, 64.

19. Jervell, *Luke and the People of God,* 64.

20. Jervell, *Luke and the People of God,* 54.

are "rejected for all times."[21] If so, "the true Israel" is now composed of the believing Jews and the believing Gentiles. Here we cannot be detained with a detailed examination of Jervell's exegesis and argument. It need only be pointed out that Jervell's view is practically the same as the traditional view as far as the composition of "the true Israel" or "the restored Israel" is concerned, in spite of his insistence that Luke reserves the designation "Israel" only for the Jewish nation or the "empirical" Israel and never uses it for the church composed of the believing Jews and Gentiles.[22]

No matter whether we follow the traditional view or Jervell's view, insofar as "the true Israel" or "the restored Israel" whom the Twelve rule (Luke 22:28-30) contains the believing Gentiles as well as the believing Jews, there is in it no room for Jewish nationalism. Therefore it is only natural for Luke to emphasize the universalistic intent of God: God "shows no partiality" among the nations (Acts 10:34-35) and seeks to create even out of the Gentiles "a people (λαόν) for his name" (15:14). Then, it is clear that with his repeated references to the redemption of "Israel" in the annunciation and infancy narratives (Luke 1–2) Luke did not envisage the restoration of the kingdom of the "empirical" Israel, which would replace the Roman Empire to rule over the nations of the world,[23] just as with his

21. Jervell, *Luke and the People of God*, 64.

22. Jervell, *Luke and the People of God*, 49-55. In some places his statements do not appear consistent: e.g., on p. 49 he says: "The 'empirical' Israel is composed of two groups, the repentant (i.e., Christian) and the obdurate. It is important for Luke to show that the Jewish Christian church is a part of Israel," but on p. 54 he says: "The unrepentant are therefore not excluded from the church which includes both Jews and Gentiles, but from the 'empirical' Israel which is made up of believing Jews." On p. 69 he says: ". . . Gentiles are saved without circumcision and belong from now on to Israel," but a little later on the same page he says: "The Gentiles, however, are not Israel, but have been associated with Israel, for which reason circumcision remains for Jews." For an evaluation of Jervell's thesis, cf. F. Bovon, *Luke the Theologian: Fifty-Five Years of Research (1950-2005)*, 2nd rev. ed. (Waco: Baylor University Press, 2006), 377-81, who says, "[Jervell's] views are perhaps less revolutionary than they seem" (p. 379). Cf. also C. K. Barrett, *A Critical and Exegetical Commentary on the Acts of the Apostles*, 2 vols., ICC (Edinburgh: T&T Clark, 1994, 1998), 1:77: ". . . the book [of Acts] as a whole makes clear that Israel, the people of God, is receiving a new definition."

23. The Hebrew version (MT) of Amos 9:12 reads: "that they [the house of David] may possess the remnant of Edom and all the nations upon whom my name has been called," whereas the Greek version (LXX) reads: "that the rest of humankind may seek the Lord, and all the Gentiles upon whom my name has been called." In Acts 15:17 Luke cites the LXX version. It is not certain whether he knows the MT version but deliberately rejects it because of its Jewish nationalistic and imperialistic overtone. If he does, his choice of the LXX version

references to Jesus' Davidic Sonship he did not envisage the restoration of the literal kingdom of David.

## Rejection of the Idea of Vengeance upon the Gentiles

In this vision of the redeemed Israel, there can be no room for a nationalistic idea of vengeance upon the Gentiles either. So, according to Luke, in Jesus' inaugural sermon (Luke 4:18-19) he cites Isa 61:1-2, omitting "the day of vengeance of our God" in Isa 61:2, which is elaborated on in the subsequent verses 5-6 with the idea of aliens and foreigners serving Israel as slaves. A similar omission is also observable in Jesus' answer to the question put by the envoys of John the Baptist, whether he was "the one who is to come" (Luke 7:18-23). Jesus points to his healings and exorcisms and answers: "Go and tell John what you have seen and heard: the blind receive their sight, the lame walk, lepers are cleansed, and the deaf hear, the dead are raised up, the poor have good news preached to them. And blessed is the one who takes no offense at me" (Luke 7:22-23). This reply is made up of echoes of several passages of Isaiah (chiefly 29:18-19; 35:5-6; 61:1) that speak of redemption of Israel from the exile. So Jesus gives himself out as the bearer of Israel's eschatological liberation and restoration. In Isa 35, the prophet presents the redemption of Israel as the result of God's coming to save his people, doing vengeance upon her enemies (Isa 35:4). It is noteworthy that in alluding to Isa 35:5-6 here Jesus takes up only the idea of salvation, omitting the connected idea of vengeance. This is consistent with what Jesus does in his inaugural sermon (Luke 4:18-19).[24] With his account

---

could be seen as part of his efforts to express his universalistic eschatological vision over against the Jewish nationalism that is prominent in some strands of the OT prophetic texts as well as in some Second-Temple Jewish literature (cf. the section immediately following).

24. In his intertextual reading of Luke-Acts, R. B. Hays appreciates that "Luke's scriptural allusions frequently depend upon the literary trope of *metalepsis,* a rhetorical and poetic device in which one text alludes to an earlier text in a way that evokes resonances of the earlier text beyond those explicitly cited," and so suggests that "in order to grasp the force of the intertextual reference, the reader must recover the unstated or suppressed correspondences between the two texts" (R. B. Hays, "The Liberation of Israel in Luke-Acts: Intertextual Readings as Resistance," paper presented at Fuller Theological Seminary, Pasadena, Calif., Jan. 26, 2006, 6). Then he wonders whether in Jesus' allusion to Isa 35:5 here we should also hear its preceding verse Isa 35:4 metaleptically: "Be strong, do not fear! *Here is your God. . . . He will come and save you.*" Discerning the metalepsis here, he argues that Luke

of how Jesus rejected his disciples' suggestion to take vengeance upon the unwelcoming Samaritans, the traditional enemies of Israel (Luke 9:51-56), Luke shows Jesus actualizing his own implicit teaching of nonvengeance upon Gentile enemies.

This rejection of the nationalistic conception of vengeance upon Gentile enemies is also consistent with Jesus' teachings on love and forgiveness, which require even forgiving and loving enemies (Luke 6:27-36/Matt 5:38-48; Luke 6:37-42/Matt 7:1-5). Further, it is consistent with Jesus' teaching about authority and lordship befitting the Kingdom of God over against the pagan conception, which we have examined above (Luke 22:24-26 pars.). Seen together with these teachings — i.e., Jesus' rejection of the idea of vengeance upon Gentile enemies, his teachings on forgiveness and love, and his definition of lordship in the Kingdom of God in terms of humble service — the Lucan contrast between Jesus and Caesar in the *inclusio* of Luke 2:1-14 and Acts 28:30-31 makes it clear that Jesus' Messiahship/Lordship is not a militaristic one like that of Caesar, and his peace and salvation is not a product of subjugation of other nations like that of the Roman Empire, but is rather a fruit of his humble service for humankind symbolized by the manger and the cross. So Jesus brings salvation to Israel not in the Roman way, i.e., not by doing vengeance upon her enemy, the Roman Empire, or subjugating her militarily to Israel, but in the way of the Kingdom of God: forgiveness and love.

## Criticism of Aspirations for a Violent Revolution

This way of Jesus was contradictory not only to the Roman way, but also to the way of some of the Jewish revolutionaries around his time. In order to

---

identifies Jesus, "the one who is to come [in the name of the Lord]" (an echo of Ps 118:26), with the God of Israel (Isa 35:4) (pp. 12-14). But this would be a curious *metaleptic* effect for Luke to expect of his readers. For Isa 35:4 reads: "Be strong, fear not! Behold, your God *will come with vengeance, with the recompense of God. He will come and save you.*" Would Luke expect his readers to get only the idea of God's coming to save Israel without the concomitant idea of his vengeance on Israel's enemies? The cases of Luke 4:18-19 and 7:23 which we are examining here demonstrate the need to substantiate critically the presence of *metalepsis* in any given text against the possibility of deliberate omission and even of atomistic allusion. Cf. also Acts 2:17-21: citing Joel 2:28-32 (3:1-5 MT), Peter also leaves out the idea of vengeance upon Gentile enemies.

understand the Jesus movement as one of the resistance or revolutionary movements against Rome and her Jewish client rulers (the Herodians and the high-priestly families), Richard Horsley paints as its background the resistance and revolutionary movements of the Galilean and Judean people, from the Jewish revolt against Herod's appointment by Rome as "king of the Judeans" in 40 B.C. to the Jewish War in A.D. 66-77 and the rebellion of Simon bar Kokhba in A.D. 132-135. Horsley points out that such resistance to alien rule and domestic oppression belonged to the very essence of Israel's tradition from the Exodus, through the prophetic movements, to the Maccabean revolt (167-164 B.C.). Drawing richly from Josephus's works, *Jewish War* and *Jewish Antiquities,* Horsley describes various types of resistance and revolutionary movements. Since Horsley is one of the leading experts on the Jewish resistance movements during the Roman occupation and has insisted, more than anybody else, on understanding Jesus in terms of the resistance movements, we will briefly summarize his description of those movements in his book *Jesus and Empire* (35-54), which is itself a brief summary of the extensive discussion in his *Jesus and the Spiral of Violence: Popular Jewish Resistance in Roman Palestine* (28-145).[25]

The first type is "the scribal resistance" movement of what Josephus calls "the fourth philosophy." It was led by Judas of Gamla and Saddok the Pharisee in A.D. 6 against the Roman census for tax assessment, since they regarded paying tributes to Caesar as a violation of Israel's duty to worship only God as their Lord, as well as enslavement to the Roman emperor. The second type that Horsley describes is the *Sicarii,* the "dagger-men," another scribal resistance movement that arose during the 50s in reaction to the brutal repressions of Roman governors against the insurgents (λῃσταί, "bandits") among the Judean and Galilean peasants suffering from famine in the late 40s. With their daggers *(sica)* they assassinated high priests and other wealthy people for their collaboration with Roman rule and exploitation of the people. Horsley terms the third type "popular resistance movements" and illustrates them with the riot in the temple at the Passover of 4 B.C. against Archelaus trying to succeed his father Herod, the riot at another Passover during the governorship of Cumanus (A.D. 48-52), the demonstration against Pilate's introduction in Jerusalem of the Roman army standards with Caesar's image, and the Galilean peasants' "labor

---

25. *Jesus and the Spiral of Violence: Popular Jewish Resistance in Roman Palestine* (San Francisco: Harper & Row, 1987; repr. Minneapolis: Fortress, 1993).

strike" against Petronius's legions advancing to Jerusalem to set up the image of Gaius (Caligula) in the temple there (A.D. 40). Then, as the fourth type, Horsley describes the three peasant revolts that broke out in Galilee, Judea, and Perea upon the death of Herod (4 B.C.) and labels them "popular prophetic and messianic movements" because they were led respectively by Judas, Athronges, and Simon, all acclaimed by their followers as "king." They had two common goals: to liberate the people from Roman and Herodian rule and to establish social-economic justice. The messianic movement of Simon bar Giora, which formed the largest fighting force during the Roman siege of Jerusalem in A.D. 69-70, as well as the Simon bar Kokhba revolt (A.D. 132-135) also belonged to this type. Finally, as the fifth type, Horsley describes "popular prophetic movements" of such prophets as Theudas, who led his followers to the River Jordan in order to reenact the Exodus, and the Egyptian Jewish prophet who took his followers to the Mount of Olives in reenactment of the fall of Jericho.

Then Horsley surveys the Q and Marcan materials and defines Jesus' work in terms of two themes: pronouncement of God's judgment on the Roman and Jewish rulers[26] and "a mission of social renewal among subject peoples."[27] Horsley concludes his study of the first theme with this affirmation:

> In all of these respects, Jesus of Nazareth belongs in the same context with and stands shoulder to shoulder with these other leaders of movements among the Judean and Galilean people, and pursues the same general agenda in parallel paths: independence from Roman imperial rule so that the people can again be empowered to renew their traditional way of life under the rule of God.[28]

He then opens his study of the second theme with this summary statement:

> Convinced that Roman rulers and their Herodian and high-priestly clients had been condemned by God, . . . Jesus acted to heal the effects of empire and to summon people to rebuild their community life. In the conviction that the kingdom of God was at hand, he pressed a program

26. Horsley, *Jesus and Empire,* 79-104.
27. Horsley, *Jesus and Empire,* 105-28.
28. Horsley, *Jesus and Empire,* 104.

of social revolution to reestablish just egalitarian and mutually support-
ive social-economic relations in the village communities that constituted the basic form of the people's life.[29]

Horsley calls this "program of social revolution" "Jesus' alternative to the
Roman imperial order."[30] Thus, he presents the Jesus movement as one of
the many revolutionary movements of his times. We cannot examine here
the details of his interpretation of Jesus' teachings and deeds. With a critical examination of his interpretation of only some relevant Gospel material (see below), we will have to be content with suggesting that his interpretation of the Jesus movement as a whole is not convincing.

However, it is noteworthy for our present purpose that in this presentation Horsley emphasizes only Jesus' similarities with his contemporary revolutionaries but does not discuss his differences from them.[31] In fact, Horsley underscores his objection to the traditional presentation of Jesus as a
pacifist who advocated enemy love (Matt 5:38-48/Luke 6:27-36) in contrast
to "the Zealots" who supposedly advocated a violent revolt against Rome
out of their zeal for the Law and Israel.[32] According to him, this traditional
concept of "the Zealots" is only an arbitrary modern construct out of disparate elements of the Jewish resistance movements,[33] and the historically real
Zealots were a band of peasant brigands who fled from the advancing Roman army in northwest Judea into the fortress city of Jerusalem in the winter of 67-68 and took part in the Jewish War as a rival party to the high-

29. Horsley, *Jesus and Empire*, 105.
30. Horsley, *Jesus and Empire*, 126.
31. See also Horsley's conclusion in *Jesus and the Spiral of Violence*, 318-26; and Horsley,
"'By the Finger of God': Jesus and Imperial Violence," in *Violence in the New Testament*, ed.
S. Matthews and E. L. Gibson (New York and London: T&T Clark, 2005), 52-53.
32. Horsley, *Jesus and the Spiral of Violence*, 149, 318-19.
33. Horsley, *Jesus and the Spiral of Violence*, 61, 121-29; "By the Finger of God," 52-53.
This view is based on his little regard for the continuity of the tradition of "zeal" or the
"zealous" holy war for God, the Torah, and Israel among the various resistance groups from
the middle of the first century B.C. to the Jewish War (A.D. 66-70) or the Bar Kokhba revolt
(A.D. 132-135) — the tradition that was powerfully shaped by the Maccabean revolt (167-164
B.C.) after the examples of Phinehas (Num 25) and Elijah (1 Kings 18:36-40; 19:10-18). Cf.
M. Hengel, *The Zealots: Investigations into the Jewish Freedom Movement in the Period from
Herod I until 70 A.D.*, trans. D. Smith (Edinburgh: T&T Clark, 1989; ET of *Die Zeloten: Unter-
suchungen zur jüdischen Freiheitsbewegung in der Zeit von Herodes I. bis 70 n. Chr.*, 2nd ed.
[Leiden: Brill, 1976]).

priestly government.[34] Furthermore, according to Horsley, there was in Palestine no movement of violent opposition to Rome at the time of Jesus so that the issue of violent or nonviolent resistance was not posed to him.[35] Finally, Horsley asserts that Jesus' teaching of enemy love was meant to be practiced within the Jewish community rather than in relationship to the Romans.[36] With these arguments, Horsley in effect makes it unnecessary to inquire whether there was any difference between Jesus and his contemporary revolutionaries, let alone whether he criticized them.

However, even while granting that the Zealots themselves emerged as a group clearly so identified only in the 60s A.D., N. T. Wright strongly counters Horsley's implicit thesis that it emerged only as the result of a group of (previously peaceful?) "social bandits" suddenly turning to become a violent military force in the war of A.D. 66-70. Thus, Wright rejects the idea that "serious violent revolution was not on the agenda in the 20s of the first century A.D.," or that therefore "Jesus could not have been speaking of, or to, such violent movements."[37]

In fact, it is an essential element of Wright's central thesis about Jesus' whole Kingdom ministry that Jesus was severely critical of his contemporaries' aspirations for a violent revolution.[38] According to him, Jesus warned Israel of failing to be true to their divine vocation to be the light to the nations (Matt 5:14-15/Mark 4:21/Luke 8:16) and of turning, instead, to nationalistic exclusivism.[39] For Jesus, the revolutionaries' nationalistic

---

34. Horsley, *Jesus and the Spiral of Violence*, 56-57.

35. Horsley, *Jesus and the Spiral of Violence*, 56-57.

36. Horsley, *Jesus and the Spiral of Violence*, 255-73, 318.

37. Wright, *Jesus and the Victory of God*, 155-60 (quotations pp. 157, 159).

38. Wright, *Jesus and the Victory of God*, 446-50, passim. Cf. also G. Theissen, "The Political Dimension of Jesus' Activities," in *The Social Setting of Jesus and the Gospels*, ed. W. Stegemann, B. J. Malina, and G. Theissen (Minneapolis: Fortress, 2002), 233-35, who shows Jesus' rejection of "the politics of physical force" in reference not only to his teaching about "enemy love" (see below, n. 42), but also to the three elements in the Jesus tradition that are often taken for the contrary view: Simon the Zealot as a disciple of Jesus (Luke 6:15; Acts 1:13; "If one is called 'the Zealot,' we may equally be sure that the others were not Zealots" [p. 234]), two swords as part of Jesus' revised directive for missionary equipment (Luke 22:35-38; "Nobody can stir up a rebellion with two swords" [p. 235]), and Jesus' temple action (Luke 19:45-46/Mark 11:15-17/Matt 21:12-13/John 2:13-16; not "an attempt to incite a political revolt" but "a prophetic symbolic action" for the destruction of this temple and building a new temple [p. 235]).

39. Wright, *Jesus and the Victory of God*, 595-96.

aspirations and military tactics were as much compromises with paganism as was the Jewish rulers' collusion with the Romans,[40] and indeed as much Satanic as the Roman oppression, insofar as they employed the same worldly method as did the latter.[41] So he offered the way of God's Kingdom — the way of love (Mark 12:30-31 pars.), even the enemy love of turning the other cheek and going the second mile (Matt 5:38-48/Luke 6:27-36).[42] But his people were rejecting his message of peace and his way of making peace (Luke 19:41-44) and were pursuing the confrontation course with Rome, with false assurance about the temple as a "talisman" of national inviolability, as in the days of Jeremiah (Mark 11:15-17/Matt 21:12-13/Luke 19:45-46). Therefore, Jesus warned Israel of God's impending judgment in the form of Rome's devastation, as Jeremiah warned Judah of God's judgment through Babylon's devastation (Mark 13/Matt 24; Luke 21).[43] And as the messianic representative of Israel, Jesus was determined to be himself what Israel was called to be but was failing to be, and to do what she ought to do but was failing to do.[44] This involved the messianic battle that he had to fight — not against Rome, as his contemporaries wanted and some revolutionaries eagerly sought, but rather against Satan himself (or evil itself) whom he saw standing behind both the Roman and the Jewish forces ranged against him.[45] And he was to fight the battle in the way he had urged Israel to fight, i.e., turning the other cheek and going the second mile:

> he was to expose his whole body to the Roman lash, and to set off on a forced march with the load the soldiers gave him to carry. And, despite all the overtones of the Maccabean martyrs which clustered around the event, as he went to his death he seems not to have responded to his pagan torturers in the time-honoured manner. Instead of hurling insults

40. Wright, *Jesus and the Victory of God,* 446-50, 596.

41. Wright, *Jesus and the Victory of God,* 595-96, 605, 608-9.

42. Wright, *Jesus and the Victory of God,* 595, 607. See also Theissen, "The Political Dimension of Jesus' Activities," 233-34, who, against Horsley, argues for the view that the injunction for enemy love has in view national enemies as well as personal enemies. Cf. also Wengst, *Pax Romana,* 68-72.

43. Wright, *Jesus and the Victory of God,* 413-28, 569-70, passim.

44. Wright, *Jesus and the Victory of God,* 595-96, 609.

45. Wright, *Jesus and the Victory of God,* 605; see 446-74 for Jesus' redefinition of the real enemy of God's people, Israel, as Satan rather than Rome, and for his battle with Satan. See pp. 124-32 below.

and threats at them, he suffered either in silence or with words of forgiveness; a startling innovation into the martyr-tradition.[46]

Jesus was convinced that through his faithfulness to his vocation unto the death on the cross "Yahweh would defeat evil, bringing the kingdom to birth,"[47] and would vindicate him.[48]

Wright is able to muster a vast amount of Gospel material to present this quite coherent picture of Jesus. For our present purpose, it is noteworthy that Wright thinks especially the material in the whole swath of Luke 11–19 supports his thesis.[49] Of course, his interpretation of several passages may be disputed. However, at least his presentation of Jesus' critique of the way of violent revolution and his warning of God's judgment through Rome is on the whole plausible. Our discussion in the preceding sections on the total absence of any call from Jesus for overthrow of the Roman rule and on Jesus' rejection of Jewish nationalism and the idea of vengeance upon the Gentiles clearly supports this picture of Jesus rather than the one that Horsley paints.[50]

## Jesus Was Declared Innocent by Pilate

With regard to Luke's representation of Jesus' attitude to the Roman rule and the Jewish revolutionaries, Werner H. Kelber presents similar views to those of Wright. In analyzing Mark's accounts of Jesus' dealings with the temple,

---

46. Wright, *Jesus and the Victory of God*, 607. Wright adds: "[This startling innovation] sent echoes across early Christianity in such a way as to be, I suggest, inexplicable unless they are substantially historical."

47. Wright, *Jesus and the Victory of God*, 609.

48. Wright, *Jesus and the Victory of God*, 595.

49. Wright, *Jesus and the Victory of God*, 330-33.

50. S. Freyne, who has discounted the picture of a Galilee engulfed by revolutionary fervor (*Galilee from Alexander the Great to Hadrian, 323 B.C.E. to 135 C.E.: A Study of Second Temple Judaism*, SJCA 5 [Wilmington, Del.: M. Glazier/Notre Dame, Ind.: University of Notre Dame Press, 1980], 208-55), also objects to depicting Jesus as a political revolutionary. According to him, inspired by the traditions of the "servant of Yahweh" group of Isa 40–66 and the *maskilim* group of Daniel, Jesus sought a path to overcoming the Herodian and Roman abuses and restoring Israel that was different from that of the political revolutionaries of first-century Palestine, who were inspired by "the triumphant Zion ideology" (S. Freyne, *Jesus, a Jewish Galilean: A New Reading of the Jesus-Story* [London and New York: T&T Clark International, 2004], 122-70, esp. 135-36).

Kelber notes how Mark relates Jesus' temple demonstration and his verbal condemnation to the abuse of its religious significance ("a house of prayer for all nations," Mark 11:17) but not to its political perversion as the epicenter of the high priestly clients of Rome (Mark 11:15-17), and how Mark presents Jesus as predicting the destruction of the temple and Jerusalem but without any criticism of Rome (Mark 13:1-37).[51] The same points can be made also for Lucan accounts of Jesus' temple demonstration (Luke 19:45-46) and his prophecies about the destruction of Jerusalem (Luke 21:5-36). So Kelber notes how in alluding several times to the Roman siege and destruction of Jerusalem (Luke 13:34-35; 19:41-44; 21:20-24; 23:27-31), the Lucan Jesus issues no complaint about Roman brutalities but criticizes only Jerusalem or the Jewish nation for having "habitually killed the prophets (13:34) and missed the appropriate time *(kairos)* of God's visitation (19:44)."[52]

In the passion narrative, Kelber sees Luke "develop[ing] the *apologia Romana,* already in existence since Mark, into a programmatic theme."[53] So, over against the Sanhedrin's accusation of Jesus as a political rebel (Luke 23:2: "We found this man perverting our nation, and forbidding us to give tribute to Caesar, and saying that he himself is the Messiah, a king"), Luke has Pilate declare three times that Jesus was innocent (23:4, 14, 22). With this, Luke makes it clear that Pilate's condemnation of Jesus was a miscarriage of justice committed under Jewish pressure. Kelber further observes how Luke omits the Marcan accounts of torture of Jesus by Pilate (Mark 15:15/Matt 27:26) and by the Roman soldiers (Mark 15:17-20/Matt 27:28-31/John 19:2-3), reporting only his torture by the Jewish guards in the courtyard of the high priest (Luke 22:63-65/Mark 14:65/Matt 26:67-68).[54] Then, Kelber sees Luke's *apologia Romana* climaxing with the centurion's pronouncement of Jesus' innocence at the foot of the cross (Luke 23:47).[55] Although Kelber brings all these data under the rubric of *apologia Romana,* he does not lose sight of the significance that through his account of Jesus' trial before Pilate Luke effectively counters the suspicion of political culpability that Jesus' crucifixion could easily raise in the minds of a Roman audience.[56] So, in the repeated declarations of Jesus' innocence by

51. Kelber, "Roman Imperialism and Early Christian Scribality," 139-40.
52. Kelber, "Roman Imperialism and Early Christian Scribality," 145.
53. Kelber, "Roman Imperialism and Early Christian Scribality," 145.
54. Kelber, "Roman Imperialism and Early Christian Scribality," 146.
55. Kelber, "Roman Imperialism and Early Christian Scribality," 146.
56. Kelber, "Roman Imperialism and Early Christian Scribality," 147.

the Roman governor Pilate and the centurion, we should also see Luke's concern for *apologia* for Jesus and Christianity to the Roman Empire. At any rate, it is reasonable to conclude with Kelber that "in effect, and probably in intention, Luke makes a case for the compatibility of Christianity with Rome."[57] Our discussions in the preceding sections lead us to believe that for this Luke has a good historical foundation in the actual ministry of Jesus. Even if this were not so, the very fact that one can speak of Lucan concerns of *apologia,* for Rome and for Christianity, argues against any attempt to see Luke as presenting Jesus as a messianic revolutionary who sought to liberate Israel from the Roman imperial rule.

Now, we may summarize the six points that we have observed so far: (1) Jesus issued no call for overthrowing the yoke of the Roman Empire; (2) there is no idea of a literal restoration of the kingdom of David; (3) the Israel that Jesus the Messiah has redeemed is redefined in terms of the eschatological people of God made up of the Jews and Gentiles who believe in the Lord Jesus; (4) Jesus rejected the nationalistic idea of vengeance upon the Gentiles, but instead taught his lordship of service as well as the requirements of forgiveness and love; (5) Jesus rejected the aspirations for a violent revolution and lamented over the Jews' rejection of his way of peace; and (6) even Pilate confirmed Jesus' innocence of political charges, although he crucified him under pressure from the Jews. These points make it clear why for Luke preaching the gospel of Jesus the Messiah is no treason against Caesar.[58]

---

57. Kelber, "Roman Imperialism and Early Christian Scribality," 147.

58. While acknowledging that Luke never presents Jesus as challenging the Roman rule, Cassidy still maintains that Jesus' care for the sick and poor, his stress on humility and service, his call for the rich to share their surplus possessions, and his rejection of the use of the sword provided a "basis for conflict" with the Roman rule. Cassidy says it is an "irony" of the Lucan story that "Pilate, the guardian and administrator of Roman rule for Judea, did not see anything in Jesus that was dangerous to Roman interests" (*Society and Politics*, 17). But it appears that not the Lucan story but Cassidy's own story presents an "irony." Which despot today or in history would condemn Jesus as a political criminal for doing such things as Cassidy summarizes, unless the despot is under pressure to frame him arbitrarily?

## 9. Jesus' Redemption: It Is a Deliverance from the Kingdom of Satan

Luke's positive presentation of Jesus' "redemption" — or better, "salvation"[1] — leads to the same conclusion, that the gospel is not treason against Caesar. For although Luke repeatedly emphasizes that Jesus the Davidic Messiah has come to redeem Israel, as we have seen, he does not actually present Jesus' redemptive work in terms of altering the political, economic, and social structures of the day to bring Israel political freedom, economic prosperity, and social justice. Rather, he presents it in terms of healing and exorcism, bringing relief for the poor and oppressed; forgiveness, restoration, and transformation of sinners; formation of a new community of the righteous, and the like.

### Exorcism and Healing of the Sick

Perhaps *Jesus' reply to the envoys of John the Baptist (Luke 7:18-23)* illustrates this point the best. Asked whether he is the Messiah who is to come, Jesus points to his healings and exorcisms. In giving his reply with words drawn from Isa 29:18-19; 35:5-6; 61:1, prophecies about Israel's deliverance and restoration, Jesus assures John's envoys that he is indeed doing the work of the Messiah according to those prophecies. But by pointing, as proof of his redemptive work, to his healing of the physically sick as well as his deliverance

---

1. Note Luke's frequent use of σωτήρ (Luke 1:47; 2:11; Acts 5:31; 13:23), σωτηρία (Luke 1:69, 71, 77; 19:9; Acts 4:12; 7:25; 13:26; 16:17; 27:34), σωτήριον (Luke 2:30; 3:6; Acts 28:28); σῴζω (x17).

of those possessed by evil spirits, he characterizes his redemptive work primarily in terms of deliverance from physical and spiritual ailments. Here he gives the impression of taking "the blind," "the lame," "lepers," and "the deaf" of the Isaianic prophecies more literally than metaphorically.[2] But the similar list of the handicapped people to be brought into the banquet of the Kingdom of God in the parable of the great banquet (Luke 14:15-24) indicates that Luke understands Jesus' (literal) healings of the variously sick people as symbolic of his eschatological realization in the Kingdom of God of the paradisial conditions that were prefigured during the restoration of the Babylonian exiles according to the Isaianic prophecies.[3]

Since Luke presents Jesus' inaugural sermon in the synagogue of Nazareth as a statement of Jesus' messianic program (Luke 4:18-19), it is natural to think that Luke would see this reply of Jesus to John's envoys in connection with Jesus' inaugural sermon. As both passages echo Isa 61:1, they share the ideas of giving sight to the blind and preaching good news to the poor.[4] But while Jesus' inaugural sermon lists further liberation of the captives and the oppressed and proclamation of the jubilee year as his messianic saving activities, Jesus' reply to John's envoys lists further exorcisms and healings.

> 4:18-19: The Spirit of the Lord is upon me, because he has anointed me to bring good news to the poor. He has sent me to proclaim release to the captives and recovery of sight to the blind, to let the oppressed go free, to proclaim the year of the Lord's favor.

> 7:22: Go and tell John what you have seen and heard: the blind receive their sight, the lame walk, the lepers are cleansed, the deaf hear, the dead are raised, the poor have good news brought to them.

So, a comparison of the two passages raises the question whether Luke identifies Jesus' exorcisms and healings presented as his messianic saving

2. Cf. I. H. Marshall, *Luke: Historian and Theologian,* enlarged ed. (Grand Rapids: Zondervan, 1989; repr. New Testament Profiles; Downers Grove, Ill.: InterVarsity Press, 1998), 121-22.

3. Marshall, *Luke: Historian and Theologian,* 126, 139. Cf. N. T. Wright, *Jesus and the Victory of God,* vol. 2 of *Christian Origins and the Question of God* (Minneapolis: Fortress, 1996), 242-43.

4. See below, pp. 139-47, for discussion about how Luke understands Jesus' messianic work of bringing the good news to the poor.

activities for John the Baptist with the acts of liberation that Jesus promised in his messianic program statement in his inaugural sermon.

At any rate, in *the Beelzebul controversy (Luke 11:14-23 pars.)*, Luke again shows Jesus concentrating his actualization/demonstration of the salvation of God's Kingdom on exorcism and healing. Since Jesus casts out demons and heals the sick (like the case of his exorcising and healing a dumb person) by "the finger of God," those activities demonstrate the presence of the saving reign of God (Luke 11:20). For our present discussion, the pericope contains two important points. First, it presents healing from spiritual and physical illness as the salvation of the Kingdom of God that Jesus has brought in. As if wanting to illustrate this point of the Beelzebul controversy as well as Jesus' reply to the envoys of John the Baptist, Luke narrates many accounts of Jesus' healing activities: giving sight to the blind (Luke 18:35-43), restoring the lame (Luke 5:17-26; cf. Acts 3:1-10; 8:7; 14:8-10), cleansing lepers (Luke 5:12-16; 17:11-19), healing the dumb (Luke 11:14), raising the dead (Luke 7:11-17; 8:40-56), and exorcism (Luke 8:26-39; 9:37-43). All these episodes of Jesus' healing activities repeatedly demonstrate the nature of salvation in the Kingdom of God that Jesus has brought.

The second point from the Beelzebul controversy is that Jesus' exorcism and healing is his liberation of the demon-possessed and sick people from the captivity of the kingdom of Satan. This is suggested by Jesus' language of the "kingdom" or "house" of Satan and his explanation of his exorcism and healing in terms of invading Satan's "palace," attacking and overpowering him, and plundering his goods (Luke 11:17-18, 21-22). It is significant that with the phrase "the finger of God" (Luke 11:20; cf. "the Spirit of God" in Matt 12:28) Jesus deliberately evokes the Exodus narrative — Moses' redemption of Israel from Egypt by "the finger of God" (Exod 8:19 [MT 15]; cf. also the "hand" of God in Exod 7:4-5; 9:3, 15; 15:6, 12) — and yet applies it not to a political redemption from the Roman Empire as from Egypt but to redemption from the kingdom of Satan.

Richard Horsley offers an exactly opposite interpretation. According to him, the political language used for Satan's "kingdom" and for Jesus' exorcism as well as the evocation of the Exodus narrative should lead us to interpret Jesus' exorcisms as meaning that Jesus was bringing about the end of the imperialistic domination of Rome.[5] According to Horsley, Gali-

5. R. A. Horsley, *Jesus and Empire: The Kingdom of God and the New World Disorder* (Minneapolis: Fortress, 2003), 101. S. Freyne, *Jesus, a Jewish Galilean: A New Reading of the*

lean peasants, as well as Qumran scribes, viewed the world as caught in a struggle between God and Satan and understood their plight under the Roman oppression as due to possession by the demonic forces of Satan. So demon possession was a "mystifying" way of explaining "the real, concrete forces that were oppressing them, the imperial Roman conquests, governors, and troops," and it was also a "self-protective explanation" of those forces because "it kept them [the Jewish peasants] from launching a suicidal revolt that would likely have evoked Roman retaliation."[6] As such, it was "the popular Galilean way of handling their subjugation to foreign forces."[7] Horsley claims that we should interpret Jesus' exorcisms in the context of this belief. So, for him, the Beelzebul discourses (Mark 3:22-27; Matt 12:22-30/Luke 11:14-23) declare that in Jesus' exorcisms God is accomplishing a victory over Satan, which, in practical terms, means his overcoming Roman rule.[8]

For his theory of demon possession, Horsley appeals to the Qumranites' belief in "the Roman armies" as "the human political forces under the power of the Prince of Darkness."[9] He thinks that the same belief is reflected in the story of the Gerasene demoniac (Mark 5:1-20/Luke 8:26-39; cf. Matt 8:28-34), where the demoniac gives his name as "legion." From this name "legion," as well as a series of words in the story that could be taken as military metaphors ("dismissed," "troop," and "charge"), Horsley concludes that "in Jesus' exorcisms . . . the demons were identified as Roman legions,"[10] that "in Jesus' exorcisms those Roman soldiers, Legion, were being sent to their destruction in the [Mediterranean] sea," just as Pharaoh's armies "drowned in the Reed Sea" at the Exodus.[11]

---

*Jesus-Story* (London and New York: T&T Clark International, 2004), 147-49, also interprets the Beelzebul controversy politically and comes to the conclusion that "Jesus' exorcisms were a serious challenge to the prevailing norms and values concerning power and control in Herodian Galilee, and those of the Roman overlords who supported those norms" (p. 148). But his arguments show some confusion in understanding the imagery of the pericope and share some of the problems with Horsley's interpretation that are pointed out here.

6. Horsley, *Jesus and Empire*, 101.

7. Horsley, *Jesus and Empire*, 101-2.

8. Horsley, *Jesus and Empire*, 101-2.

9. Horsley, *Jesus and Empire*, 101-2 (quotation p. 102).

10. Horsley, *Jesus and Empire*, 100-102 (quotation p. 102).

11. Horsley, *Jesus and Empire*, 101. For a similar interpretation, cf. K. Wengst, *Pax Romana and the Peace of Jesus Christ*, trans. J. Bowden (Philadelphia: Fortress, 1987), 65-66, who refers

However, quite besides the fact that the exorcism of the Gerasene demoniac is the only place in the entire Gospel tradition where exorcism evokes an association of the Roman military,[12] and the fact that this episode is located in the region of the Gentile Gerasenes rather than in a region of the Jews,[13] there is a serious logical difficulty in Horsley's interpretation: if demon possession was a "self-protective" explanation of subjugating forces that the Jews developed to keep from launching a suicidal revolt against the Romans, what was then the meaning of Jesus' exorcising the demon of "legion" and making the demoniac return to "his right mind" (Mark 5:15/Luke 8:35)? Horsley concentrates on the imagery of the destruction of the "legion" demon(s), but does not pay much attention to the man healed.[14] On Horsley's scheme, should we not say that Jesus blew his cover of the self-protective explanation for him to face the reality of the Roman legions and disclosed that the moment the Jews like the Qumranites had been waiting for — the moment of God's eschatological battle with Belial in which God's people, the sons of light, should join on

---

to G. Theissen, *The Miracle Stories of the Early Christian Tradition,* ed. J. Riches, trans. F. McDonagh, SNTW (Edinburgh: T&T Clark/Philadelphia: Fortress, 1983), 255. Horsley further elaborates on his theory of demon possession and on his interpretations of the Beelzebul controversy and the healing of the Gerasene demoniac in Horsley, "'By the Finger of God': Jesus and Imperial Violence," in *Violence in the New Testament,* ed. S. Matthews and E. L. Gibson (New York and London: T&T Clark, 2005), 63-68, appealing to the work of the psychiatrist Frantz Fanon and treating the story of the Gerasene demoniac almost as an allegory.

12. So C. Bryan, *Render to Caesar: Jesus, the Early Church, and the Roman Superpower* (Oxford: Oxford University Press, 2005), 48. In fact, R. H. Gundry, *Mark: A Commentary on His Apology for the Cross* (Grand Rapids: Eerdmans, 1993), 260, objects to seeing a "covert reference to the occupation of Palestine by Roman legions" even in our passage, pointing out that the text (Mark 5:9/Luke 8:30) itself "explicitly associates Legion with numerousness." R. D. Aus, *My Name Is "Legion": Palestinian Judaic Traditions in Mark 5:1-20 and Other Gospel Texts,* Studies in Judaism (Lanham, Md.: University Press of America, 2003), 15-17, shows that the Latin word *legio* was often used as a loan word in Hebrew and Aramaic simply for a great number — e.g., legions of angels (e.g., in interpretation of Ps 91:7; *Midrash on Psalms* 17.8 on Ps 17:8), a "legion of olives" (*Genesis Rabbah Bereshith* 20.6 on Gen 3:16) — as well as a reference to Roman troops.

13. As Gundry (*Mark,* 260) hints, it would indeed be most extraordinary that with their explicit location of Jesus' exorcism of the Legion demon(s) in the region of the Gentile Gerasenes, Mark and Luke wanted to convey the sense of Jesus' liberation of the *Jews* from Roman legions.

14. Cf. Bryan, *Render to Caesar,* 48: in the story "the only thing that we see Jesus actually *doing* is healing the man, restoring him to 'his right mind' (Mark 5.15)" (italics original).

the side of God against Kittim, the sons of darkness (cf. 1QM) — had at last arrived? With his exorcisms, was Jesus then convincing the Jews that he or God was in the process of destroying the oppressive Roman forces, so that they should now join in the (military) struggle against them? When Jesus sent the healed demoniac home, asking him to tell his friends "how much the Lord has done for you, and how he has had mercy on you" (Mark 5:19; cf. Luke 8:39), did he commission the healed demoniac to herald this good news and thereby rally the people of Decapolis for Jesus' anti-Roman campaign? Apart from this interpretation, is there any evidence that Jesus viewed his work in terms of a military struggle against the Roman forces and encouraged his audience to take off the cover of their self-protective understanding of the Roman forces and join in his military struggle against them? No such evidence is apparent. Therefore, Horsley's interpretation of Jesus' exorcisms seems quite strange.

Apparently Horsley is uneasy about his own interpretation of Jesus' exorcism of the Gerasene demoniac. So, in his essay "By the Finger of God," he says: "The revelation that behind the mystification of demon-possession lay the Roman military as the real agent of their possession, however, was frightening to the community. They desperately begged Jesus to leave. It was difficult, indeed impossible, to face the real political-economic situation of imperial violence. Even though the hearers of Mark's story were hearing in this episode and others the 'gospel' of God's liberation from Roman rule, they too would likely have felt uneasy and ambivalent about facing the concrete political-military forces that controlled their lives."[15] But what about the Gerasene demoniac himself who came to "his right mind"? Did Jesus' exorcisms result only in awakening fear of Roman troops in the minds of the poor Jews and the later readers/hearers of the Gospels? Or did they also result in arousing faith in Jesus' victory over Roman oppressors and resolution to join Jesus in the victorious struggle against them? If the latter was not involved, how would they have heard Jesus' exorcism stories as "the 'gospel' of God's liberation from Roman rule"? If the latter was also involved, did many hearers of the Gospel stories of Jesus' exorcisms join in the Jewish fight against the Romans during A.D. 66-70? If they did not, why not? Did they not think like the Qumranites, after all, as Horsley suggests? Or did they not have as much faith in their Messiah Jesus as the followers of Simon bar Giora had in him (Josephus, *Jewish War* 4.508-10) — in spite of Jesus' proven "victory" over Romans in exorcisms? How would the hearers of the Gospel stories of Jesus' exorcisms have thought of the disaster of A.D. 70? Above all, how would they have thought of Jesus' crucifixion by the Romans? For

15. Horsley, "By the Finger of God," 68.

what purpose, then, did the Synoptists include the stories of Jesus' exorcisms in their post-70 situations? Regardless, given Horsley's theory of demon possession and his interpretation of Jesus' exorcisms, and especially given his statement about the effects of Jesus' exorcisms that is quoted above, it is difficult to comprehend how he can say in the same essay that "[according to Q and Mark, Jesus] was pursuing a renewal of Israel in resistance and opposition to Roman rule and its client high priestly rulers. Central to his movement of resistance and renewal were *attempts to heal the effects of violence, particularly possession by alien demonic spirits* and the disintegration of the fundamental form of society, the village life."[16] How did Jesus' exorcisms "heal the effects of [Roman] violence" upon the Jews? Were the Gerasene people "healed" when they were left, according to Horsley, in a newly awakened fear of Roman legions as a result of Jesus' exorcism?

Werner H. Kelber rejects Horsley's kind of interpretation of demon possession in general as the modern anthropological and psychological insight that an ancient audience probably did not have, and yet views the case of the Gerasene demoniac as an exception and adopts Horsley's interpretation of it.[17] In spite of his avoidance of Horsley's concept of a "self-protective" device in understanding demon possession, Kelber's interpretation also does not resolve completely the difficulties that we have raised with regard to the effects of the exorcism on the demoniac and the Gerasene people in Horsley's interpretation. In fact, Kelber deals only with the first half of the episode (Mark 5:1-13) and ignores its second half (Mark 5:14-20) completely. Further, the champions of this interpretation usually ignore the logical incongruence involved in seeing the demons (Roman "legion") entering into the "swine" (Roman troops) to drive them into the sea. Or do they think that here mass suicide of Roman troops or self-destruction of the evil Empire is envisaged as a result of the Messiah Jesus' campaign?

Roger D. Aus argues that the story of the Gerasene demoniac goes back to the pre-Marcan tradition which a Palestinian Jewish Christian narrator developed by combining "some terminology and structural elements" taken from a "pre-Marcan, Semitic form" of Jesus' exorcism in Mark 1:21-28 with "Judaic haggadic traditions on Samson [Judg 13–16], including the term 'legion' and the Egyptians' rushing down . . . to drown in the Reed Sea (Exod 15:4)"[18] and that Mark then combined the pre-Marcan tradition with elements drawn from Jewish interpreta-

16. Horsley, "By the Finger of God," 74 (my italics).

17. W. H. Kelber, "Roman Imperialism and Early Christian Scribality," in *Orality, Literacy, and Colonialism in Antiquity*, ed. J. A. Draper, SemeiaSt 47 (Atlanta: Society of Biblical Literature, 2004), 138-39. See also S. D. Moore, "Mark and Empire: 'Zealot' and 'Postcolonial' Readings," in *The Postcolonial Biblical Reader*, ed. R. S. Sugirtharajah (Oxford: Blackwell, 2005), 194-96.

18. Aus, *My Name Is "Legion,"* 1-99 (quotation p. 91).

tions of Ps 91.[19] While arguing that the Jewish haggadic traditions of labeling Pharaoh as a swineherd and the legions of Egyptians drowned in the Reed Sea as swine were the *Vorlage* for the herd of about 2,000 swine rushing to drown in the Sea of Galilee in Mark 5:13,[20] Aus sees no anti-Roman sentiment beyond at most an allusion here.[21] Instead, he stresses that the exorcized demoniac in Mark 5:18-20 is modeled after the Pharaoh who in the Jewish haggadah survived drowning in the Reed Sea and went to Nineveh and proclaimed the Lord's name there.[22] Aus's interpretation of the story of the Gerasene demoniac in the light of the Jewish haggadic traditions is interesting, but his use of late and disparate Rabbinic materials prevents us from putting much confidence in his interpretation. However, he at least tries to account for the climax of the story, namely the healing of the demoniac and his subsequent preaching mission in the Decapolis, whereas Horsley, Kelber, and Moore neglect it.

Horsley also interprets Jesus' healings in terms of liberation of the people from the Roman oppression. For him, "each healing story was both a healing of a particular person and a continuing 'healing' of the social 'body' of subsequent communities of hearers," and since the individuals healed in these stories are "representative figures," their healing stories are not just about healing of their individual persons but also about Jesus' liberation of Israel from the Roman imperial rule.[23] Horsley believes that the story of the healings of the two women in Mark 5:21-43/Luke 8:40-56/Matt 9:18-26 illustrates this point:

> Both the woman who had been hemorrhaging for twelve years and the nearly dead twelve-year-old girl clearly represent the people of Israel, which consisted symbolically of twelve tribes. The original hearers of the Gospel would have known tacitly and implicitly — and we can reconstruct by historical investigation — that both the individual and the social hemorrhaging and near death were the effects of the people's subjection to imperial forces. Thus as the woman's faith that special powers are working through Jesus, leading her to take the initiative in touching his garment, results in her healing, so also the people's trust that God's restorative powers are working through Jesus is leading to their recovery

---

19. Aus, *My Name Is "Legion,"* 11-16, passim.
20. Aus, *My Name Is "Legion,"* 45, 47, 95.
21. Aus, *My Name Is "Legion,"* 98.
22. Aus, *My Name Is "Legion,"* 96.
23. Horsley, *Jesus and Empire,* 108.

from the death-dealing domination by Roman imperial rule. When Jesus brings the seemingly dead twelve-year-old girl back to life just at the time she has come of age to produce children, he is mediating new life to Israel in general. In these and other episodes Jesus is healing the illness brought on by Roman imperialism.[24]

But Christopher Bryan designates this as a "highly subjective" reading as there is no mention of Rome in the narrative.[25] Then he counters this interpretation with the episode of Jesus' healing of a centurion's servant (Matt 8:5-13/Luke 7:1-10), in which Jesus not only avails his healing power for that representative of Roman occupation forces,[26] but even commends his faith as one whose quality he has found "not even in Israel" — the faith that the centurion expresses with an illustration of "his behavior as a *military agent of imperial rule:* 'for I too am a person subject to authority, with soldiers subject to me. And I say to one, Go, and he goes, and to another Come, and he comes' (Matt 8:9//; Luke 7:8)."[27] As it is likely that "the original hearers of the gospel" would have seen the centurion as a representative of Roman rule, Bryan asks, "what would *that* identification have to say about 'Jesus and Empire'?"[28] As far as Luke is concerned, we may also ask: what message was he trying to convey to "Theophilus" with the accounts of Jesus' healings of the Gerasene demoniac (Luke 8:26-39) and the two women (Luke 8:40-56) by including them in the Gospel dedicated to him (Luke 1:1-4)? Was Luke trying to convince the Roman nobility that Jesus was about to destroy the Roman legions and liberate Israel? Is this plausible?[29]

Unfortunately, except for this one case of Mark 5:21-43/Luke 8:40-56/Matt 9:18-26, Horsley does not seek to further demonstrate his anti-Roman reading of Jesus' healings.[30] Therefore, one wonders how he would

---

24. Horsley, *Jesus and Empire,* 109.

25. Bryan, *Render to Caesar,* 50. We may add that it is also a fairly allegorical reading.

26. How may this be understood in terms of Horsley's interpretation of Jesus' healings as liberation from Roman imperial oppression? Jesus healed the servant of a Roman centurion in order to signify that he was liberating Israel from the Roman forces?

27. Bryan, *Render to Caesar,* 46 (his italics).

28. Bryan, *Render to Caesar,* 50 (his italics).

29. Since it is Luke who uses the "liberation" language most prominently among the Evangelists, I suppose that it is not easy to get around this question with the often popular tactic of declaring that Luke has distorted (or "spiritualized") the original "revolutionary" meanings of the two accounts.

30. On his interpretation of Mark 2:1-12 pars., see p. 138, below.

interpret, for example, *Jesus' healing of a crippled woman on the Sabbath in Luke 13:10-17.* The woman is said to have had "a spirit of infirmity for eighteen years." Jesus explains her infirmity in terms of her "bondage" to Satan for eighteen years and his healing of her as "liberation" (ἀπολέλυσαι, v. 12; λυθῆναι, v. 16) from that "bondage" (ἀπὸ τοῦ δεσμοῦ) to Satan. Does this exorcism and healing also symbolize Jesus' liberation from Roman imperial oppression? Does Luke give any hint that he understands the episode in that sense? If there is any "hint" here with regard to our present concern, it points in the opposite direction. For Luke shows the healing as giving rise to a Sabbath controversy with the ruler of the synagogue, rather than to any discussion that might imply a socio-political liberation.[31] Furthermore, we have already noted how in Luke 13 — even while mentioning, uniquely among the Evangelists, Pilate's brutality (vv. 1-5) and Herod's slyness (vv. 31-33) — Luke does not have Jesus call for a fight against their evil rules or for redemption of their victims but rather has Jesus warn Israel of divine judgment for refusing to repent and listen to his message. It is noteworthy that between these two pericopes Luke places this special material about Jesus' healing of the crippled woman on the Sabbath, explaining it explicitly as liberation from her eighteen-year bondage to Satan (Luke 13:10-17). Thus the three passages of Luke 13 (1-5, 10-17, 31-35) illustrate the point here rather effectively: Jesus fights the kingdom of Satan and redeems the sick out of it, but he does not fight the Roman imperial system and does not redeem the victims of its evil rulers.

As we have seen, it is by no means certain that the identification of the demon(s) as "legion" in the episode of the Gerasene demoniac (Mark 5:1-20/Luke 8:26-39; cf. Matt 8:28-34) points to Roman military oppression. Even if it does, we have to evaluate its significance in view of the Evangelists' overall presentation of Jesus as fighting the kingdom of Satan rather than the Roman Empire, as well as in view of the actual climax of the episode relating the effects of the exorcism on the demoniac and the Gerasenes (Mark 5:14-20/Luke 8:34-39/cf. Matt 8:33-34). Thus we can say at most that Jesus or the Evangelists, seeing Satan's rule as the fundamental

---

31. Cf. C. Dietzfelbinger, "Vom Sinn der Sabbatheilungen Jesu," *EvT* 38 (1978): 281-98; W. Grimm, *Der Ruhetag: Sinngehalte einer fast vergessenen Gottesgabe,* ANTJ 4 (Frankfurt: Lang, 1980), 62-77, for Jesus' healing activities on the Sabbath as symbolic of the redemption of creation from the power of Satan and its restoration to the original state of perfection under the reign of God. So the Sabbath theme in this passage coheres well with the theme of redemption from Satan.

problem, perceive the Roman oppression as one of its various ills. But Jesus does not focus only or chiefly on that manifestation of Satan's rule as did many of his contemporary insurgents. Rather, as the bearer of the Kingdom of God, Jesus seeks to deal with the fundamental problem of evil and to defeat Satan, its source.[32] So his redemption, being a comprehensive redemption from the kingdom of Satan, deals with the many manifestations of Satan's rule, such as sins, various forms of suffering (mental and physical illness, poverty, alienation, injustice, oppression, etc.), and death. His exorcisms, healings, and fellowship meals are a proleptic realization of this redemption, and as such they anticipate or promise the full redemption at the eschaton when God's Kingdom fully comes. The episode of the Gerasene demoniac may demonstrate this anticipatory character of Jesus' redemption with regard to political oppression,[33] just as Jesus' healings on

32. This point is made by N. T. Wright effectively when he argues from three passages — the Beelzebul controversy (Luke 11:14-23/Matt 12:22-30/Mark 3:22-27), the real object to fear (Luke 12:4-7/Matt 10:28-31), and the seven other demons (Luke 11:24-26/Matt 12:43-45) — that contrary to many of his contemporary anti-Roman insurgents Jesus identified the real enemy facing Israel (and the world) as Satan (Evil) rather than Rome and redefined the battle for the Kingdom of God in terms of a conflict with Satan rather than with Rome (*Jesus and the Victory of God*, 451-59). Wright further argues that Jesus regarded "the tradition and symbol" of "the 'zealous' holy war" (p. 448) or "nationalistic militarism" (p. 450) that many of his contemporaries were upholding, as well as Roman oppression, as part of Satan's work (pp. 448-50, 462, 595, 605-9). Thus, Wright objects to the interpretations of Horsley and others that present Jesus as one of the Jewish anti-Roman insurgents: "Not only does the argument fail for lack of evidence and inner logic, as has often been shown. It goes in the diametrically opposite direction to the whole course of Jesus' ministry as we have plotted it so far" (p. 450). According to Wright, having struggled with Satan and won his initial victory over him immediately after his baptism (pp. 457-59), Jesus implemented that victory in his ministry of exorcisms, propounded turning the other cheek or taking up the cross, i.e., the way of love, as the right way of fighting the real enemy Satan (Evil), and fought the battle himself in that way to overcome the kingdom of Satan and bring in the Kingdom of God (pp. 463-74; see further, 605-11). Inasmuch as all this is quite convincing, it is curious how having interpreted Jesus in this way, Wright can interpret Paul in terms of anti-Roman struggle while at the same time affirming the essential unity between Jesus and Paul (see N. T. Wright, *Paul: In Fresh Perspective* [Minneapolis: Fortress, 2005], 154-61).

33. Since the climax of the episode relating the effects of the exorcism on the demoniac and the Gerasenes (Mark 5:14-20/Luke 8:34-39/cf. Matt 8:33-34) does not call for the hearers/readers of the episode to join in Jesus' *present* struggle against the Roman imperial oppression, a political interpretation of the episode seems to lead at most to the conclusion that it anticipates the full redemption from political oppression at the eschatological consummation of the Kingdom of God.

the Sabbath demonstrate it with regard to physical suffering, and just as his meal fellowship with sinners demonstrates it with regard to sins and alienation (e.g., Luke 5:27-32 pars.; 19:1-10).

In Part One, it was pointed out how Horsley and others tend to argue deductively from the assumption of a pervasive imperial cult in Paul's mission fields in order to present Paul's teaching as a resistance to imperial ideology and cult, and how their interpretations run aground on the actual texts of the Pauline Epistles. Horsley displays the same method in his interpretation of Jesus, and so faces the same kind of criticism. In his *Jesus and Empire*, Horsley describes at length, first of all, the brutal oppression and exploitation of the Roman Empire and the ceaseless uprisings of the Jews against Roman rule. Then he assumes that since Jesus carried out his Kingdom ministry in this context, his gospel and ministry must be interpreted in terms of Roman oppression and Jewish resistance. This assumption leads Horsley to seek a political or anti-Roman meaning wherever possible in Jesus' deeds and sayings in Q and Mark. But in reality Horsley relies mainly on a couple of exorcism and healing episodes as well as Jesus' temple action to demonstrate his thesis, which is deduced from his assumption. As our examination here shows, however, even Horsley's chosen few cases of the actual Synoptic texts do not support his thesis.[34]

Horsley's proclivity to argue from assumptions is well illustrated in the following statement:

> While the violence of imperial conquest and economic exploitation has previously often been accepted or ignored, such violence constituted the very conditions for Jesus and the movement(s) he catalyzed as well as the many contemporary Judean and Galilean movements that resisted Roman rule. This is manifested most vividly in the generally accepted historical fact of Jesus' execution: by the Romans by means of crucifixion, a form of torturous execution reserved mainly for rebellious slaves and rebel leaders among subject peoples. Recognition of the brutal realities of the imperial situation and its effect on the Judean, Samaritan, and Galilean peoples, moreover, opens toward the further recognition that Jesus' mission and movement(s) were fundamentally similar in most respects to other, contemporary resistance and renewal movements among the Judeans and Galileans.[35]

Here, Horsley deduces that Jesus' movement was one of the many Jewish anti-Roman resistance movements from the fact of Jesus' crucifixion, as well as from the fact that imperial oppression and Jewish resistance were the conditions for Jesus' movement. Horsley does not bother with the Evangelists' unanimous witness

---

34. See further pp. 138-39 below.
35. Horsley, "By the Finger of God," 54.

that Jesus was wrongly condemned as a rebel leader, just as he does not bother to examine the teachings and deeds of Jesus beyond a few sayings and stories. For the former, he may point to his discussion in his *Jesus and the Spiral of Violence*, in which he conveniently dismisses the Evangelists' witnesses as due to their "apologetic concerns vis-à-vis the Romans."[36] Horsley's method is remarkable here: he argues for the revolutionary character of the Jesus movement from the Evangelists' accounts of Jesus' temple action, Jesus' recognition as an anointed king, and his "stirring up" of the people, as well as his condemnation of the rulers and lamentation over the temple and Jerusalem. Horsley contends such material proves that the charge that Jesus was a rebel leader was not false, and yet, out of their apologetic concerns, the Evangelists designated the charge as false. Were all the Evangelists so foolish as to give away in the body of their Gospels so much evidence for the charge that they would seek to deny in vain at the end? Unfortunately, it does not seem to occur to Horsley to ask why, in spite of those teachings and deeds of Jesus, the Evangelists were still insisting that Jesus was not a rebel leader. Does this not constitute another piece of evidence that Horsley is driven by his assumption and deductive argumentation? Be that as it may, it is amazing to see how Horsley nevertheless concludes his presentation of Jesus only as a "social revolutionary" in contradistinction from a "political revolutionary," as one who worked for a "social revolution" ("renewal of local community") in anticipation of the "political revolution" that God himself would imminently bring about with the judgment of the oppressive regimes and the restoration of Israel.[37] If so, was it right to condemn such a Jesus as a rebel "king" (Messiah)?

Against Horsley's deductive argumentation from assumption, Bryan has a very effective counter:

> In my prologue to this book, I quoted Horsley's comment that 'trying to understand Jesus' speech and action without knowing how Roman imperialism determined the conditions of life in Galilee and Jerusalem' is rather like 'trying to understand Martin Luther King without knowing how slavery, reconstruction, and segregation determined the lives of African-Americans in the United States.' I agree. The comparison is valid. But for the very reason it may be pressed further. If one were to study some other American preacher, a contemporary of King in

---

36. Richard A. Horsley, *Jesus and the Spiral of Violence: Popular Jewish Resistance in Roman Palestine* (San Francisco: Harper & Row, 1987; repr. Minneapolis: Fortress, 1993), 160-64 (quotation p. 164).

37. Horsley, *Jesus and the Spiral of Violence*, 321-26. Cf. Wright, *Jesus and the Victory of God*, 296-97, 449-50, against Horsley's distinction and his thesis, which Wright calls a "softer version" of the thesis of S. G. F. Brandon, *Jesus and the Zealots: A Study of the Political Factor in Primitive Christianity* (New York: Charles Scribner's Sons/Manchester: Manchester University Press, 1967).

the southern United States, whose recorded teaching seldom even *mentioned* slavery, reconstruction, or segregation, and when it did, did so in a way that was, to say the least, ambiguous or unclear, what conclusion would one be obliged to draw from that? Surely, either that the preacher was not interested in those questions or else that he had a view of them very different from King's. And that, *mutatis mutandis,* is exactly what happens when we set the remembered teachings of Jesus alongside those of heroes of Jewish resistance to Rome such as Eleazar b. Ari, even as they appear in the pages of such a lukewarm advocate as Josephus. Moreover, the more we might incline to think that Horsley is right (over against, say, Cohen, Neusner, or Freyne) in his analysis of the *general* situation of anti-Roman unrest and resistance in first century Galilee and Judea, the weaker, in this connection, Jesus' words sound.[38]

*Peter's testimony about Jesus' healing activities in Acts 10:34-43* must give Horsley as much a trouble as the episode of Jesus' healing of a centurion's servant (Luke 7:1-10/Matt 8:5-13) does for his interpretation of Jesus' healings in terms of liberation from Roman imperial oppression. In the passage, summarizing the messianic ministry of Jesus as part of the gospel that Peter preached to Cornelius, Luke says: "how God *anointed* Jesus of Nazareth with the Holy Spirit and with power; how he went about doing good and *healing all that were oppressed by the devil,* for God was with him" (Acts 10:38). As in Luke 11:14-23 and 13:10-17, so also in Acts 10:38 it is plain that Luke understands sickness as oppression by Satan, and Jesus' healing of sick persons as his liberation of them from the bondage of Satan. We have already noted that Acts 10:36-43 is Luke's own summary of what he wrote in his first volume, the Gospel of Luke. Therefore, we can see here Luke interpreting all the healing activities of Jesus reported in that first volume in terms of Jesus liberating those oppressed by Satan. Further, as in Luke 7:18-23, so also in Acts 10:38 it is plain that Luke understands Jesus' healing activities as his messianic acts. Luke makes this quite unmistakable with his repeated emphasis on Jesus' Messiahship here: "how God anointed Jesus of Nazareth" (v. 38); "he is the one ordained by God to be judge of the living and the dead" (v. 42); and "to him all the prophets bear witness" (v. 43). We have already noted the significance of Luke's stress on the universal Lordship of Jesus Christ in our passage: "This one is the Lord of all" (v. 36), that Luke is making this emphatic statement in deliberate contrast to the rival claim of Caesar: Jesus Christ and not Caesar is the uni-

---

38. Bryan, *Render to Caesar,* 47 (his italics).

versal Lord who has brought the "gospel" (εὐαγγέλιον) of "peace" (εἰρήνη).[39] So it is highly significant that even in the context of presenting to a Roman officer and his friends Jesus as the Messiah and the universal Lord in conscious contrast to Caesar, as well as Jesus' "gospel of peace" in deliberate contrast to the Caesar's "gospel of peace," Luke points to Jesus' activities of redemption from the kingdom of Satan (healings in v. 38 and forgiveness of sins in v. 43)[40] rather than from the empire of Caesar.

Here both points need to be appreciated: one, that even before Caesar's officer and loyal subjects Luke does not flinch from proclaiming the truth of the gospel that Jesus Christ and not Caesar is the true Lord and Savior, and two, that Luke interprets the Lord Jesus Christ's salvation in terms of redemption from the kingdom of Satan and forgiveness of sins. These two points are made throughout Luke-Acts, as we have been observing. They naturally raise the question, isn't the empire of Caesar or its oppression also related to Satan's kingdom and his oppression? But this question is not addressed in the passage. Instead, only sins and ailments, physical and spiritual, are specified as the "oppression" of the devil. In view of all the points that have been observed in chapter 7 above, it is impossible to say that Luke is making an implicit contrast between Jesus Christ and Caesar here without being conscious of the oppression of the Roman Empire as part of the devil's oppression. So, shall we say that with his implicit contrast between Jesus Christ and Caesar Luke "alludes" to the imperial oppression? Perhaps this is the most we can say. Anyway, that Luke avoids referring to imperial oppression alongside the other aspects of the oppression of the Satanic kingdom here is consistent with the fact that nowhere in his Gospel does Luke present Jesus as acting to liberate the politically imprisoned or oppressed. This is also consistent with Luke's dedication of both volumes to "Theophilus," a (real or symbolic) member of the Roman nobility.[41]

39. See above, pp. 81-84.

40. On its margin, the Nestle-Aland Greek text (*Novum Testamentum Graece*, 27th ed. [Stuttgart: Deutsche Bibelgesellschaft, 1993]) notes Acts 10:40-41 as parallel to 1 Cor 15:4-7. But it seems better to see Acts 10:39-43 as parallel to the whole of 1 Cor 15:3-7 (what Paul claims to be the common apostolic "gospel"; cf. 1 Cor 15:11). Although in Acts 10:39 Luke does not explicitly formulate Christ's death as having been "for our sins" as Paul does in 1 Cor 15:3, with his concluding summary of the benefits of Christ's work as "forgiveness of sins through his name" for "everyone who believes in him" in Acts 10:43, Luke does reflect the formulation that Paul gives in 1 Cor 15:3.

41. Apparently Luke does not want to convey the impression that with this testimony

Just like Acts 10:34-43, *Paul's apostolic commission in Acts 26:15-18* also provides clear evidence that Luke understands Jesus' redemption in terms of liberation from the kingdom of Satan rather than from a socio-political state. In Acts 26:15-18 Luke narrates the Lord Jesus' commissioning of Paul as an apostle to the Gentiles "to open their eyes, that they may turn from darkness to light and *from the power of Satan to God,* that they may receive forgiveness of sins and a portion among those who are sanctified by faith in me" (v. 18). In agreement with Paul's own understanding of his apostolic commission (2 Cor 4:6; Gal 1:15-17),[42] this Lucan word of Paul's apostolic commission echoes the call of the Servant of Yahweh in Isa 42, especially verses 7 and 16:

> to open eyes that are blind, to free captives from prison and to release from the dungeon those who sit in darkness (v. 7)

> I will lead the blind . . . I will turn the darkness into light. . . . (v. 16)

These verses of Isa 42 originally referred to liberation of the Jewish people from their Babylonian captivity. But here in Acts 26:18 Luke interprets them in terms of liberation from captivity to Satan rather than from a political enslavement or oppression. This is highly significant for our present discussion. Quite probably, Luke likewise understands the words of Isa 61:1-2 and 58:6 (originally references to liberation from the Babylonian captivity), referred to in Jesus' inaugural sermon (Luke 4:18-19), in terms of liberation from captivity to Satan rather than from a political captivity.

This is made very likely by the fact that Isa 42 and 61:1-3, both concerning the commissioning of the Servant of Yahweh,[43] are very similar in content. Compare Isa 42:1 with 61:1:

> He is my servant, whom I uphold, my chosen one in whom I delight; I will pour my Spirit on him. . . . (42:1)

---

about Jesus' "healing all that were oppressed by the devil" to the Roman centurion Cornelius and his friends Peter was really trying to say, "Thus Jesus went about liberating (or promising to liberate) the Jews from the Roman oppression," as Horsley might want to have it. How could the Roman centurion Cornelius or the Roman nobleman "Theophilus" accept it?

42. See S. Kim, "Isaiah 42 and Paul's Call," in *Paul and the New Perspective: Second Thoughts on the Origin of Paul's Gospel* (Grand Rapids: Eerdmans/Tübingen: Mohr Siebeck, 2002), 101-27.

43. Cf. I. H. Marshall, *The Gospel of Luke: A Commentary on the Greek Text*, NIGTC (Grand Rapids: Eerdmans, 1978), 183, and the literature cited there.

The Spirit of the Sovereign LORD is on me, because the LORD has anointed me. . . . (61:1)

Compare also Isa 42:7 with 61:1b (especially in their LXX versions):

to open eyes that are blind, to free captives from prison and to release from the dungeon those who sit in darkness (LXX: ἀνοῖξαι ὀφθαλμοὺς τυφλῶν ἐξαγαγεῖν ἐκ δεσμῶν δεδεμένους καὶ ἐξ οἴκου φυλακῆς καθημένους ἐν σκότει; 42:7)

to proclaim freedom for the captives, and release from darkness for the prisoners (LXX: κηρύξαι αἰχμαλώτοις ἄφεσιν καὶ τυφλοῖς ἀνάβλεψιν; 61:1b)

The close similarity between Isa 42 and 61:1-3 makes us wonder, on the one hand, whether the reference to Isa 61:1 in Jesus' inaugural sermon (Luke 4:18-19) might also echo Isa 42:7.[44] This echo is plausible since Luke, like his fellow Synoptists, alludes to Isa 42:1 in his account of Jesus' messianic commission at his baptism: like the Servant in Isa 42:1, Jesus is commissioned as God's Son in whom God "is well pleased" and on whom God's Spirit has descended (Luke 3:22/Mark 1:10-11/Matt 3:16-17). This is further supported as Luke has Simeon echo Isa 42:6 (//Isa 49:6) to describe Jesus as the bearer of the light of divine revelation to the Gentiles (Luke 2:32). The close similarity between Isa 42 and 61:1-3 makes us wonder, on the other hand, whether in the allusion to Isa 42 in Paul's apostolic commission (Acts 26:18), Isa 61:1 may not also be echoed. Such an echo is made plausible by the fact that the motif of "sending" in Acts 26:17 (ἀποστέλλω σε) seems to come directly from the phrase ἀπέσταλκέν με ("he has sent me") in Isa 61:1, while summing up the content of the commissioning of the Servant in Isa 42.

In fact, it is highly likely that Luke formulated Paul's apostolic commission in Acts 26:18 at least partially in parallel to Jesus' inaugural sermon in Luke 4:18. For Luke shows the parallelism of Paul's apostolic commission to Jesus' messianic commission by alluding to the call of the Servant of Yahweh in Isa 42 for both (Luke 3:22 — Isa 42:1; Acts 26:16-18 — Isa 42:7,

44. Cf. Marshall, *Gospel of Luke*, 184, who takes the phrase καὶ τυφλοῖς ἀνάβλεψιν in Luke 4:18 as an allusion to Isa 42:7 as well as Isa 61:1 (where in the LXX the phrase καὶ τυφλοῖς ἀνάβλεψιν stands for ולאסורים פקח־קוה in the MT).

16). This is part of the well-known feature of Luke's presentation of Paul's mission in close parallelism to the mission of Jesus, whereby Luke shows the apostle Paul carrying on the work of his Lord Jesus Christ.[45] If thus Paul's apostolic commission (Acts 26:18) is formulated in parallel to Jesus' inaugural sermon (Luke 4:18), the motif of liberation from the power of Satan in the former would be equivalent to the motif of liberation of the captives and the oppressed in the latter. This consideration makes it significant that in Acts 26:18 turning from the power of Satan is seen as bringing about ἄφεσιν ἁμαρτιῶν. Ἄφεσις, which appears twice in Jesus' inaugural sermon as a key word (Luke 4:18), is used here. However, it is not used for liberation from a political captivity and oppression but for forgiveness of sins.[46] This again shows that Luke interprets Jesus' redemption (ἄφεσις) promised in his inaugural sermon in terms of redemption from captivity to Satan and concretely in terms of forgiveness of sins.

Thus (a) the material similarity between Isa 42:1, 7 and Isa 61:1; (b) the possibility of an echo of Isa 42:1, 7 in the reference to Isa 61:1 in Jesus' inaugural sermon as well as the possibility of an echo of Isa 61:1 in the allusion to Isa 42:7, 16 in Paul's apostolic commission; and (c) the likelihood that Luke formulated the wording of Paul's apostolic commission in Acts 26:18 in parallel to Jesus' inaugural sermon in Luke 4:18 converge in pointing to this fact: Luke understands the liberation of the captives (expressed primarily through a reference to Isa 61:1-2) in Jesus' inaugural sermon (Luke 4:18-19) in terms of liberation from captivity to Satan, just as he understands the redemption (expressed primarily through an allusion to Isa 42:7, 16) in Paul's apostolic commission (Acts 26:18) in terms of liberation from captivity to Satan.

In Acts 26:18, turning from darkness and turning from the power of Satan are equivalent, and by doing that the Gentiles are to receive forgiveness of sins. Turning to light and turning to God are also equivalent, and by doing that they are to receive a portion among the people of God. So Paul is commissioned to bring the light of divine revelation by preaching the gospel to the Gentiles (Isa 42:6-7), so that they may convert from their sins committed in ignorance and under the reign of Satan toward the

---

45. See below, p. 153, n. 2.

46. This is quite in line with the fact that except for the two apparent exceptions in Luke 4:18 the terminology ἀφίημι/ἄφεσις is used throughout in Luke-Acts unmistakably for forgiveness of sins, but never for liberation of political captives. See below, p. 136, n. 53.

knowledge of and obedience to God, in order to receive forgiveness and inheritance as members of God's holy people. Here, then, we can see how Luke understands opening blind eyes and liberating from captivity metaphorically in terms of knowing God and liberation from Satanic control, respectively,[47] and how Luke understands forgiveness of sins as a result of liberation from Satanic control.

All these observations from Luke 7:18-23; 11:14-23; and 13:10-17 and from Acts 10:34-43 and 26:15-18 make it clear that Luke understands the liberation of the captives and the oppressed in Jesus' inaugural sermon (Luke 4:18-19) to mean deliverance from the power of Satan, who forces us to sin and afflicts us with spiritual and physical illness.

This understanding is in line with Luke's presentation of Jesus' ministry as a struggle with the kingdom of Satan rather than with any political kingdom, in spite of his contrast of Jesus Christ with Caesar in the *inclusio* of Luke 2:1-14 and Acts 28:30-31 and in his account of Jesus' messianic inauguration (Luke 3:1-22). Luke presents Jesus entering into a conflict with Satan (Luke 4:1-13) rather than with Caesar or his representatives right after his messianic installation as the Son of God (Luke 3:21-22). With his successful overcoming of Satan's temptations or attacks, Jesus launched his messianic mission in the power of the Spirit (Luke 4:14-30) and immediately began to heal sick people by liberating them from demon possession (Luke 4:31-41).[48]

But Luke gives the impression that Jesus' ministry of the Kingdom of God was a continual struggle with Satan right to the end (Luke 22:3, 22).

---

47. In this also Luke agrees with Paul: cf. 2 Cor 4:4-6.

48. Note the sequence in Luke 3–4: Jesus' inauguration as the Christ and Son of God (3:1-22); [3:23-38: Jesus the true Son of David and Son of God in fulfillment of the Davidic covenant (2 Sam 7:12-14), who would truly represent God's kingship vitiated by the Davidic dynasty of the line of Solomon as well as by Adam]; overcoming Satan's attacks (4:1-13); Jesus' inaugural sermon at the synagogue of Nazareth (4:14-21); Jesus' criticism of Israel and inclusion of the Gentiles (4:22-30); Jesus' healing of a man by subjugation of a demonic spirit (4:31-37); Jesus' healing of many people and subjugation of demons (4:38-41). Note here how Luke has the promise of liberation of the captives and the oppressed in Jesus' inaugural sermon (4:18-19) immediately followed by an account of Jesus' rejection of Jewish nationalism and by the two accounts of Jesus liberating those in demonic captivity. With this sequence, is Luke trying to orient his readers right away to understand Jesus' messianic liberation of the captives and the oppressed, promised in his inaugural sermon, in terms of healing and liberation from the oppression of demons, the underlings of Satan (Luke 11:15-18), i.e., in terms of liberation from the kingdom of Satan, rather than in terms of the nationalistic liberation of Israel?

This is evident not only in Luke 11:14-23 and 13:16, which we have examined, but also in Luke's account of the mission of the Seventy: Jesus sends out the seventy disciples to impart peace, "heal the sick," and proclaim that "the Kingdom of God has come near to you" (Luke 10:5-9). The Seventy return and report, "Lord, even the demons are subject to us in your name" (v. 17). To them Jesus says, "I saw Satan fall like lightning from heaven" (v. 18). Here the progress of the Kingdom of God on earth bringing healing and deliverance from the demons is linked with the dethronement of Satan in heaven (cf. Isa 14:12-15), and Jesus and his disciples as the bearers of the Kingdom of God (cf. Luke 10:16) are presented as subduing Satan and his demons as their "enemy" (Luke 10:19). In other words, the disciples' proclamation of the Kingdom of God and their healing activities are linked with the subjugation of the demonic spirits, and the latter are presented as the sign of Satan's downfall from heaven. This means that in his account of the mission of the Seventy as well as in Luke 11:14-23 and 13:16, Luke presents exorcism and healing as deliverance from the kingdom of Satan. Here it is important to note that the Kingdom ministry of Jesus and his disciples is said to be "attacking and subduing" Satan (11:22), bringing about the "downfall" of Satan (10:18), and "loosening from the bond" of Satan (13:16). Isn't it significant that Luke uses such language for the effects of Jesus' Kingdom ministry with regard to the kingdom of Satan but not with any political kingdom, neither with Caesar's nor with Herod's?

Thus, our examination of Luke's accounts of Jesus' redemptive activities suggests that for Luke Jesus' exorcism and healing and his forgiveness of sins were the messianic liberation of the captives and the oppressed that Jesus promised in his inaugural sermon (Luke 4:18-19), and that therefore Jesus' bringing about the "downfall" of Satan through his Kingdom ministry was the fulfillment of Mary's hope of the downfall of the mighty (Luke 1:52) and Zechariah's prophecy about redemption from enemies (Luke 1:71-74).

## Restoration of Sinners

As we have already seen, in Acts 26:18 (cf. also 10:38, 43) Luke suggests his understanding that sinners are in captivity to Satan[49] and that therefore

---

49. So also C. K. Barrett, *A Critical and Exegetical Commentary on the Acts of the Apostles*, 2 vols., ICC (Edinburgh: T&T Clark, 1994, 1998), 2:1161.

forgiveness of sins is also redemption from Satanic captivity. By "turn[ing] . . . from the dominion of Satan to God," which appears to be a good definition of repentance,[50] sinners receive forgiveness (ἄφεσις, i.e., redemption from the kingdom of Satan) and a portion among the sanctified people of God (i.e., restoration to the Kingdom of God).[51] Luke presents Satan as tempting Jesus to follow his will rather than God's (Luke 4:1-14), as inciting Judas to betray Jesus (Luke 22:3) and Ananias to lie to the Holy Spirit (Acts 5:3), and as controlling Elymas the magician to be an "enemy of all righteousness, full of all deceit and villainy" (Acts 13:10). Thus Luke thinks of sinners as enslaved to follow the dictates of Satan. Therefore, we can see how natural it is for him to think of forgiveness of sins as liberation from Satanic captivity. Then, when Jesus says, "Those who are well have no need of a physician, but those who are sick; I have come (ἐλήλυθα) to call not the righteous but sinners to repentance" (Luke 5:31-32), Jesus is not enunciating a new messianic mission different from the one he enunciated in his inaugural sermon (Luke 4:18-19). Just like his healing the sick, his imparting forgiveness (ἄφεσις) to sinners and restoring them to God is also his redemption (ἄφεσις) of the captives and the oppressed, which he spoke about in his inaugural sermon.

This is why Jesus concentrates on bringing about restoration of sinners as well as on healing the sick. Jesus characterizes his ministry as seeking out sinners as the lost sheep among God's flock (Luke 15:1-32; 19:10), imparting forgiveness of sins (Luke 5:17-26; 7:36-50), and enjoying table fellowship with sinners and tax collectors (Luke 5:27-32; 15:1-2). In these activities, Jesus functions as the shepherd of God's flock[52] on behalf of God (i.e., as God's fully empowered agent). Jesus' meal fellowship with sinners and tax collectors is a sign-act whereby he conveys to them God's forgiveness of their sins and assures them of their participation in the messianic banquet

50. Cf. H. Merklein, "μετανοέω/μετάνοια," in *Exegetical Dictionary of the New Testament,* ed. H. Balz and G. Schneider, 3 vols. (Grand Rapids: Eerdmans, 1990-93), 2:416. For the importance of repentance in Lucan theology, especially for its being the precondition for forgiveness, see pp. 417-18.

51. Thus Acts 26:18 is a close parallel to Col 1:12-14: ". . . the Father, who has qualified us to *share in the inheritance of the saints* in *light.* He has *delivered* us from the *dominion* of *darkness* and transferred us to the kingdom of his beloved Son, in whom we have *redemption,* the *forgiveness of sins.*"

52. Marshall, *Luke: Historian and Theologian,* 139, sees here Jesus acting as the shepherd of God's flock in Ezek 34:16.

or the eschatological salvation of the consummated Kingdom of God. So, it is a sign-act of their restoration to God.

In the parable of the great banquet (Luke 14:15-24), the poor, the maimed, the blind, and the lame are brought in for the banquet of the Kingdom of God (v. 15). Although this list does not contain an explicit reference to sinners, the parable of the prodigal son (Luke 15:11-32) suggests that repentant sinners would be restored to God the heavenly Father as his children (heirs) and so would participate in his rich feast. This parable demonstrates that forgiveness of sins is salvation not only because it frees sinners from condemnation at the last judgment (cf. Luke 10:13-15; 12:4-5; 13:1-5, 22-30; 16:19-31) but because it is, positively, restoration to God and his abundant life. Jesus' work of restoring repentant sinners is illustrated by the story of Zacchaeus, who on repentance is restored as "a son of Abraham" (i.e., as a member of God's people) and is given the salvation of the Kingdom of God that Jesus has brought in (Luke 19:1-10). Pointing to the restoration and salvation of Zacchaeus, Jesus declares that he, the Son of Man, "came [ἦλθεν] to seek and save the lost" (v. 10).

This ἦλθεν-saying in Luke 19:10, together with the ἐλήλυθα-saying in 5:32 ("I have come [ἐλήλυθα] to call not the righteous but sinners to repentance"), raises the question of how Luke understands Jesus' mission declared in this solemn formula vis-à-vis his inaugural sermon (4:18-19). It is instructive to compare the four definitions of Jesus' messianic mission in Luke:

4:18-19: The Spirit of the Lord is upon me, because he has anointed me to bring good news to the poor. He has sent me to proclaim release to the captives and recovery of sight to the blind, to let the oppressed go free, to proclaim the year of the Lord's favor.

7:22: Go and tell John what you have seen and heard: the blind receive their sight, the lame walk, the lepers are cleansed, the deaf hear, the dead are raised, the poor have good news brought to them.

5:31-32: Those who are well have no need of a physician, but those who are sick; I have come to call not the righteous but sinners to repentance.

19:10: For the Son of Man came to seek and save the lost.

Cf. two passages from Acts:

10:38:   . . . how God anointed Jesus of Nazareth with the Holy Spirit and
with power; how he went about doing good and healing all who
were oppressed by the devil, for God was with him.

26:17-18:   I [the Lord Jesus] am sending you [Paul] to open their eyes so that
they may turn from darkness to light and from the dominion of
Satan to God, so that they may receive forgiveness of sins and a
place among those who are sanctified by faith in me.

Above, from a comparison between Luke 4:18-19 and 7:22, we have inferred
that Luke identifies Jesus' exorcisms and healings as his messianic activities
of liberation (cf. Acts 10:38). Now a comparison between Luke 4:18-19 on
the one hand and Luke 5:32 and 19:10 on the other leads to a similar conclusion, namely, that Luke identifies Jesus' restoration of sinners as his messianic activities of liberation (cf. Acts 10:43). In the absence in the main body
of Luke's Gospel of any statement about Jesus' mission or activities to liberate Israel from the Roman rule, this repeated and emphatic statement about
the purpose of Jesus' mission conveys the same impression as the statement
in Acts 26:18: namely, Luke wants his readers to understand that Jesus' forgiveness of sins and restoration of sinners to God is his redemption of the
captives and the oppressed, and his enactment of the jubilee remission,[53]

---

53. The reference to "the acceptable year of the Lord" (= Isa 61:2: MT: שנת־רצון ליהוה,
"the year of the LORD's favor") in Luke 4:19, has led J. H. Yoder, *The Politics of Jesus: Vicit Agnus Noster*, 2nd ed. (Grand Rapids: Eerdmans/Carlisle: Paternoster, 1994), 28-75, to adopt the
interpretation of A. Trocmé, *Jesus and the Nonviolent Revolution*, trans. M. H. Shank and
M. E. Miller (Scottdale, Pa.: Herald, 1974), and explain the whole message of Jesus' inaugural
sermon and much of Jesus' kingdom preaching and ministry in terms of implementation of
the three provisions of "the year of jubilee" (Lev 25): letting the fields fallow, liberating
slaves, and remitting debts. Yoder focuses especially on the use of the word group ἀφιέναι in
the Synoptic Gospels for his view, as it is often used in the LXX for release of captives and
slaves and remission of debts. But this interpretation has found little endorsement (see
Yoder's own report on its reception among NT scholars in the second edition of his *Politics
of Jesus*, 72-75). For, as R. T. France, "Liberation in the New Testament," *EvQ* 58 (1986): 9-10,
notes, all but two of the total 17 occurrences of it in the NT refer to the forgiveness of sins,
and even the two exceptions, which are both in Luke 4:18, turn out, in our present examination, to be understood by Luke himself as referring to liberation from the power of Satan,
i.e., healing and forgiveness. See further nn. 73 and 76 below. Cf. the conclusion of J. S.
Bergsma, *The Jubilee from Leviticus to Qumran: A History of Interpretation*, VTSup 115
(Leiden: Brill, 2007), 304: "Finally, a shift occurs in Second Temple literature concerning the
type of debt the jubilee addresses. While the original legislation was clearly concerned with

which he promised in his inaugural sermon.[54]

It is then no wonder that Luke concludes his first volume as follows, highlighting its main message and building a bridge to his second volume:

> Then he said to them, "These are my words that I spoke to you while I was still with you, that everything written about me in the law of Moses, the prophets, and the psalms must be fulfilled." Then he opened their minds to understand the scriptures, and he said to them, "Thus it is written, *that the Messiah is to suffer and to rise from the dead on the third day, and that repentance for forgiveness of sins is to be proclaimed in his name to all nations, beginning from Jerusalem.* You are witnesses of these things. And see, I am sending upon you what my Father promised; so stay here in the city until you have been clothed with power from on high." (Luke 24:44-49)

Then, in his second volume Luke shows how Jesus' apostles carried out this commission to proclaim in his name "repentance for forgiveness of sins" to all nations (Acts 2:38; 3:19; 5:31; 10:42-43; 13:38; 26:18), while also bringing healing to the spiritually possessed and the physically sick (3:1-10; 5:16; 8:7; 9:32-35, 36-43; 14:8-10; 19:11-16; 20:7-12). But nowhere in Acts does Luke show them engaged in political liberation. It is especially noteworthy that in Acts 2:29-39 and 13:32-41 he lets both Peter and Paul declare the consequence of the fulfillment of the Davidic covenant (cf. 2 Sam 7:12-14; Ps 2:7) in Jesus through his resurrection (cf. Rom 1:3-4) in terms of forgiveness of sins (ἄφεσις ἁμαρτιῶν) (Acts 2:38; 13:38; cf. also 5:30-31), rather than a literal restoration of the Davidic kingdom or a political redemption (ἄφεσις) of the oppressed nation Israel.[55]

---

monetary debt, the later texts apply the jubilee to moral-spiritual debt, i.e., sin. This is implicit in many documents (cf. Dan 9:24; T. Levi 17:10-11; 18:9) but is made explicit in 11QMelchizedek, where the liberty (דרור) proclaimed for the men of the lot of Melchizedek is 'to free them from [the debt of] all their inequities' (11 Q Melch 6)." I owe this reference to Steve Young.

54. Cf. J. Jervell, *The Theology of the Acts of the Apostles*, NTT (Cambridge: Cambridge University Press, 1996), 99: "When Luke sums up what salvation is all about, the most important element is 'the forgiveness of sins', *aphesis hamartion*, . . . which means that God has cancelled the 'debt of guilt incurred by their evil conduct.'"

55. In the case of Paul's sermon in Acts 13:32-41, note how Luke elaborates on "forgiveness of sins" with a statement reflecting the Pauline doctrine of "justification" (δικαιωθῆναι) by faith but not by the Mosaic law (vv. 38-39), and also how thereby Luke summarizes Paul's

It is ironic that in his book *Jesus and Empire* Horsley ignores almost entirely the rich Gospel material about Jesus' forgiveness of sins and association with sinners while he sees everywhere in Mark and Q Jesus' campaign to liberate the Jews from Roman imperialism, even though in the two documents there is no explicit reference to such a campaign, only the ambiguous reference to "legion" in the story of the Gerasene demoniac (Mark 5:1-20/Luke 8:26-39; cf. Matt 8:28-34). Since in his book *Jesus and the Spiral of Violence* Horsley makes valiant efforts to explain away most of the references to sin/sinners in the Synoptic Gospels and assign only marginal importance to forgiveness of sins in Jesus' ministry,[56] it is no surprise that he makes only one substantive reference to Jesus' forgiveness of sins in *Jesus and Empire:*

> [T]his covenantal renewal speech [= the Sermon on the Mount/Plain] addressed the symptoms of the disintegration of the people's communities under the pressures of Roman imperialism and exploitation by the local Roman client rulers. . . . The speech does this in the bold declarations of new deliverance that open the covenant renewal: 'Blessed are the poor, for yours is the kingdom of God,' and so on (Q 6:20-26). There are indications elsewhere in Jesus traditions that the people, precisely because they were rooted in covenant tradition, may have been blaming themselves. Insofar as they were suffering hunger, disease, and poverty, it was because they had sinned, by breaking the covenant laws. They were therefore now receiving the curses. This is surely what Jesus was addressing in his forgiveness of sins in connection with healings (as in Mark 2:1-12). In addressing the people's self-blame and despair, therefore, Jesus transforms the blessings and curses into a new declaration of God's assurance of deliverance for the poor and hungry and condemnation of those who were wealthy, almost certainly because they were expropriating the goods of the peasantry.[57]

Apart from his apparent assumption that everything in Jesus tradition should be interpreted in terms of Roman oppression and exploitation, what ground does Horsley have to read this sort of politico-economico-psychological meaning into

---

gospel as Paul himself defines his gospel in Rom 1:3-4 + 16-17: the gospel concerns the Seed of David/Son of God raised in fulfillment of the Davidic covenant (2 Sam 7:12-14) and means justification of sinners, i.e., their deliverance from God's wrath, by faith but not by the Mosaic law (cf. Rom 1:18–5:21). For the unity of the double definition of the gospel in Rom 1:3-4 and 16-17, see S. Kim, *Paul and the New Perspective: Second Thoughts on the Origin of Paul's Gospel* (Grand Rapids: Eerdmans/Tübingen: Mohr Siebeck, 2002), 94-95, 200-202; S. Kim, *The Origin of Paul's Gospel*, WUNT 2.4 (Tübingen: Mohr Siebeck, 1981, 2nd ed. 1984/ Grand Rapids: Eerdmans, 1982), 132-36.

56. Horsley, *Jesus and the Spiral of Violence*, 182, 217-24.

57. Horsley, *Jesus and Empire*, 118.

such an episode as Jesus' healing/forgiving of the paralyzed in Mark 2:1-12 pars.?[58] If sinners are so identified with those who became poor, sick, and despairing because of oppression and exploitation by the Roman rulers and their Jewish accomplices, how can we explain the frequent association (and even identification) of tax collectors with sinners and Jesus' forgiving acceptance of both in the Gospel tradition (Mark 2:15-17 pars.; Luke 7:34/Matt 11:19; Luke 15:1; cf. Matt 9:9; 21:31-32; Luke 18:9-14; 19:1-10)? Tax collectors were serving the Roman Empire, either directly or indirectly (through the client king, Herod), and were neither poor people themselves nor friends of the poor people.[59]

## Good News Preached to the Poor

In the parable of the great banquet (Luke 14:15-24), the list of people who are brought in to the feast of the Kingdom of God includes the poor (v. 21). In a similar list of people who receive Jesus' saving benefits in his answer to the envoys of John the Baptist (Luke 7:22),[60] again the poor are mentioned. This corresponds to their inclusion in the list of Jesus' inaugural sermon (Luke 4:18). In 4:18 and 7:22, the statements "to preach good news to the poor" and "the poor have the good news preached to them," respectively, appear as part of an allusion to or echo of Isa 61:1. It is well known that Luke stresses Jesus' particular concern for the poor. In Luke, who are the poor? What is the nature of the good news preached to them? And may Jesus' activities for them be seen as redemptive?

A comparison of the Lucan version (Luke 6:20-26) of the Beatitudes with the Matthean version (Matt 5:3-12) clearly indicates that Luke presents the poor starkly as the materially poor who suffer from physical hunger and therefore are in sorrow, while Matthew stresses the spiritual poverty of those who feel needy and yearn for God's help rather than being content with their own resources. The parable of the rich fool (Luke 12:16-21) shows that Luke does not neglect this connotation,[61] which is traditional also in

---

58. Cf. Horsley, *Jesus and the Spiral of Violence*, 183-84.

59. Cf. Horsley, *Jesus and the Spiral of Violence*, 212-23, for an attempt to deny Jesus' association with tax collectors as well as the latter's Roman connections; see Wright, *Jesus and the Victory of God*, 266-67, and Bryan, *Render to Caesar*, 42-43, against this attempt.

60. Marshall, *Luke: Historian and Theologian*, 139, notes the similarity of the two lists.

61. So Marshall, *Luke: Historian and Theologian*, 142, recognizing the key in the concluding verse: "So is he who lays up treasure for himself, and is not rich toward God" (Luke 12:21).

some strands of the Old Testament and Judaism (e.g., Psalms).[62] But although Matthew may count among "the poor" such people as Joseph of Arimathea (Luke 23:50-53); Barnabas (Acts 4:36-37); and Mary Magdalene, Joanna (the wife of Herod's steward), Susanna, and others who materially supported Jesus in his Kingdom ministry (Luke 8:2-3), Luke would not identify them as such. The parable of the rich man and Lazarus (Luke 16:19-30), which is Lucan special material, appears to be a parabolic illustration of the contrast between the poor and the rich here and now, and of the reversal of their lots in the Kingdom of God set out in the Lucan Beatitudes and Woes (6:20-26). So, like the latter, the parable also makes it clear that Luke designates the materially deprived people as "the poor." It is likely that Luke also counts widows (cf. Luke 7:11-17; 18:1-8; 21:1-4) and many handicapped and sick people (cf. especially Luke 18:35) among "the poor."

Luke has Jesus warn against idolatry of Mammon (Luke 12:13-21; 16:13)[63] and exhort a complete trust in God's fatherly provision of our daily needs (12:22-31). He has Jesus issue a command: "Sell your possessions, and give alms," so as to have "a treasure in the heavens" (12:33). Luke also has Jesus pronounce woes to the rich while pronouncing blessings to the poor in his Beatitudes and Woes (6:24-26) and criticize the rich man for enjoying his luxurious life while neglecting to care for the poor Lazarus in the parable of the rich man and Lazarus (16:19-30). But Luke does not present Jesus condemning the rich *ipso facto*, as he presents Jesus rather relying on the support of some of his rich friends for his Kingdom ministry (8:2-3; 10:1-12, 38-42; 23:50-53).[64] Nor does Luke present Jesus attempting to question, let alone change, the socio-economic system of the day, when he presents Jesus using the picture of rich households with servants for parabolic illustrations of the Kingdom of God (e.g., 14:15-24; 15:11-32; 19:11-27) or of his mission (20:9-19).[65] Luke shows that the fault that Jesus finds with some

---

62. Cf. W. D. Davies and D. C. Allison, *A Critical and Exegetical Commentary on the Gospel according to Saint Matthew,* 3 vols., ICC (Edinburgh: T&T Clark, 1988-97), 1:442-45.

63. For the Jesus that Horsley, *Jesus and Empire,* presents, this word of Luke 16:13 (// Matt 6:24), "No servant can serve two masters. . . . You cannot serve God and Mammon," is rather strange. Should he not rather say: "You cannot serve God and Caesar"?

64. Cf. G. Theissen, *Sociology of Early Palestinian Christianity,* trans. J. Bowden (Philadelphia: Fortress, 1978), 17-23; G. Lohfink, *Jesus and Community: The Social Dimension of Christian Faith,* trans. J. P. Galvin (Philadelphia: Fortress/New York: Paulist, 1984), 31-32, 53-54.

65. Cf. M. Hengel, *Property and Riches in the Early Church: Aspects of a Social History of*

rich people is their idolatry of Mammon and their neglect of caring for the poor.

This is well illustrated by the contrasting stories of the rich ruler (Luke 18:18-30) and Zacchaeus (19:1-10). In the former, the rich ruler asked Jesus how he might inherit "eternal life," the life of the age to come, i.e., the life of the Kingdom of God. Jesus points him to the commandments of the second table of the Decalogue which were all concerned with love of neighbor. This is consistent with Jesus' discussion with a lawyer in which he commended the lawyer's summary of the law in terms of the two commands, love God (Deut 6:5) and love your neighbor (Lev 19:18), and insisted that the lawyer should practice them in order to "inherit eternal life" (Luke 10:25-28), especially emphasizing the need to practice neighbor love (Luke 10:29-37: the parable of the good Samaritan). In order to obtain "eternal life," the life of the age to come/the Kingdom of God, the two commands must be kept because they are the law of the Kingdom of God, or because God's kingly reign comes to human beings concretely with the twofold demand to love God and to love your neighbor.

For a proper understanding of Jesus' teaching in the stories of both the rich ruler and the lawyer, we should bear in mind that Jesus sets love of Mammon as the chief opposite of love of God (Luke 16:13; 12:13-21) and that Mammonistic idolatry, the attempt to secure one's well-being by accumulating wealth, inevitably leads to exploitation of neighbor. This is why Jesus teaches to trust in God's fatherly provision (love of God) instead

---

*Early Christianity*, trans. J. Bowden (London: SCM Press/Philadelphia: Fortress, 1974), 28. Contra Horsley's implausible, and, in fact, quite opaque interpretation of the parable of the wicked tenants (Luke 20:9-19/Mark 12:1-12/Matt 21:33-46) in his *Jesus and Empire*, 95: "Jesus' followers and other peasants would thus have sympathized with the behavior of the tenants, who they would have understood as just trying to reassert claims to what was rightfully theirs in the first place, as confirmed by the traditional Mosaic covenantal provisions of prohibition of interest on loans and of seventh-year cancellation of debts. Yet they also knew well that they dared not risk acting on their resentments lest their powerful absentee landlords take retaliatory action to destroy them. Palestinian peasants had firsthand knowledge of the slice of life portrayed in the parable of the tenants. They would have felt vindicated to hear this story clearly signaling that God would take action against the predatory priestly rulers of Israel, the tenants of God's vineyard, and give the vineyard to others — that is, give it back to its rightful heirs, the peasant families to whom it had been given as an inheritance in the first place. The peasant hearers in the crowd would have related to the parable only after they recognized its application, that is, once they recognized that the devious and violent tenants were the Jerusalem elite."

of being covetous out of anxiety about daily needs (Mammonism), and to give alms (love of neighbor) instead of exploiting neighbors (12:22-34). The summary exhortation in Luke 12:33, "[Trusting in the Father who is pleased to give you the Kingdom], sell your possessions, and give alms; [so] provide yourselves . . . with a treasure in the heavens," is echoed in the advice that Jesus gave to the rich ruler: "Sell all that you have and distribute to the poor, and you will have treasure in heaven" (18:22). Thus, to the rich ruler who asked how he might obtain the life of the Kingdom of God, Jesus answered that he could have it ("you will have treasure in heaven") by accepting God's kingly reign — by loving (i.e., trusting in) God rather than his possessions ("sell all that you have") and loving his neighbor ("and distribute to the poor"). But the poor rich ruler chose his Mammon rather than God, the life that Mammon could provide rather than the "eternal life" that God could give, and rejected the way of loving his neighbors, contrary to his claim that he had kept all the commandments from his youth.

Luke narrates the story further: Looking at the rich ruler's failure to enter the Kingdom of God that he offered, Jesus said: "How hard it is for those who have riches to enter the Kingdom of God! For it is easier for a camel to go through the eye of a needle than for the rich to enter the Kingdom of God." Those who heard it said, "Then, who can be saved?" But he said, "What is impossible with human beings is possible with God" (Luke 18:24-27).

This assurance of Jesus is demonstrated in the story of Zacchaeus (Luke 19:1-10). As a "chief tax collector" of Jericho, Zacchaeus was a "rich" man. From Luke's description of his eager efforts to see Jesus (vv. 3-4), we may assume that Zacchaeus had heard about Jesus' message of God's Kingdom and his forgiveness of sins and perhaps even of his acceptance of tax collectors. Jesus proposed for Zacchaeus to have him as a guest at his house. Moved by this gracious initiative of Jesus, Zacchaeus told Jesus that he would give half of his goods to the poor and restitute fourfold anyone he had extorted. For Jesus, this declaration was an adequate sign of Zacchaeus's repentance of his sins and entrance into the Kingdom of God: repenting of his life of extorting his neighbors because of his Mammonistic idolatry, he was now going to serve the poor with half of his goods and repay his former victims fourfold, trusting in God's fatherly provision of his own needs. Thus, Zacchaeus was declaring his resolve to love God (rather than Mammon) and love his neighbors (rather than extorting them). This was a clear sign that he had entered the Kingdom of God and was submitting to God's kingly reign. So Jesus declared, "Today salvation has come to this house, since he also is a son of Abraham," a member of God's people (v. 9). Whereas the rich ruler turned his back to the Kingdom of God that Jesus offered, Zacchaeus accepted it. Hence, whereas the rich ruler forfeited "eternal life," Zacchaeus received "salvation." Thus, a rich man, Zacchaeus, entered the Kingdom of God, and this was made possible by God's prevenient grace delivered through Jesus, his fully empowered agent.

The contrasting stories of these two rich men have further lessons. The fact that Jesus did not demand for Zacchaeus to give all his possessions to the poor suggests that when Jesus demanded that of the rich ruler he did not do so because he demonized wealth or rejected the legitimacy of private property. He was interested only in redeeming the rich ruler from the idolatry of Mammon. When a rich man showed sufficiently clear repentance of Mammonism and entrance into the Kingdom of God, Jesus was not interested in laying down figures as to how much he must give up for the sake of the poor. He was not a proto-Communist! Further, seen from the currently popular politico-socio-economic perspective, "the apolitical nature" of the Zacchaeus story is striking, as R. S. Sugirtharajah notes.[66] This is in line both with the apolitical treatment of the centurion at Capernaum (Luke 7:1-10) and with the absence of politico-socio-economic critique in Jesus' parables of the Kingdom that use the picture of rich households with servants (e.g., Luke 14:15-24; 15:11-32; 19:11-27; 20:9-19), as we have noted above.

Many rich people who responded to Jesus' gospel of the Kingdom of God positively like Zacchaeus must have been moved by Jesus' insistence on practicing the double command of love and his special compassion for the poor and made efforts to share their goods with the poor. This influence may have initiated the primitive church's communal life of believers' sharing their goods (Acts 2:41-47; 4:32-37). Luke presents this sharing as the fulfillment of Jesus' ideal of the common life of God's people (cf. also Acts 11:27-30; Gal 2:10).[67] He paints the primitive church in Jerusalem as one in

---

66. R. S. Sugirtharajah, *Postcolonial Criticism and Biblical Interpretation* (Oxford and New York: Oxford University Press, 2002), 90; cf. also Bryan, *Render to Caesar*, 42.

67. Cf. Hengel, *Property and Riches in the Early Church*, 32-34. It is quite conceivable that in the Spirit-generated enthusiasm and especially in view of their imminent eschatology the early Christians attempted to follow Jesus' teaching about God's Kingdom and

which the believers held all things in common (Acts 2:44; 4:32). He indicates that this came about as the believers with means sold their property and distributed the proceeds to the needy (Acts 2:45; 4:34-35), and illustrates this with the example of Barnabas (Acts 4:36-37). Luke seems to be stressing this fact in order to lead his readers to hear the intertextual echo and recognize that the rich believers in the primitive church in Jerusalem followed the direction that Jesus gave to his disciples (Luke 12:33) and to the rich people (Luke 18:22; 19:8-9): "Sell your properties, and distribute to the poor."

According to Birger Gerhardsson, the Shema of Deut 6:5 underlies Acts 4:32, in that the "whole heart and whole soul" of the Shema are rephrased as the "one heart and soul" in Acts 4:32a and the "whole strength" of the Shema is referred to as "his possessions" in Acts 4:32b in accordance with the usual Jewish understanding. So Luke is saying that the Jerusalem church loved God with all three elements of their whole being according to the Shema and that this loving of God not only with their "whole heart and whole soul" but with their "whole strength," or possessions, meant their sharing their possessions with one another, which was then the fulfillment of the commandment of neighbor love in Lev 19:18 as well.[68] Thus, according to Luke, the believers in the primitive church were united in loving God according to the Shema and in loving one another as a consequence of their love of God, and they expressed their love for God and for one another concretely by sharing their wealth together. This reading supports the view here propounded that in Acts 2:41-47 and 4:32-37, by evoking the intertextual echo of such passages as Luke 10:25-37; 12:29-34; 18:25; 19:1-9, Luke seeks to say that the believers in the primitive church in Jerusalem faithfully carried out Jesus' instruction to practice the double command of love, love of God (Deut 6:5) and love of neighbor (Lev 19:18), especially the latter. The wonderful result of this discipleship was: "There was no poor person [ἐνδεής] among them" (Acts 4:34).

By narrating the cheating done by Ananias and Sapphira (Acts 5:1-11) and the dispute between the Hellenists and the Hebrews about the daily

---

wealth and realize this ideal, which was also cherished both in the Jewish sectarian movements like the Qumran Essenes and in the idealized circles of friends in Hellenism — see some references conveniently in Barrett, *Acts*, 2:167-69; also Hengel, *Property and Riches in the Early Church*, 9.

68. B. Gerhardsson, "Einige Bemerkungen zu Apg 4,32," *ST* 24 (1970): 144-46; this interpretation is endorsed by Barrett, *Acts*, 1:153.

distribution (Acts 6:1-6), Luke himself shows that the ideal of the common life was not entirely practicable when human sins of greed and jealousy had not been completely overcome even in the Spirit-guided church. The ideal could not be realized completely. Yet apparently it was not given up but rather was continually pursued in the early church, perhaps with some realistic modifications. Apparently in Pauline churches also rich believers donated their wealth to the common fund of their church, so that poor members like widows may benefit from it (cf. 1 Tim 5:9-16; 6:17-19). The problem of the idlers in the Thessalonian church (ἄτακτοι in 1 Thess 5:12-14; 2 Thess 3:6-12; cf. ἀργαί in 1 Tim 5:13) seems to have arisen out of this noble institution, as some members exploited the common fund, spending all their time as gossipers and busybodies in the church (i.e., among the Christian community) rather than working to earn their living or make contribution to the common fund.[69] By referring twice to the fellowship of goods in his summary reports of the Jerusalem church (Acts 2:41-47; 4:32-37), Luke stresses its positive value, in spite of some inevitable aberrations, and expresses his desire for the church of his time to emulate it. This evaluation and this desire must be related to his widely recognized deep concern for the poor. He seems to think that the church must work towards the ideal, even though it is not completely attainable, because only in this way can the poor ("the needy," 2:45; 4:34-35) be properly taken care of.

If Luke is indeed presenting the Jerusalem church's fellowship of goods as a fruit of Jesus' teaching for the rich to share their goods with the poor out of their obedience to the double command of love, as we have interpreted here, that fellowship of goods would be the only concrete evidence in Luke's two-volume work for Jesus' messianic ministry of the Kingdom of God being "good news for the poor" (Luke 4:18) in this world. Although Luke has Jesus proclaim the jubilee year with the inauguration of his messianic ministry as well as explicitly define his messianic mission in terms of preaching good news to the poor and liberating the captives (Luke 4:18-19), Luke does not show anywhere in his two-volume work Jesus — the earthly or the risen — working literally to cancel debts and restore lands for the poor and to free slaves and captives.[70] Therefore, the

---

69. For the possibility that the idlers in the Thessalonian church misunderstood Jesus' teaching in Luke 12:22-34(//Matt 6:25-34 + 19-21) which Paul had delivered to the church along with the eschatological sayings in Luke 12:35-38, 39-40, 41-48, cf. S. Kim, "The Jesus Tradition in 1 Thess 4.13–5.11," *NTS* 48 (2002): 225-42 (esp. p. 242 n. 34).

70. See n. 53 above.

blessings that Jesus promised for the poor in the Beatitudes (Luke 6:20-23) may be interpreted as meant not for this world but entirely for the age to come, for the time when the Kingdom of God is consummated.[71] If so, the "good news for the poor" that Jesus' messianic ministry represented would be only raising hope for the future consummation of the Kingdom of God. But it is difficult to think that Luke would exclude only the poor from the benefits of his proleptic soteriology, from the salvation of the Kingdom of God that has already been proleptically realized through the Christ-event.[72] It would be odd if Luke stressed the sick already benefiting from Jesus' proleptic realization of the salvation of God's Kingdom and yet sought to say that for the poor there was no such benefit, especially as many of the sick would actually be poor as well. Therefore, it seems better to conclude that Luke regards the fellowship of goods in which the poor had their needs met as a concrete sign of the "good news" that Jesus' messianic ministry brought to the poor. If Zacchaeus's giving half of his goods to the poor in his obedience to the Kingdom of God demonstrated the presence of salvation (the blessing of the Kingdom of God) with his household (Luke 19:8-9), how should the material benefit that the poor received as a consequence of Zacchaeus's obedience be understood? Should it not also be regarded as a benefit from the Kingdom of God, i.e., as sharing in the salvation of the Kingdom of God? Thus, Luke seems to suggest that Jesus' messianic ministry was "good news to the poor" not only because it assured them that they would eventually receive the Kingdom of God in full measure, but also because where Jesus' gospel of the Kingdom of God was preached, the rich were moved to share their goods with the poor, so that the poor were delivered from their dire needs — at least partly — already here and now.[73]

71. Cf. Marshall, *Luke: Historian and Theologian*, 144: "Although our previous discussion has established that for Luke 'now' is the era of salvation and the associated blessings, the reversal of conditions for the rich and the poor is associated with the future. In the Beatitudes it is those who suffer *now* who will be recompensed *then*. The afflicted on earth will have treasure in heaven."

72. For the proleptic structure of Lucan soteriology, cf. Marshall, *Luke: Historian and Theologian*, 116-44; F. Bovon, "Das Heil in den Schriften des Lukas," in *Lukas in neuer Sicht: Gesammelte Aufsätze*, trans. E. Hartmann, A. Frey, and P. Strauss, Biblisch-Theologische Studien 8 (Neukirchen-Vluyn: Neukirchener Verlag, 1985), 68-69. See below, pp. 151-55.

73. Cf. Wright, *Jesus and the Victory of God*, 294-95: "the jubilee-language" in Luke 4:18 does not have in view a literal enactment of the three Jubilee provisions, but expresses rather Jesus' intention for "his cells of followers to live 'as if' the Jubilee were being enacted," i.e., to

This view of the fellowship of goods as a mechanism of deliverance of the poor and therefore as a concrete fruit of Jesus' messianic ministry for the poor entails a negative verdict on all those attempts to interpret Lucan theology as a sort of socialist ideology of revolution, let alone an anti-imperial ideology. In Luke there is only the demand for people to share their wealth with the poor in obedience to the double command of the Kingdom of God, but no actual attempt at a politico-socio-economic revolution.[74] Luke has Jesus disclaim even the role of "a judge or divider" between the two brothers in their inheritance dispute (Luke 12:13-15 — Lucan special material). It is remarkable that in this little episode Luke has Jesus refuse to lend his support for the disadvantaged brother but only warn him of the covetousness born of the Mammonistic idolatry with the parable of the rich fool (Luke 12:15 + 12:16-21 — also Lucan special material). So, according to Luke, Jesus does not encourage the disadvantaged to *fight* to get their justice. Jesus delivers the poor from their dire needs — an affliction of the kingdom of Satan — not by a politico-socio-economic struggle but by liberating the rich from the idolatry of Mammon and the sin of exploitation through which Satan reigns. So the fellowship of goods is the result of Jesus' liberation of both the rich and the poor from the kingdom of Satan.

## Conclusion

To conclude our discussions in chapters 8 and 9: according to Luke, Jesus' redemptive work did not consist in altering the political, economic, and social structures of the day to bring Israel political freedom, economic prosperity, and social justice. It consisted rather in exorcism and healing, forgiveness of sins and restoration of sinners, and bringing relief for the poor through formation of a new commonwealth. According to Luke, Jesus was critically aware of the evils of the Roman imperial system. Yet he did not regard it as the only manifestation of Satan's rule but rather as one of the many diverse forms, such as physical and spiritual illness, various forms of sin (Mammonistic idolatry, greed, self-seeking, oppression and

---

live by "the Jubilee principle" among themselves, forgiving not only sins but also debts; and "[t]his may help to explain the remarkable practice" of the fellowship of goods in the early church (Acts 2:41-47; 4:32-37). Cf. n. 53 above.

74. On such personalization of the issue, see below, pp. 147-49.

exploitation of others, hypocritical piety without true trust in and obedience to God and without love of neighbor, etc.), social alienation, and poverty. Therefore, as the messianic bearer of the Kingdom of God Jesus was determined to overcome the reign of Satan, the root cause of all these forms of evil and suffering. Hence, he concentrated on delivering the people from various spiritual and physical ailments and on calling sinners out of the kingdom of Satan and restoring them to the right relationship to God and to the community.[75] Shunning the nationalistic revolutionary method of some of his contemporaries because it was as much a Satan-inspired method of self-assertion and domination as the Roman imperial system, Jesus aimed at gathering and forming a new community of God's people who would live by the law of the in-breaking Kingdom of God, namely, the double command of love for God and for neighbor, a community where therefore the needs of the poor and the oppressed would be met. Thus, healing the sick, restoring sinners, and forming a new community of God's people were the chief work of redemption or liberation of the people from the kingdom or bondage of Satan that Jesus did in anticipation of the full realization of God's Kingdom.

According to Richard T. France, this stance of Jesus expresses his being concerned more fundamentally to alter human beings' attitudes and relationships towards God and towards one another than to bring changes to systems.[76] R. S. Sugirtharajah, a proponent of postcolonial hermeneutics,

---

75. This may be compared with the concept of Christian warfare in Eph 6:10-20: "Be strong in the Lord and in the strength of his might. Put on the whole armor of God, so that you may be able to stand against the wiles of the devil. For we are not contending against flesh and blood, but against the principalities, against the powers, against the world rulers of this present darkness, against the spiritual hosts of wickedness in the heavenly places. Therefore take the whole armor of God: . . . truth, . . . righteousness, . . . the gospel of peace, . . . faith, . . . salvation, . . . the Spirit, . . . the word of God, . . . praying . . . with all perseverance."

76. Cf. France, "Liberation in the New Testament," 8-9: "And yet [Jesus] talked about 'good news to the poor', 'release', 'liberty'. If he was not preaching political liberation, what did he mean? At the risk of sounding hopelessly traditional, I can only say that the liberation he proclaimed was from something far more deep-rooted than the political oppression of the Roman empire. He did not expect, and certainly did not advocate, a reestablishment of Jewish national freedom; indeed, he went out of his way to pour cold water on any such hopes. His concern was with men's attitudes and relationships towards one another and towards God. In the latter respect he looked for liberation from sin, from hypocrisy, from alienation from God; in the former respect he attacked pride, greed, injustice, and the barriers of class, race, wealth and respectability which divide man from man. These are all mat-

also recognizes this and designates such a stance as personalization of the issues. Noting the "apolitical nature" of Jesus' encounter with Zacchaeus (Luke 19:1-9), Sugirtharajah observes:

> Jesus did not call upon Zacchaeus to give up his profession nor did he request him to work against the system, the very system which had made him rich. Instead, Jesus believed in a person's, in this case Zacchaeus's ability to transform things from within, beginning with his own change of heart. Jesus's response to an oppressive structure had more to do with personalizing the issue and appealing directly to individuals to act fairly than with calling for a radical overhaul of the system. Jesus challenged the system by appealing to the moral conviction of individuals, and raising their consciousness.[77]

Indeed, Jesus seems to have trusted in the power of God's kingly reign to change individuals' hearts as they submit to its demand to turn from the Satanic self-seeking or Mammonistic idolatry to loving God and neighbors out of trust in his fatherly care, and he seems to have seen such personal changes as essential and effective for any real change in the system.

In this context, Seán Freyne's explanation of Jesus' stance in connection with his creative interpretation of the Kingdom of God is also helpful.[78] Freyne relates Jesus' understanding of the Kingdom of God to his "faith that was grounded in a trust in the goodness of the creation as he had experienced it and reflected on its mysterious but hidden processes," a faith "that had been nourished by the apocalyptic imagination that this creator God was still in charge of his world and had the power to make all things new again."[79] Further, Freyne believes that Jesus drew inspiration from the Servant of Yahweh in Isa 53 who led people to righteousness through his teaching and his voluntary suffering and death, and from the *maskilim* in Daniel who likewise taught people righteousness and dissuaded them from assimilating to foreign ways, while remaining faithful to the covenant values, even accepting persecution and death and expecting ultimate vindication from God during the crisis of Antiochus IV, in con-

---

ters of attitudes and values, of a man's spiritual and social orientation, and it is here that Jesus' programme of liberation centred."

77. Sugirtharajah, *Postcolonial Criticism*, 90.

78. Freyne, *Jesus, a Jewish Galilean*, 121-70.

79. Freyne, *Jesus, a Jewish Galilean*, 149.

trast to the Maccabean freedom fighters and the *Hasidim* who operated with the triumphant Zion ideology.[80] On the basis of such a faith and such an understanding of the Kingdom of God, and inspired by such models, Jesus eschewed the violent way of resistance to the Roman Empire and its Jewish client rulers, but instead "chose the way of the *maskilim*, teaching the many righteousness and trusting in God to make things right. He would render to God what was God's, and leave it to the creator God to make all things new."[81]

These insights of Freyne, Sugirtharajah, and France — Jesus' faith in the real, though hidden, reign of the creator God over the world and in history, his adoption of the Servant of Yahweh and the *maskilim* as his models, his rejection of the triumphant Zion ideology, and his personalization of issues — should be brought into the framework formed on one side by Jesus' view of Satan's reign in sin as the fundamental problem, and on the other by his belief in the imminent consummation of the Kingdom of God.[82] And Jesus' revolutionary teaching on love — even enemy love (instead of vengeance) that goes much beyond the ethos of the Servant and the *maskilim* — should also be mixed in. Then we can go a long way to understanding Jesus' stance or the characteristics of his ministry that have been sketched above.

---

80. Freyne, *Jesus, a Jewish Galilean*, 129-30, 169.

81. Freyne, *Jesus, a Jewish Galilean*, 170. Cf. also G. Theissen, who concludes his essay "The Political Dimension of Jesus' Activities," in *The Social Setting of Jesus and the Gospels*, ed. W. Stegemann, B. J. Malina, and G. Theissen (Minneapolis: Fortress, 2002), similarly and yet with somewhat different stress: "Jesus and his movement envision a humane rulership, and Jesus expects that God will establish this rulership. Only God can realize a way of ruling without the use of force and coercion. This process is as nonviolent as the growth of plants. Yet Jesus and his adherents did not espouse political quietism. They do not remain passive. They participated in the realization of the kingdom of God by an explicit renunciation of force, by political symbolic actions, and by an in-group exercise of humane rulership" (p. 243).

82. Cf. G. Bornkamm, *Jesus of Nazareth*, trans. I. and F. McLuskey (London: Hodder & Stoughton/New York: Harper & Row, 1960), 121, who sees Jesus' imminent expectation of the Kingdom of God as the reason why "the problem of the state appears [only] at the margin of Jesus' preaching."

# 10. The Apostles' Campaign against the Kingdom of Satan and Witness to the Kingdom of God

## The Exalted Lord Jesus Christ Continues His Redemptive Work through His Apostles

The healings and exorcisms that constitute Jesus' work of redemption from Satan's reign were prolepsis and symbols of the complete salvation, "eternal life," in the future consummated Kingdom of God.[1] While the consummated Kingdom of God is still outstanding, the risen and exalted Lord Jesus Christ continues this redemptive work in the power of the Spirit and through his apostolic church. So, in the second volume of his work, the Acts of the Apostles, Luke shows how the exalted Lord empowers and directs his apostolic church through the Holy Spirit to carry on this saving work (cf. Acts 1:1-2).

Having shown, uniquely among the Evangelists, Jesus' ascension to heaven (Luke 24:50-53; Acts 1:9-11), Luke stresses Jesus' exaltation to the right hand of God to be the "Lord" or God's viceroy in fulfillment of Ps 110:1 (Acts 2:32-36; 5:30-31), that is, that Jesus now exercises God's lordship on his behalf. Luke expresses this also by combining "the Kingdom of God" with "the name of Jesus Christ" or with "the Lord Jesus Christ" in his summaries of the gospel that Philip and Paul preached (Acts 8:12; 28:23, 31), as well as by making the object of the verbs *euangelizomai* (εὐαγ-γελίζομαι, "preach the good news") and *kēryssō* (κηρύσσω, "proclaim") not only the Kingdom of God (Acts 8:12; 20:25; 28:31) but also the Lord Jesus

---

1. Cf. F. Bovon, "Das Heil in den Schriften des Lukas," in *Lukas in neuer Sicht: Gesammelte Aufsätze*, trans. E. Hartmann, A. Frey, and P. Strauss, Biblisch-Theologische Studien 8 (Neukirchen-Vluyn: Neukirchener Verlag, 1985), 69.

Christ, the Son of God (Acts 5:42; 8:5, 35; 9:20; 10:36; 11:20; 17:18; 19:13; cf. 15:35; 17:3, 7) in his other summaries of the apostolic preaching. The Lord Jesus Christ is the present regent of the Kingdom of God and he executes the divine work of salvation (Acts 2:21; 3:16; 4:12, 30; 10:42-43; 22:16), and hence to preach him is to preach the gospel of the Kingdom of God.

Therefore, in Acts, Luke shows how the exalted Lord Jesus heals a lame man through Peter and John at the gate of the temple (3:15-16); receives the spirit of Stephen at the right hand of God (7:54-60); converts Paul and commissions him as his apostle (9:1-19; 22:6-11; 26:12-18), and directs Ananias to be instrumental in his commissioning of Paul as his apostle (9:10-18); heals the paralytic Aeneas through Peter (9:34-35); helps Peter overcome his inhibition about "unclean" food as part of his direction of him to Cornelius (10:9-16); gives the scattered Hellenists success with their gospel preaching in Antioch (11:19-21); sends his angel to rescue Peter from Herod's prison (12:6-11, 17); punishes Elymas the magician and leads Sergius Paulus to faith through Barnabas and Saul/Paul (13:6-12); bears "witness to the word of his grace, granting signs and wonders to be done by [the] hands" of Paul and Barnabas (14:3); opens Lydia's heart to receive Paul's gospel (16:14-15); assures Paul of his protection before the Jewish opposition at Corinth (18:5-11); lets Paul escape from Jerusalem and sends him to the Gentiles (22:17-21); and sends Paul to Rome to bear witness to him there (23:11).

As is well known, Luke also speaks of the Spirit directing and empowering the apostles' mission (e.g., 8:29; 10:19; 11:12, 28; 13:2-4; 15:28; 16:6-7; 19:6, 21; 20:22, 23; 21:4, 11). So there is a close parallelism between the statements about the activities of the exalted Lord Jesus Christ and those about the activities of the Holy Spirit. That the two kinds of statements really refer to the same reality is suggested in 16:6-7: the Holy Spirit who directs Paul to leave Asia for Macedonia is explicitly identified as "the Spirit of Jesus." Therefore, they may be combined as meaning that the Lord Jesus Christ exalted in heaven directs and empowers his apostolic church through his Spirit on earth. The identification of the Holy Spirit as the Spirit of Jesus is clearly related to the important interpretation of the Pentecostal outpouring of the Spirit: having been installed as the "Lord" or God's vicegerent at God's right hand, Jesus "has received from the Father the promised Holy Spirit and has poured (the Spirit) out" to his church (Acts 2:33). This explains why the Holy Spirit, which is the Spirit of God the Father, is the Spirit of Jesus the Lord as well (cf. Rom 8:9-17). This fact may be affirmed in reverse also: the Holy Spirit, which is the Spirit of Jesus, is really the Spirit of God the Father. For this reason, Luke concludes his account of Paul's experience of direction by the Holy Spirit (i.e., the Spirit of Jesus) away from Asia into Macedonia thus: "*God* had called [him] to preach the gospel" to the Macedonians (16:10). Thus 16:6-10 implies the trinitarian structure of divine lordship exercised in regards to the church's mission: the exalted Lord Jesus Christ executes God's direction of his church through the Spirit, which is both God's and his.

During his earthly existence Jesus preached the gospel of the Kingdom of God and actualized God's saving reign through the power of the Holy Spirit (Luke 11:20; Acts 2:22; 10:38). Now, having been properly installed as "Lord" or God's vicegerent at God's right hand, he has received the Holy Spirit from the Father and poured the Spirit out to his church (Acts 2:33). So, now while remaining at the right hand of God in heaven until his (second) coming for "the restoration of all things" or the consummation of the Kingdom of God (3:19-21), the Lord Jesus Christ directs and empowers through the Holy Spirit (i.e., his Spirit) his apostles or the apostolic church to actualize his saving reign, which is really God's saving reign (11:20-24; 16:6-10). So the apostles perform "signs and wonders" "in the name of Jesus Christ" (3:6, 16; 4:10, 30; 8:6-12; 16:16-18; cf. 19:13-20) and through the power of the Holy Spirit (1:8; 2:33; 4:29-31; 6:3-8; 8:5-19), which are really the "signs and wonders" that God (15:12; 19:11-13) or the Lord Jesus Christ (14:3) enables them to perform.

Thus, the apostolic church actualizes the Lord Jesus Christ's saving reign through the Holy Spirit, and the redemption of the Lord Jesus Christ's saving reign that she actualizes is the same as that which the earthly Jesus actualized: by preaching the gospel of the Kingdom of God and the Lord Jesus Christ (Acts 8:12; 14:22; 17:17; 19:8; 20:25; 28:23, 31), the apostles bring about exorcisms (5:16; 8:7; 16:18; 19:11-16), healings (3:1-10; 9:32-35; 9:36-43; 14:8-10; 19:11-12; 20:7-12; cf. also 2:43-47; 4:30; 5:12-16; 6:8; 8:7, 13; 14:3; 15:12),[2] and forgiveness of sins through the name of Jesus (2:38; 3:19; 5:31; 10:43; 13:38; 22:16; 26:18), which are all understood as redemption from the oppression of Satan (10:38; 26:18), as well as formation of the community of sharing in which the needs of the poor are met (2:41-47; 4:32-37; 6:1-6; 11:27-30; 20:35; 24:17).

---

2. Cf. B. D. Ehrman, *The New Testament: A Historical Introduction to the Early Christian Writings,* 2nd ed. (New York and Oxford: Oxford University Press, 2000), 128, for parallelism between Jesus' work in Luke and the apostles' work in Acts.

This unity of the redemptive work of the earthly Jesus and the exalted Lord Jesus Christ means that just as the earthly Jesus waged a campaign to subvert the empire of Satan rather than the Roman Empire, so also the exalted Lord Jesus Christ does the same through his apostles or apostolic church. Therefore, in his second volume, the Acts of the Apostles, Luke does not show the apostolic church engaged in waging a revolutionary work against the Roman imperial system. The exalted Lord Jesus Christ, the present regent of the Kingdom of God, directs his church to carry on only what he did while on earth, and does not direct his church to open up a new front against the empire of Satan and fight the imperial political (or any political) form of its manifestation.

According to Klaus Wengst, Luke presents Jesus' ascension as his enthronement as king and has Jesus designated as "king" at the triumphal entry (Luke 19:38) because the event is the beginning of Jesus' heavenly enthronement. However, since the Kingdom of God is not to appear immediately (Luke 19:11-17; Acts 1:4-11) and Jesus is to enter upon his rule on earth only at his *parousia*, Luke holds that his kingship applies only to heaven for the moment. Wengst believes that this is the reason why at the triumphal entry Jesus' disciples cry "Peace *in heaven* and glory in the highest" (Luke 19:38), whereas at his birth the angels cried "Glory to God in the highest, and *on earth* peace among people with whom he is pleased!" (Luke 2:14).[3]

As Wengst insists, the two "peace" cries as well as the two acclamations of Jesus' Messiahship/kingship in Luke 2:10-14 and 19:38 must be understood in mutual reference. But precisely because they should be seen together, Wengst's interpretation of the "peace" cry in Luke 19:38 as a contradiction to that in Luke 2:14 cannot be accepted. If Luke is to end his account of Jesus' messianic work with affirming his realization of peace only in heaven, why does he let the angels cry "peace on earth" at Jesus' *birth*? Surely Luke would not mean to imply that Jesus unfortunately failed to accomplish his mission on earth. Or is he in 2:14 letting the angels cry for what will be realized on earth only at Christ's second coming? But then it would be odd that Luke lets the angels sing the song of praise on the occasion of his *first* coming for what really befits his *second* coming. More seriously, then, how are we to regard all the saving activities that Luke depicts the earthly Jesus as having performed and those that he depicts the church as performing on earth in the name of the exalted Lord Jesus Christ or through the power supplied by his Spirit? Do they not constitute the "peace" or salvation that Christ Jesus has brought and is bringing *on earth*? If Jesus is understood to bring "peace" only in heaven at pres-

---

3. K. Wengst, *Pax Romana and the Peace of Jesus Christ*, trans. J. Bowden (Philadelphia: Fortress, 1987), 103-4.

ent, this will have to be denied. For this difficulty, Wengst's interpretation has to be rejected along with the view held in some quarters that the Lucan Christ is only in heaven and inactive on earth during the interim period between his ascension and *parousia*.

Jesus' triumphal entry to Jerusalem as "king" is indeed an anticipatory celebration of his enthronement in heaven and not a real celebration of his enthronement on earth. And with his ascension and enthronement in heaven peace is established in heaven, but insofar as his kingship is rejected on earth, peace is not established on earth. Luke shows this by immediately following the account of Jesus' triumphal entry (Luke 19:28-40) with his narrative of Jesus lamenting over Israel's rejection of "the things that make for *peace*" (i.e., Jesus' teachings about the Kingdom of God) and weeping over the impending destruction of Jerusalem and the people by foreign enemies (Luke 19:41-44). So in 19:38 Luke could not let the disciples cry "on earth peace," but only "in heaven peace." However, in so doing, he does not mean to limit the redemptive kingship of the enthroned Jesus only to heaven and deny its peace-bringing effects on earth. For he is going to show in his second volume how the King or Lord Jesus Christ enthroned in heaven, in fact, brings about "peace" or salvation on earth through his Spirit and his apostolic church. The angels' cry at Jesus' birth, "on earth peace," in Luke 2:14 has in view the complete course of his ministry as the Messiah and Lord, from his earthly ministry through his heavenly enthronement to his *parousia* and consummation of God's Kingdom (Acts 3:19-21). The disciples' cry at the triumphal entry, "in heaven peace," has in view only what is to happen immediately, namely, Jesus' enthronement in heaven, which, however, will involve his further struggle with the Satanic forces through his Spirit and his church until his *parousia* — to establish "peace" on earth.

## To Persuade the Rulers to Submit to the Kingdom of God and the Lord Jesus Christ?

We have also seen above how Luke implies in his account of Jesus' temptation by Satan that the Roman emperor and other kings of this world derive their authority from Satan and exercise it for their own benefit as he wills (Luke 4:1-13), and how Luke has Jesus criticize the pagan kings for lording it over their subjects, i.e., for exercising their authority in a way that befits Satan's kingdom (Luke 22:24-27).[4] This line of thinking demands that Jesus' and his apostolic church's campaign against the kingdom of Satan

4. See above, pp. 88-90.

should include not only healing the sick, restoring sinners, and building a community of sharing, but also struggling against the oppressive rules of Caesar, Pilate, Herod, and others. Indeed, Luke clearly sees that ultimately their lordship of oppression will have to be abolished and replaced by Jesus' lordship of service (Luke 22:26-27), so that the people suffering from injustice and oppression under their lordship may be redeemed, i.e., the captives and the oppressed may be liberated. The *inclusio* of Luke 2:1-14 and Acts 28:30-31, together with the account of Jesus' messianic inauguration (Luke 3:1-22), and passages such as Luke 4:1-13; 22:24-27; Acts 10:36-43, suggest that Caesar's kingship will eventually be replaced by the kingship of Jesus, the Son of David and the Son of God, as the kingdom of Satan will be replaced by the Kingdom of God. All these passages clearly envision Jesus, the real Lord *(kyrios)* and the real Savior *(sōtēr),* replacing Caesar, his mere parody, and bringing the real "peace," a universal shalom, to replace *pax Romana,* its mere parody.

But we have repeatedly noted that Luke does not show Jesus and the apostles actually working to materialize here and now this political dimension of redemption from the kingdom of Satan or the Roman Empire. While concentrating on realizing redemption from the kingdom of Satan in the form of healing the sick, restoring sinners, and building a community of love and service, nowhere do Jesus or the apostles work to subvert or even correct the Roman imperial rule, or any local political rule, and liberate God's people from such a rule of injustice and oppression. Is this so because, unlike the other aspects of redemption from the kingdom of Satan, this political dimension is completely postponed until the time of the "renewal" and "restoration" of the whole creation, which the *parousia* of the Lord Jesus Christ will usher in (Acts 3:20-21)? In fact, this seems to be suggested by the programmatic statement in Acts 1:6-8. The conversation between Jesus and his apostles in the passage reveals that the universal proclamation of the gospel is prior to the "restoration of the kingdom to Israel," that the latter belongs to the eschaton (i.e., the time of "restoration of all things," 3:21), the timing of which is reserved for the sovereign decision of God the Father, and that therefore, leaving concerns for it aside for the moment, the apostles should concentrate on bringing the gospel to the ends of the earth. Thus this programmatic statement postpones until the eschaton the "restoration of the kingdom to Israel," the restoration of the political fortunes to "Israel" (whether the physical Israel or the redefined Israel of the Jewish and Gentile believers in Christ). And it clearly reveals that Luke is going to narrate the course of the apostolic mission in the Book of Acts from the viewpoint of the progress of the gospel rather than that of the "restoration of the kingdom to Israel." Hence, the absence of any report in the book about the apostles working to bring about greater freedom, justice, and peace in the name of the Lord Jesus Christ.

Does this mean that Luke abandons even a mere suggestion that the church in the meantime must try to persuade individual rulers to accept the Kingdom of God and the Lord Jesus Christ (i.e., God's kingship and Jesus' lordship) for realization of greater shalom, just as Jesus tried to persuade rich people to accept the Kingdom of God and live by its demand, the double command of love, in order to materialize at least a proleptic redemption of the poor?

It may be possible to interpret Luke 21:12-13 as containing such a suggestion. In the passage Jesus predicts that as part of their persecution at the end time his disciples "will be brought before kings and governors for my name's sake" (ἀπαγομένους ἐπὶ βασιλεῖς καὶ ἡγεμόνας ἕνεκεν τοῦ ὀνόματός μου), and then adds, "this will turn out to be your opportunity to bear witness" (ἀποβήσεται ὑμῖν εἰς μαρτύριον; NRSV: "this will give you an opportunity to testify"). The latter sentence is the Lucan rephrasing of the Marcan phrase εἰς μαρτύριον αὐτοῖς (Mark 13:9). This Marcan phrase already has the positive sense of "in order to bear witness before them," and Matthew (10:18) strengthens it by adding to the Marcan phrase καὶ τοῖς ἔθνεσιν, which seems to be drawn from Mark 13:10, the verse that speaks of the need for the gospel to be preached to all nations before the end time. With his use of the word ἀποβήσεται, Luke strengthens the positive sense even more than Matthew does, by implying that the (negative) trials will turn out to be (positive) opportunities (cf. Phil 1:19); the disciples' trials before kings and governors would turn out to be opportunities for them to bear witness to Jesus or the Kingdom of God.[5] This interpreta-

---

5. H. Strathmann, "μάρτυς, κτλ," *TDNT,* 4:502-4, wrongly interprets all the εἰς μαρτύριον αὐτοῖς phrases of Mark 1:44/Matt 8:4/Luke 5:14; Mark 13:9/Matt 10:18; Matt 24:14 in the negative sense of "for a testimony against them" (i.e., for proof for indictment) at the last judgment rather than in the positive sense of "to testify to them." Even so, Strathmann thinks that with the phrase ἀποβήσεται ὑμῖν in Luke 21:13 Luke has turned the negative sense of Mark 13:9 into the positive sense of "the opportunity to bear witness." For our present purpose, affirming this is enough. However, it must be pointed out that the phrase εἰς μαρτύριον πᾶσιν τοῖς ἔθνεσιν in Matt 24:14 has clearly the positive sense, and that by reflect-

tion is supported by Acts 9:15, which reports the Lord's word to Ananias concerning Paul at the latter's call on the Damascus road: "Go, for he is a chosen instrument of mine to carry my name before the Gentiles and *kings* and the sons of Israel," and again by Acts 27:24, in which Paul reports the word of an angel to him in the midst of the shipwreck on the way to Rome: "Do not be afraid, Paul; you must stand before Caesar," clearly in order to bear witness to the Lord Jesus Christ (cf. Acts 23:11). It would be too restrictive an interpretation to think that bearing witness to Christ before kings and governors has only the purpose of proving the political harmlessness of the gospel and so securing the freedom to preach it. In fact, all the passages discussed in this paragraph clearly suggest that it has rather the purpose of persuading the kings and governors to accept the gospel of the Kingdom of God and the Lord Jesus Christ (cf. Acts 28:23, 31, esp. διαμαρτυρόμενος τὴν βασιλείαν τοῦ θεοῦ in v. 23),[6] or to put it in the words of Paul, to "bring about [their] obedience of faith for the sake of his name" (Rom 1:5).

So, Luke actually shows how Peter and John used their trials before the Sanhedrin as opportunities to bear witness to the Lord Jesus Christ (Acts 4:1-22; 5:17-42), and how Stephen did the same (6:8–7:60). Especially in Acts 24–26 (cf. also 22:1-21), Luke repeatedly shows how Paul turned the trials before the Roman governors and the king Agrippa into opportunities to bear witness to the Lord or preach the gospel. It is noteworthy that

---

ing both verses 9 and 10 of Mark 13 together in Matt 10:18, Matthew clearly took the phrase εἰς μαρτύριον αὐτοῖς in Mark 13:9 in the positive sense. In Mark 1:40-45 pars. Jesus sends the leper whom he has cleansed to the priest for inspection and for the rites and sacrifices prescribed by Moses (Lev 14:1-32), so that he may obtain the "health clearance" necessary for a proper restoration to the community at large. Thus Jesus sends the cleansed leper to the priest περὶ τοῦ καθαρισμοῦ σου ἃ προσέταξεν Μωϋσῆς, εἰς μαρτύριον αὐτοῖς (Mark 1:44), i.e., in order to demonstrate his cleansing to the priest and the society at large, or "for a proof to the people" (RSV). It is quite perverse for Strathmann to understand the phrase εἰς μαρτύριον αὐτοῖς here in the sense of "Belastungszeugnis" (witness to make them guilty) for their unbelief.

6. This positive sense is especially clear when all the passages concerning Paul's Roman journey are seen together: Acts 19:21 (Paul's resolution *in the Spirit* to go to Rome); 23:11 (the Lord's direction for Paul to "bear witness" at Rome); 27:24 (the Lord's direction for Paul to stand before Caesar); 28:14, 23, 31 (having, at last, arrived at Rome, Paul "bears witness [διαμαρτυρόμενος] to the Kingdom of God" [v. 23] and teaches about the Lord Jesus Christ — something that he would surely do also before Caesar when the trial before him takes place).

Luke has Paul not only preach about the resurrection of Jesus Christ (24:21; 25:19; 26:8) but also preach about "faith in Christ Jesus" (24:24); argue "about justice [δικαιοσύνη] and self-control and future judgment" (24:25); explain about redemption from the power of Satan, forgiveness of sins, and incorporation into the people of God (26:18); call for repentance and conversion to God (26:20); testify from the Scriptures that Christ must suffer and rise again from the dead to bring revelation both to Israel and the Gentiles (26:22-23); and even try to convert Agrippa (26:27-29). Earlier Luke also showed how Paul was able to convert Sergius Paulus, the proconsul of Cyprus, with "the teaching of the Lord" backed up by his demonstration of power (13:4-12). In the light of all these examples, it is not difficult to surmise that Paul appealed to Caesar to be tried before him, not just for the purpose of securing liberty to preach the gospel, but also to bear witness to the Kingdom of God and teach about the Lord Jesus Christ (28:23, 31).

Why is witnessing to the Kingdom of God and the Lord Jesus Christ before kings and governors and converting them important? If this question is put to Luke, he may answer as he has Paul imply in his answer to King Agrippa (Acts 26:29): it is important for the sake of their own salvation. Further, Luke may answer that it is important for the sake of the freedom of Christian mission. Would Luke also add that it is especially intended to make them good rulers who seek justice, peace, and freedom of their people, in obedience to the Lord Jesus Christ? Is this hinted at in his report of Paul's discussion before Felix "about justice [δικαιοσύνη] and self-control and future judgment" (24:25)? It may be. But even if it is, it is only a hint.

Although Luke does not have Jesus or Paul say to the rulers or officers the equivalent of what he has John the Baptist say to tax collectors and soldiers — "Collect no more than is appointed to you" and "Rob no one by violence or by false accusation, and be content with your wages" (Luke 3:12-14) — would it be possible that Luke assumes Paul to have admonished Sergius Paulus to be a just and caring proconsul when he converted him with "the teaching of the Lord" (Acts 13:4-12)? Or is this implied in Luke's description of the proconsul as "astonished at the teaching of the Lord" (Acts 13:12), or in his description of Paul's charge of Elymas the magician, who was trying to dissuade the proconsul from converting to the Christian faith: "You son of the devil, you enemy of *all righteousness* [δικαιοσύνη], full of all deceit and villainy" (Acts 13:10)? Luke nowhere explicitly says that part of Paul's purpose in witnessing to Christ before the rulers was to make them exercise their authority in the spirit of justice and service in obedience to the teaching of the Lord (Luke 22:24-27). We have to surmise it from such flimsy pieces of evidence as the passages that have been surveyed here, bearing in mind Luke's particular concerns for the poor and the oppressed, or about injustice and oppression.

All the discussion so far has turned out, somewhat disappointingly, only to highlight the paucity of evidence in Luke-Acts that Jesus and his apostles made an effort to materialize the *political* dimension of redemption from the kingdom of Satan here and now, in contrast to the abundant evidence that they attempted to materialize other dimensions, such as healing the sick, restoring sinners, and building a community of love and service.

## 11. Reasons for Lack of Concern for the Political Materialization of Redemption

Why is there such a dearth of concern in Luke-Acts for the redemption of the Kingdom of God to materialize politically in the present?

### Eschatology

Above we have observed how Paul's expectation of the imminent end of this age/world and the imminent consummation of the Kingdom of God gave him little motivation for changing the social and political status quo. May Luke have a similar eschatological motivation for his lack of concern about the socio-political changes in the present? According to Hans Conzelmann, in Luke's case it is not the expectation of the imminent *parousia* of the Lord Jesus Christ but rather the opposite, the sense of the delayed *parousia*, that leads him to seek an adjustment to the Roman world. Now that the end is no longer expected to be imminent and therefore the empire and the world are here to stay, the church needs to arrange a long-term settlement as to her relationship to the empire and the world. So in Luke-Acts, Luke seeks to make a political apologetic toward the Roman Empire that Christianity is a loyal movement posing no threat to order.[1] If this is indeed a purpose of Luke's writing, it is understandable that he does not stress how the gospel of the Kingdom of God and the Lord Jesus Christ is to bring about changes to the Roman imperial system at present.

1. H. Conzelmann, *The Theology of St. Luke*, trans. G. Buswell (London: Faber and Faber/New York: Harper & Row, 1960), 137-49.

However, Jacob Jervell objects to Conzelmann's concepts of the de-layed *parousia* and political apologetic. Jervell summarizes the Lucan es-chatology in this formula: "The kingdom of God is always present after Je-sus, but the day of his coming lies in the future."[2] That is, with Jesus' ministry, resurrection, and ascension, and the outpouring of the Spirit, the eschaton has arrived, and therefore the church already lives in the end of times, although it has to await Christ's *parousia* for the consummation of salvation, the "times of refreshing" and "the restoration of all things" (Acts 3:19-21).[3] Luke ties the consummation with the gospel reaching "the ends of the earth" (Acts 1:6-8; 3:19-21; Luke 24:47). According to Jervell, the fact that Luke retains expressions of an imminent *parousia* (Luke 3:7, 9; 9:27; 10:9, 11; 18:7-8; 21:32-33, 36) suggests that he does not see too long a post-ponement of it; in fact, since he regards the gospel as having reached most of the Jews (including the Diaspora), it is likely that he regards the *parousia* and the consummation as imminent.[4]

If this view of Luke's eschatology is correct, then, like Paul, Luke may be uninterested in any political changes in the short interim period of the present because he expects the kingdoms of the world under the sway of Satan to be soon replaced by the consummated Kingdom of God at the im-minent *parousia*. Jervell does not say this, but still he affirms: "It is an issue in itself that the state and the Roman Empire are never dealt with in prin-ciple."[5] And with this statement he argues against the theory that in Luke-Acts Luke is presenting an *apologia* for the church to Roman authorities in order to court their favorable treatment of the church.[6] For such a view Jervell finds far too much negative presentation of Roman authorities in Luke-Acts. As far as the Roman Empire is concerned, "Luke's intention is to show Christians that the empire cannot mean any serious threat to the church, cannot obstruct the proclamation of the gospel and is forced to serve the will of God, even if it joins with the Jews in persecuting the church."[7] But, for our purpose, it is regrettable that Jervell does not raise the question of why, in spite of Luke's idea of the church as the restored Is-

---

2. J. Jervell, *The Theology of the Acts of the Apostles*, NTT (Cambridge: Cambridge University Press, 1996), 109.

3. Jervell, *Theology of the Acts of the Apostles*, 106-15.

4. Jervell, *Theology of the Acts of the Apostles*, 111-12, 114-15.

5. Jervell, *Theology of the Acts of the Apostles*, 102.

6. Jervell, *Theology of the Acts of the Apostles*, 100-106.

7. Jervell, *Theology of the Acts of the Apostles*, 105.

rael, his Christology of Jesus as the Messiah-king, and his eschatology about the Kingdom of God,[8] he does not relate the claims of the Lord Jesus Christ to the Roman Empire in any way, but instead emphasizes only the political harmlessness of the church and the innocence of her leaders.[9]

However, Stephen G. Wilson observes that the Gospel of Luke contains both the strand that allows for a delay in the *parousia* (Luke 19:11; 21:20-24; 22:69; Acts 1:6-8) and the strand that expects the imminent *parousia* (Luke 9:27; 10:9, 11; 12:38-48; 12:54–13:9; 18:8; 21:32).[10] Wilson thinks that Luke affirms both in order to meet the needs of his pastoral situations, i.e., to resolve the two opposite problems that can arise out of disappointment at the delayed *parousia:* with the former strand, Luke tries to prevent a renewed fanatical apocalypticism and impatient attempts to force the Kingdom of God in by human efforts, while with the latter he tries to prevent people from giving up the hope for the *parousia* altogether.[11] So Wilson insists that for the Gospel of Luke both strands should be affirmed and neither should be ignored or overrated.[12] However, he thinks that in Acts Luke develops only the notion of the delayed *parousia,* neglecting the belief in an imminent end. Luke does this by schematizing the eschatological timetable to allow "a hiatus between the Resurrection and the Parousia in which the Church can exist and grow," and by "substitut[ing] Ascension theology, the present activity of the exalted Lord in his Church, for belief in an imminent end."[13]

It is true that although in Acts Luke maintains the expectation for the *parousia* of Christ (Acts 1:11; cf. 2:19-21) for the eschatological consummation (3:19-21) and the last judgment (10:42; 17:30-31), the note of imminence is absent. Luke's appreciation of the ascension of the risen Jesus as the presently reigning Lord (Luke 24:51; Acts 1:9-11; 2:32-36) and of the Pentecostal outpouring of the Holy Spirit as the inauguration of the last days (Acts 2:16-21), as well as his depiction of the church's expansion from Jeru-

---

8. Jervell thinks that all these contain obvious political concerns (*Theology of the Acts of the Apostles,* 104).

9. This emphasis is recognized by Jervell himself (*Theology of the Acts of the Apostles,* 105-6).

10. S. G. Wilson, *The Gentiles and the Gentile Mission in Luke-Acts,* SNTSMS 23 (Cambridge: Cambridge University Press, 1973), 67-77.

11. Wilson, *Gentiles and the Gentile Mission,* 83-85.

12. Wilson, *Gentiles and the Gentile Mission,* 85.

13. Wilson, *Gentiles and the Gentile Mission,* 80.

salem to Rome, do indeed suggest that he takes the delayed *parousia* for granted. However, it is not certain that by the time Luke comes to write Acts his eschatology has changed, as Wilson thinks [14] so as to abandon the expectation of an imminent *parousia* that he maintained alongside the notion of a delayed *parousia* in his Gospel. For in Acts not only are such hopes for an imminent *parousia* absent, but so also are such expressions of a delayed *parousia*. In Acts Luke simply does not show much interest in the timing of the *parousia*.

In Acts 1:6-11 it is simply said that the timing of the end-time consummation cannot be known or the apostles should not be anxious to know it as it is reserved for the sovereign decision of God the Father. But modern interpreters tend to read into the text a delayed *parousia,* thinking that the commission for the church to take the gospel from Jerusalem to "the end of the earth" (1:8) involves a long time and therefore necessarily presupposes a delay. However, for Luke, Rome may be "the end of the earth,"[15] as he appears to structure the course of the church's mission in Acts in accordance with the programmatic scheme of 1:8 and see Paul's preaching of the gospel in Rome (28:16-31) as the fulfillment of that program. If so, as Jervell argues,[16] Luke may think that the gospel has reached the end of the earth and so the *parousia* is not far away. Even if "the end of the earth" refers to the land further beyond Rome, say, to Spain, or refers to Rome as the representative of the world rather than as an end in itself,[17] since Luke's notion of evangelization appears to be closer to Paul's provincial conception (Rom 15:15-24)[18] than to our modern individualistic conception, he may be thinking that the commission of Acts 1:8 can be completed in a short time, perhaps within his generation. So Luke could still expect the *parousia* soon. In fact, Acts 1:7-8 may express no more than the belief that it cannot be known

14. Wilson, *Gentiles and the Gentile Mission,* 86.

15. C. K. Barrett, *A Critical and Exegetical Commentary on the Acts of the Apostles,* 2 vols., ICC (Edinburgh: T&T Clark, 1994, 1998), 2:80.

16. Jervell, *Theology of the Acts of the Apostles,* 111-12, 114-15; see p. 162, above.

17. So Barrett, *Acts,* 2:80.

18. Paul reports that he has "fully preached the gospel" to the whole regions "from Jerusalem as far around as Illyricum" (Rom 15:19), so that there is for him "no more room to work in those regions" (v. 23), and expresses his eagerness to go to Spain (v. 24) as part of his mission to "all the nations" (Rom 1:5; cf. Mark 13:10; Rev 14:6) or the end of the earth. Apparently this language is possible because he regards his gospel preaching completed in a province when he has won first converts from it and offered them as the "firstfruits" of its Gentile nation to God (cf. Rom 11:16; 15:16; 16:5; 1 Cor 16:15).

whether the *parousia* will be delayed for a considerable period or may happen soon, and therefore that instead of being anxious about its date, the apostles must concentrate on taking the gospel to the end of the earth and bringing people to repentance and faith if they want the *parousia* to take place soon (Luke 24:47; Acts 3:19-21).

Precisely because in his second volume Luke has decided to write about the history of the church, or the Lord's continuous work of salvation in the power of his Spirit and through his apostolic church (Acts 1:1-2),[19] he may be concentrating on that task without much concern about the imminence or delay of the *parousia*.[20] But Conzelmann assumes that Luke's decision to write the history of the church involves his theological appreciation of the present, the period of the church, as a stage within God's plan of salvation, and this appreciation is motivated by the delay of the *parousia*.[21] But why should we assume that this appreciation of the present is motivated by the delay of the *parousia?* Could someone who believes in an imminent end not have appreciated Christ's work of salvation that was done during his earthly ministry and is being done through his Spirit since his ascension? Writing in the 80s and entertaining the possibility of the *parousia* within his own generation, could Luke still not appreciate what the Lord had been doing in and through his church since his ascension and write an account of it in order to strengthen the faith of Christians of his generation and attract others to the Christian faith? Why should we assume he could have done that only when he was resigned to a long-term delay of the *parousia?* After all, even Mark, who apparently thought more in terms of an imminent *parousia* than a delayed one, wrote an account of Jesus Christ's saving work around A.D. 70, in order to help his generation evangelistically or catechetically. Why is it strange, then, that Luke decided to do the same, only strengthen-

---

19. Cf. I. H. Marshall, *Luke: Historian and Theologian,* enlarged ed. (Grand Rapids: Zondervan, 1989; repr. New Testament Profiles; Downers Grove, Ill.: InterVarsity Press, 1998), 87, 157, 179-82; Barrett, *Acts,* 2:lxxxv; S. Kim, "Kingdom of God," in *Dictionary of the Later New Testament and Its Developments,* ed. R. P. Martin and P. H. Davids (Downers Grove, Ill.: InterVarsity Press, 1997), 629-32.

20. This seems a more plausible supposition than to posit a change of mind in Luke between his two volumes, as Wilson claims (see p. 163, above). It is unlikely that within the short period intervening between the Gospel and Acts, Luke changed his eschatology so substantially. Furthermore, as argued here, it is not easy to prove that in Acts Luke has indeed abandoned the belief in the imminent *parousia.*

21. Conzelmann, *Theology of St. Luke,* esp. 13-14.

ing his cause by adding an account of the Lord Jesus Christ's continuing work in and through the church (cf. Luke 1:1-4; Acts 1:1-2)? Further, even Paul, who believed in an imminent *parousia* (cf. Rom 13:11-14; 16:20), wrote to the Roman Christians of his apostolic mission thus:

> In Christ Jesus, then, I have reason to boast of my work for God. For I will not venture to speak of anything except what Christ has accomplished through me to win obedience from the Gentiles, by word and deed, by the power of signs and wonders, by the power of the Spirit of God, so that from Jerusalem and as far round as Illyricum I have fully proclaimed the gospel of Christ. Thus I make it my ambition to proclaim the gospel, not where Christ has already been named. . . . This is the reason that I have so often been hindered from coming to you. But now, with no further place for me in these regions, I desire, as I have for many years, to come to you when I go to Spain. For I do hope to see you on my journey and to be sent on by you, once I have enjoyed your company for a little while. At present, however, I am going to Jerusalem in a ministry to the saints. (Rom 15:17-25)

Is not much of the second half of Acts essentially an unfolding of these words of Paul about "what Christ has accomplished through [him] to win obedience from the Gentiles, by word and deed, by the power of signs and wonders, by the power of the Spirit of God" (Rom 15:18-19), in the various provinces of the eastern hemisphere of the Roman Empire, and about his long-desired journey to Rome? Why should we then over-interpret Luke's writing of "what Christ has accomplished" through Peter, Paul, and other preachers of the gospel as an attempt to solve the problem of the delayed *parousia* by providing the present with a salvation-historical meaning? What is disputed here is not that Luke provides such a meaning, but that he does so because he is pressed by the problem of the delayed *parousia*. Rather, he appears to find this salvation-historical meaning quite naturally as he looks at what the Lord Jesus Christ has been doing in and through the church since his ascension after the decisive saving event of his ministry, death, and resurrection.[22]

This brief discussion on Lucan eschatology leads us to the conclusion that he holds out both possibilities, that the *parousia* can take place soon,

---

22. Cf. B. Witherington III, *The Acts of the Apostles: A Socio-Rhetorical Commentary* (Grand Rapids: Eerdmans/Carlisle: Paternoster, 1998), 185.

perhaps within his generation, or that it can be delayed. Even in Acts, he does not take its delay for granted. Furthermore, even when Luke thinks of a possible delay, it is doubtful that he thinks the wait will be many generations, not to mention many centuries. Concerning Lucan eschatology on the whole, therefore, it appears more reasonable to say that he expects the *parousia* to take place *soon*, though he cannot say *how soon*, than to say that he believes it to be not imminent but delayed indefinitely.[23]

Nevertheless, it is undeniable that in Acts this expectation of the imminent *parousia* remains in the background as Luke concentrates on recounting the present work of the exalted Lord Jesus Christ in the power of the Spirit in and through his church. It has been argued above that Luke does this to strengthen his testimony about the saving work of the Lord Jesus Christ by writing about his continuous work beyond the Christ-Event, rather than to adjust to the situation created by the delayed *parousia*. But then, precisely because he seeks to show the exalted Lord Jesus Christ as continuing his saving work in the apostolic church, should Luke not try to show how the Lord Jesus Christ implements the salvation of the Kingdom of God politically as well as physically, spiritually, and socially (healing, forgiveness, and a new community of love and service)? Precisely because Luke, more than any other Evangelist, draws the contrast between the kingdoms of the world (including the Roman Empire) and the Kingdom of God and presents Jesus' messianic work in terms of deliverance from oppression,[24] should we not expect him to be interested in how the work of the Lord Jesus Christ brings about deliverance in the political as well as other realms?

If, though we are not stressing it here, the sense of the delayed *parousia* has also contributed to Luke's concentration on the present saving work of the Lord Jesus Christ, given such contrast between the Kingdom of God and the Roman Empire and such stress on deliverance from oppression, that sense should not lead Luke to accommodate to the Roman imperial order

---

23. Cf. "imminent rather than immediate," the formulation of Marshall, *Luke: Historian and Theologian*, 136. Wilson summarizes Luke's eschatology in the Gospel thus: "although he made ample room for the delay of the Parousia Luke still thought it a possibility, and a real one, that the End would come soon" (*Gentiles and the Gentile Mission in Luke-Acts*, 77). It is argued here that there is no reason to see a change in this eschatology in Acts.

24. Cf. R. B. Hays, "The Liberation of Israel in Luke-Acts: Intertextual Readings as Resistance," paper presented at Fuller Theological Seminary, Pasadena, Calif., Jan. 26, 2006, 8, who criticizes Conzelmann for neglecting the infancy narratives of Luke in his *Theology of St. Luke*.

(contra Conzelmann), but, on the contrary, to seek to bring about positive changes to it in the name of the presently reigning Lord Jesus Christ. Suppose that Luke, who is strongly concerned about the deliverance of God's people from the oppression of the Roman Empire, has realized that the fervent hope for the imminent consummation of God's Kingdom and imminent deliverance of God's people is fading, and yet has found a new joy in learning that the exalted Lord Jesus Christ is already implementing the redemption of God's Kingdom through the power of the Holy Spirit. Would he then advise the church simply to acquiesce to the Roman imperial order and seek an accommodation with it now, finding solace in the belief that when the *parousia* takes place in a remote future they will have their ultimate redemption? Or would he advise the church to see how the presently reigning Lord Jesus Christ may be trying to bring about changes to the imperial order for greater justice and freedom already now through their obedience to him? Isn't the latter much more logical than the former?

Thus, no matter whether Luke's concentration on the present redemptive work of the exalted Lord Jesus Christ in the power of the Spirit in and through his church is caused by the sense of the delayed *parousia* or by Luke's decision to strengthen his testimony about the saving work of the Lord Jesus Christ, we would expect that precisely because of that concentration and his strong concern for the liberation of God's people Luke would demonstrate the political dimension of the Lord Jesus Christ's present redemptive work. But Luke does not do that — why?

Below we will consider some other factors for this unexpected absence, such as political realism, Luke's relative appreciation of *pax Romana,* and so on. But none of them provide an adequate explanation in themselves. It appears that these factors need to be combined with Luke's fundamental belief that the *parousia* and the eschatological consummation are not too far away, though they may be delayed for a while.

### An Apology for the Church to the Empire?

There are certainly elements in Luke-Acts that give the impression that Luke is eager to demonstrate the political innocence of the church and the Roman officials' recognition of it. As we have seen above, in his Gospel Luke shows Jesus as presenting no threat to the Roman imperial order and as rather critical of the aspirations of his contemporary revolutionaries.

Therefore, it is no surprise to see Luke stressing that although Jesus was accused by the Sanhedrin of perverting the Jewish nation, *forbidding the payment of tribute to Caesar, and claiming to be the Messianic king,* he was declared innocent again and again during his trial, by Pilate (three times: Luke 23:2-4, 13-14, 22) and by Herod (23:15), and even at the moment of his crucifixion, by the centurion, probably a leader of the execution squad (23:47). It is indeed striking that Luke alone among the Evangelists reports the Sanhedrin's charges against Jesus in these sharpest political terms and then has them emphatically denied by both Pilate and Herod.

In his Acts of the Apostles Luke also presents Paul as repeatedly proven not guilty of any political crime. So the Philippian magistrates apologize to Paul and Silas for having wrongly jailed them (Acts 16:39). In Thessalonica, although the Jews accuse Paul, Silas, and Timothy of "acting against the decrees of Caesar" by proclaiming "another king, Jesus" (17:7) the *Politarchs* there took no more action than requesting money as security from their host, Jason — thus apparently disregarding the serious charge (17:1-9). In Corinth the Jews accuse Paul of teaching contrary to the law, but the proconsul Gallio refuses even to take up the charge, declaring that it concerns only an internal Jewish dispute and not "a matter of wrongdoing or vicious crime," which a transgression of Roman law would be (18:12-17). In Ephesus, a silversmith stirs up a riot of fellow traders against Paul's anti-idolatry teaching, but the *Asiarchs* there protect Paul as his "friends," and the town clerk dismisses the riotous assembly, saying that there is no cause to justify the riot (19:23-41).

In Jerusalem the Jews from Asia stir up a riot with the charges that Paul taught against the Mosaic law and the temple and defiled the temple, but the Roman tribune Claudius Lysias rescues him from mob lynching and sends him to the procurator Felix in Caesarea under military escort with a letter stating that Paul is charged by the Jews with violation of their law but with nothing deserving imprisonment (Acts 21:27-39; 22:22-30; 23:12-30). Representing the Jews, Tertullus accuses Paul before Felix for agitating the Jews as a leader of the sect of the Nazarenes and for trying to profane the temple (24:1-9), but Felix does not take the charges seriously and treats Paul well, although his opportunism prevents him from releasing Paul (24:22-27). Felix's successor, Festus, ascertains that the Jews were charging Paul not of such evils as might concern him as a Roman governor but only of disputes about Judaism and Jesus (25:13-21), and confirms at least the last element of Paul's defense: "Neither against the law of the Jews, nor against the temple, *nor against Caesar* have I committed any wrong" (25:8; cf. vv. 25-26). So Festus and King Agrippa agree that Paul is innocent and could have been released but for his appeal to Caesar (26:30-32).

All these accounts form a clear and impressive pattern. After all these repeated notes of Paul's innocence, Luke ends his second volume (Acts 28:16-31) with an account of Paul staying in his rented home in Rome and "preaching the Kingdom of God and teaching about the Lord Jesus Christ with all openness and without hindrance" to many guests (v. 31), while waiting for the trial before Caesar. Thus in Luke's presentation it is mostly the Jews who bring charges against Paul to Roman or local authorities for transgressing the Jewish law, but the authorities repeatedly ignore them. Where the charges include also transgression of Roman law, the authorities find them groundless. These elements in the Lucan presentation of Jesus and his apostolic church have led some commentators to see that part of Luke's purpose in writing Luke-Acts was to present an apology for the church toward Roman authorities, i.e., to persuade them of the political harmlessness of Christianity.[25]

If this view is correct, then it is understandable that Luke would be careful not to present Christianity as a challenge to the imperial order. However, scholars who object to this view point out the marginal significance of these elements within the total presentation of Luke-Acts as well as material in Luke-Acts that presents a critical view of the Roman imperial system.[26] In this connection, C. K. Barrett's terse comment is often quoted: "no Roman court could be expected to wade through so much Jewish religious nonsense in order to find half a dozen fragments of legally significant material."[27] We have already seen that the material in Luke 1–4

25. E.g., besides Conzelmann (*Theology of St. Luke,* 137-49), classically H. J. Cadbury, *The Making of Luke-Acts* (New York and London: Macmillan, 1927), 308-15; F. F. Bruce, *The Acts of the Apostles: The Greek Text with Introduction and Commentary,* 3rd rev. and enl. ed. (Grand Rapids: Eerdmans/Leicester: Apollos, 1990), 23-25; R. F. O'Toole, "Luke's Position on Politics and Society in Luke-Acts," in *Political Issues in Luke-Acts,* ed. R. J. Cassidy and P. J. Scharper (Maryknoll, N.Y.: Orbis, 1983), 4-8; J. D. Crossan and J. L. Reed, *In Search of Paul: How Jesus' Apostle Opposed Rome's Empire with God's Kingdom* (San Francisco: HarperSanFrancisco, 2004), 32-34; cf. also K. Wengst, *Pax Romana and the Peace of Jesus Christ,* trans. J. Bowden (Philadelphia: Fortress, 1987), 98-100, 105.

26. E.g., R. Maddox, *The Purpose of Luke-Acts,* FRLANT 126 (Göttingen: Vandenhoeck & Ruprecht, 1982), 93-96; Hays, "The Liberation of Israel in Luke-Acts," 8.

27. Barrett, *Acts,* 2:xlviii; cf. its earlier version in his *Luke the Historian in Recent Study* (London: Epworth, 1961; repr. FBBS 24; Philadelphia: Fortress, 1970), 63.

(also Acts 10:36) would not have been taken by Roman authorities as politically innocent. In Acts 4:27-30, the Roman governor Pontius Pilate and the Roman client-king Herod are charged along with the Jews for having killed the Messiah Jesus and for continuing to threaten his church (cf. also Acts 2:23; 13:28).[28] Furthermore, in spite of the Lucan efforts to present Paul and his team as innocent victims of misunderstanding and mistreatment, agitated mostly by the Jews but sometimes also by a non-Jewish pro-Roman populace, it is questionable whether Roman authorities would always take in a positive light the accounts of them causing civil disturbance in so many cities: Antioch (13:45-50), Iconium (14:4-6), Lystra (14:8-20), Philippi (16:16-40), Thessalonica (17:5-9), Berea (17:13), Corinth (18:12-17), Ephesus (19:23-41), and Jerusalem (21:27-36).[29]

## An Apology for the Empire to the Church?

Some scholars appreciate basically the same material in Luke-Acts as do the advocates of an apologetic purpose for the church toward the Roman Empire, but argue for the opposite perspective, namely an apology for the empire to the church.[30] First of all, they point out how in the passion narrative Luke softens Mark's very negative pictures of Pilate and the Roman soldiers: Luke presents Pilate as finding Jesus innocent but being forced to act against him by the Jewish leaders and mob, and he omits the account of the Roman soldiers' abuse of Jesus, weakening the impression of their direct involvement in the crucifixion (compare Luke 23 with Mark 15).[31] They also argue that Luke's accounts of Paul's treatment by Gallio, the Thessalonian *Politarchs,* the Ephesian *Asiarchs,* the tribune Lysias, and even Felix and Festus

28. Cf. Jervell, *Theology of the Acts of the Apostles,* 100-103: "Acts 4:27f. is a . . . most unlikely introduction to an appeal to Roman authorities for a friendly attitude towards Christians" (p. 103).

29. Cf. S. Walton, "The State They Were In: Luke's View of the Roman Empire," in *Rome in the Bible and the Early Church,* ed. P. Oakes (Carlisle: Paternoster/Grand Rapids: Baker, 2002), 25-26.

30. E.g., P. W. Walaskay, *'And So We Came to Rome': The Political Perspective of St Luke,* SNTSMS 49 (Cambridge: Cambridge University Press, 1983), 58-63; Wengst, *Pax Romana,* 90-105; H. W. Tajra, *The Trial of St. Paul: A Juridical Exegesis of the Second Half of the Acts of the Apostles,* WUNT 2.35 (Tübingen: Mohr Siebeck, 1989), 199; cf. also Maddox, *Purpose of Luke-Acts,* 96-97.

31. See above, pp. 112-13.

make the officials and judicial system of the Roman Empire appear in a favorable light, as these are presented as protecting Paul from the Jewish and Gentile mobs and giving him the due process of the law (cf. esp. Acts 25:16).

Furthermore, these scholars point to Luke's positive presentation of the various centurions: the centurion of Capernaum whose exceptional faith is praised by Jesus (Luke 7:1-10); the centurion who at the foot of the cross praised God and confessed that Jesus was innocent (Luke 23:47); Cornelius, a devout God-fearer and liberal alms-giver (Acts 10:1-43); and Julius of the Augustan Cohort, who treated Paul kindly and protected him during the voyage to Rome (Acts 27:3, 43). Along with Cornelius, Sergius Paulus, the proconsul in Cyprus, who is described as "a man of intelligence" (Acts 13:4-12), and the Philippian jailor (Acts 16:16-40) were actually converted to the Christian faith. Publius, the chief of the island Malta, extended hospitality to Paul's entourage for three days and experienced God's healing grace for his father through Paul (Acts 28:7-10). Paul is presented as making good use of his Roman citizenship to receive the protection of Roman law (Acts 16:37-39; 22:25-29; 25:10-12). Pointing to these examples, some scholars argue that Luke is trying to advise the church to appreciate the Roman imperial order and so adjust to it positively.

Like the view that Luke's purpose is an apology for the church to the empire, this view also would explain why Luke is not interested in showing Christians as trying to bring changes to the imperial order. But this view is also countered by the fact that in Luke-Acts these examples are balanced by other elements that show the Roman imperial order in a negative light. In spite of Walaskay's valiant efforts to explain otherwise,[32] a critical presentation of the Roman rulers and officials is undeniable in such accounts as John the Baptist's exhortation to tax collectors and soldiers (Luke 3:13-14), the devil's second temptation of Jesus (Luke 4:6), Pilate's brutality (Luke 13:1), and Jesus' characterization of Gentile rulers (Luke 22:24-25), not to mention the implicit background of Roman oppression in the annunciation, birth, and inauguration narratives (Luke 1–4). If the Lucan passion narrative makes Pilate appear at best as a weak governor who commits a miscarriage of justice (Luke 23:1-25), Acts 4:27-30 clearly indicts him as responsible along with Herod and the Jews for the death of Jesus. Felix and Festus are also portrayed as opportunists failing to administer justice (Acts 24–27), and the former is even characterized as a corrupt governor (Acts 24:26).

---

32. Walaskay, 'And So We Came to Rome,' 15-49.

## The Purpose of Legitimation

Thus, just like the theory of an apology for the church to the empire, so also the theory of an apology for the Roman Empire to the church as part of Luke's purpose is on the whole not sustainable. Yet, just as it is impossible to deny the Lucan emphasis on the innocence of Jesus and his apostles, so also it is impossible to miss the Lucan appreciation of some Roman officials and the positive side of Roman justice in spite of some corrupt officials flouting it. It is especially striking how Luke presents the centurion of Capernaum (Luke 7:1-10), the centurion at the foot of the cross (Luke 23:47), Cornelius (Acts 10:1-43), and Sergius Paulus (Acts 13:4-12). Therefore, Philip F. Esler's view appears quite plausible, that Luke seeks to reassure Roman soldiers and administrators in the church that their allegiance to the empire and Christian faith are quite compatible, and thus helps legitimate their faith.[33] This view agrees well with Luke's dedication of his book to the "most excellent" Theophilus (Luke 1:3) and the stated purpose in that dedication (Luke 1:1-4; Acts 1:1-2). Esler considers the Lucan report of Jesus' reference to the Aramean general Naaman (Luke 4:27; cf. 2 Kings 5:1-19) as a confirmation of this theory of "legitimation," as the story includes the prophet Elisha's tacit approval of the converted Naaman's attendance at his king's worship in the temple of Rimmon.[34] Bryan also interprets the Lucan accounts of Paul's appeal to his Roman citizenship thus: "Here we are shown the great apostle of Christ actually claiming to be a citizen, and being protected by the empire (Acts 22.23-29, 23.12-35)"; these accounts could assure Romans

---

33. P. F. Esler, *Community and Gospel in Luke-Acts: The Social and Political Motivations of Lucan Theology,* SNTSMS 57 (Cambridge: Cambridge University Press, 1987), 201-19. This view is endorsed by C. Bryan, *Render to Caesar: Jesus, the Early Church, and the Roman Superpower* (Oxford: Oxford University Press, 2005), 96; so also by Walton, "Luke's View of the Roman Empire," 31-32, albeit with some reservation. A. Neagoe also acknowledges this as an element of what he calls Luke's overall purpose of an *apologia pro evangelio* (*The Trial of the Gospel: An Apologetic Reading of Luke's Trial Narratives,* SNTSMS 116 [Cambridge: Cambridge University Press, 2002], esp. 90, 214-15, 222). Esler supports this view further by observing Luke's efforts to present Christianity as an ancestral religion (*Community and Gospel in Luke-Acts,* 213-17).

34. Esler, *Community and Gospel in Luke-Acts,* 218-19. Endorsing this, Bryan, *Render to Caesar,* 100, comments: "What better news, or what better precedent, could have been offered for the comfort of a converted soldier like Cornelius, or a converted civil servant such as Sergius Paulus, both of whom, virtually as a part of their work, would from time to time need to be present at pagan imperial ceremonies?"

like Cornelius and Sergius Paulus that "as Christians they do not need to re-ject the empire and can even, on occasion, claim to be part of it and look to it for protection from God's enemies."[35]

Therefore, along with the main theological purpose of proclaiming the truth of the gospel or the greatness of God's saving work in and through Jesus Christ,[36] there seems to be at least secondarily also this pur-pose of reassuring Roman Christians that their new Christian faith is com-patible with their allegiance to the empire as well as perhaps encouraging the seekers among Roman officials to make a commitment to the Lord Je-sus Christ like Cornelius and Sergius Paulus.[37] This purpose seems to be one reason that Luke refrains from stressing how the Lordship of Jesus Christ has to be realized here and now in the political realm as well as in other areas, although he does not hesitate to state clearly that Jesus rather than Caesar is the real Lord and Savior.

## Jesus' Example

As we have seen, Luke clearly thinks that the Roman Empire has its evil side, as it essentially represents the reign of Satan, and therefore has to be replaced by the Kingdom of God at the *parousia* of the Lord Jesus Christ. But in this the Roman Empire is not alone. *All* the kingdoms of the world have the same character (Luke 4:5-7; cf. also 22:24-27). According to Luke,

---

35. Bryan, *Render to Caesar,* 103; similarly also Esler, *Community and Gospel in Luke-Acts,* 210.

36. Cf. Barrett, *Acts,* 2:xlix-liv. L. Alexander argues that Luke's chief apologetic interest lies in presenting the gospel to the Diaspora Jews: "Acts is a dramatized narrative of an intra-communal debate, a plea for a fair hearing at the bar of the wider Jewish community in the Diaspora, perhaps especially in Rome" ("The Acts of the Apostles as an Apologetic Text," in *Apologetics in the Roman Empire: Pagans, Jews, and Christians,* ed. M. Edwards, M. Good-man, and S. Price [Oxford: Oxford University Press, 1999], 15-44, quotation p. 43).

37. In this context, it is significant that Luke makes the Roman officer Cornelius's con-version through Peter (Acts 10:1–11:18) the official beginning of the church's Gentile mission and the inclusion of Gentiles in the people of God. Cf. Bryan, *Render to Caesar,* 95-96: "Luke would have been happy to persuade respectable Romans of the middle or upper rank that there was nothing subversive about Christianity, if only so that such considerations need not be a barrier to their conversion or to their continuing loyalty to their new faith" (p. 96). Bryan calls this the "classic" view, and cites a long list of scholars supporting it (pp. 160-61 n. 7).

Jesus was opposed to his contemporary Jewish revolutionaries because he saw that the kingdom of David or Israel that they aspired to establish through their fight against the Roman imperial system would be no exception.[38] Therefore, Jesus pursued the way of peace, the way of love rather than retaliation, in his Kingdom ministry, and eventually submitted to the trial and execution by the Roman governor, even if it was unjust, and so realized the divine plan of salvation. Therefore, it is no surprise that Luke presents Jesus' apostles as carrying out their mission in a way consistent with this stance of Jesus vis-à-vis the Roman Empire. Thus, the example of Jesus is surely a great factor in Luke's presentation of his apostles' concentration on proclaiming the gospel of the Kingdom of God and the Lord Jesus Christ without engaging in political struggles.[39]

## Political Realism

Presumably realism also plays a part in this political "conservatism." According to Rev 13:3-4, when Vespasian's accession to the Roman throne brought to an end within a year the chaos of the four emperors that ensued from Nero's suicide in A.D. 68, the whole world submitted to the emperor with a sense of wonder: "Who is like the beast, and who can fight against it?" This slogan well expresses the perception of the subjugated peoples of the empire about the invincibility and irresistibility of the Roman military might (cf. also, e.g., Josephus, *Jewish War* 2.362; 5.366-67). With Richard Horsley's attempt to explain demon possession among the Jews during the New Testament period in terms of a "self-protective explanation" of the oppression by the Roman military forces which was devised to keep the Jews from launching a "suicidal" revolt,[40] even he endorses the sentiment that any revolt against the Roman Empire at that time was really suicidal. In A.D. 70 the Jews tragically confirmed this. Now, writing most probably

---

38. See above, pp. 109-10.

39. However, there is not enough evidence for us to say, with Robert Maddox, that with the politically innocent example of Jesus and Paul as well as a positive presentation of the imperial government Luke is trying to encourage Christians "to live at peace with the sovereign power, so far as possible, and not to play the hero," by challenging the imperial order and courting martyrdom (*Purpose of Luke-Acts,* 96-97). Cf. O'Toole, "Luke's Position on Politics and Society in Luke-Acts," 9-13, for the theme of imitation of Jesus in Luke-Acts.

40. See pp. 116-17.

not long after that disaster and under the overwhelming impression of its tragedy (cf. Luke 21:20-24; 23:28-31), Luke would have been sensitive to the danger of the budding Christian movement appearing to be rebellious. How suicidal would it be for such a tiny movement to appear subversive?[41] How could the small band of believing Jews and Gentiles who were harassed by the majority of both the Jews and the Gentiles survive, let alone carry out its mission, if they antagonized the Roman authorities? Should this movement not rather seek Roman protection from the Jewish and Gentile persecutors? Should it not take advantage of the *pax Romana* by cooperating with the Roman authorities?

When we consider this political *Sitz im Leben* of Luke, it is amazing to see how he nevertheless maintains intact the claims of Jesus' gospel of the Kingdom of God and the apostles' gospel of the Kingdom of God and the Lord Jesus Christ; how he presents Jesus as proclaiming the Kingdom of God over against the kingdom of the devil, which is manifested in the kingdoms of the world, and as promising deliverance from the latter; how he presents Jesus' apostles as proclaiming Jesus as the true Lord and Savior who has brought the true gospel of peace; how he therefore presents Jesus in contrast to Caesar Augustus; and how he ends his book by hinting at the eventual triumph of the Kingdom of God and the Lord Jesus Christ in the seat of Caesar's Empire. Luke is well aware that this gospel proclamation can be taken as treasonous (e.g., Luke 23:1-5, 37-38; Acts 17:7). But he does not flinch from laying the claims of the gospel bare.

Yes, Luke does present the claims of the gospel boldly. Yet his political realism born of the keen awareness of the irresistible might of the Roman Empire on the one hand and the tiny beginning of the Christian movement on the other seems to prevent him from taking the next logical step of urging Christians to materialize the claims of the gospel in political terms here and now. For otherwise it would only be logical for Luke to urge Christians to work to materialize the salvation of the Kingdom of God/Lordship of Jesus Christ in political terms, i.e., in terms of greater justice and freedom, just as he urges Christians to work to materialize God's Kingdom in socio-economic terms by taking care of the poor through a community of sharing. Luke must be drawing support for his political re-

---

41. May we infer from Luke 14:31-32 Luke's political realism, even if the parabolic saying appears in the context of teaching on discipleship, with no clear allusion to the Roman Empire?

alism from historical realism, i.e., the actual ministries of Jesus and his apostles, which are the subject matter of his historical reporting, as Jesus and his apostles did not attempt to subvert the imperial order or bring about changes to it.[42] Luke does not think that in order to urge the Christians of his generation to bring about changes to the imperial order he has to go beyond the historical data and present Jesus and his apostles as if they had done these things. When Christians are so few and so insignificant that they have access to kings and governors only when they are brought to trial before them (Luke 21:12-13; Acts 9:15; 27:24; cf. Luke 23:1-25; Acts 23:33–26:32), how unrealistic would it be for Luke to present Christians on trial as trying to persuade the rulers to extend freedom and justice in obedience to the Lordship of Jesus Christ? It is quite realistic that in his accounts of the various trials of Paul in Acts, Luke shows him mainly trying to defend Christianity, with only some hints at his efforts to win rulers over for the Christian faith. Thus his political realism seems to lead Luke to look forward to the day of the consummation for the Kingdom of God to replace the kingdoms of the world or the empire of Satan, without being greatly concerned about its proleptic realization in the political realms here and now.

## An Appreciation of *Pax Romana*

Now, even if Luke understands that all the kingdoms of this world are essentially diabolic, apparently he does not think that therefore they have no positive side at all. For, as we have observed, he does not present the Roman imperial order and its officers only in a negative light as the Revelation of John does, but frequently in a positive light as well. Thus, it is conceivable that he evaluates various kingdoms of the world differently and considers the Roman Empire *relatively* better than some other kingdoms. In view of his presentation of Jesus opposing the Jewish revolutionary activities, it is also conceivable that, for Luke, although the *pax Romana* is only a dialectical phenomenon that soon has to be replaced by the *pax Christi*, it is still better than its opposite, be it wars between nations or anarchy and suffering that would result from revolutionary upheavals. It is

---

42. We can say this confidently at least with the case of Paul, since it is borne out by his own writings (see above Part One).

difficult to know whether Paul's confinement of his mission to the Roman Empire and Luke's confinement of reporting the Christian mission only to that carried out within the Roman Empire suggest this relatively higher appreciation of the Roman imperial order. But at least Luke's reports of the imperial military, administration, and judiciary sometimes functioning to protect Christian missionaries, and his reports of Paul's use of his citizenship, his insistence on the proper execution of Roman law (Acts 16:19-39; 25:9-10), and his appeal to Caesar (Acts 25:10-12) seem to reflect Luke's relative appreciation of the Roman imperial order, in spite of its essential diabolic nature and occasional failures.[43]

Luke's belief that before the *parousia* the gospel has to be preached to all the world (Luke 24:47; Acts 1:6-8; 3:19-21) seems to contribute to his relative appreciation of the Roman imperial order. Above we have observed in Acts 1:6-8 how Luke presents the risen Jesus as directing his apostles to concentrate on bringing the gospel to the end of the earth, setting aside concerns for the "restoration of the kingdom to Israel" for the moment, as it belongs to the end-time days of the "restoration of all things" (Acts 3:21). We have noted that with this programmatic statement Luke declares his intention to narrate the course of the apostolic mission from the viewpoint of the progress of the gospel rather than that of the political fortunes of "Israel." An implication of this intention, then, is that Luke's attitude to the Roman Empire can be determined by the former viewpoint rather than the latter.

So, from the viewpoint of this primary concern about the progress of the gospel, Luke seems to evaluate the Roman imperial order or *pax Romana* as relatively superior to other states, as it provides an environment in which Christian mission can progress, even if with some difficulty at times, whereas other states may not provide even such an environ-

---

43. Commenting on Luke's account of Paul's appeal to Caesar (Nero!) in reaction to Festus's suggestion for him to stand trial in Jerusalem (Acts 25:1-12), Maddox says that "the imperial court was to be trusted rather than the Sanhedrin in Jerusalem" (*Purpose of Luke-Acts,* 95), and Conzelmann goes even further to say that "in the end it is confidence in the justice of the Emperor that forms the great climax of the narrative" (*Theology of St. Luke,* 144). Cf. Wengst, *Pax Romana,* 89-105, for an insightful and critical presentation of Luke as a writer thoroughly committed to *pax Romana.* But it is somewhat one-sided, as it fails to pay adequate attention to the contrary evidence in Luke 1–4 and elsewhere (see above, pp. 77-93). Surely on Wengst's own showing, Luke's attitude cannot be compared with that of Clement of Rome (see pp. 61-62, above). See below, pp. 182-90.

ment.[44] Of course, nowhere in his writings does Luke refer to the conditions of the empire such as the political unity and peace of the Mediterranean world, the networks of good and safe roads and sea routes, free movements of peoples and mixing of cultures, tolerance of foreign cults, and so on, which must have been conducive to Christian mission. Yet it is true that in Acts Luke presents at least the Roman administration and justice as functioning more to aid Christian mission than to obstruct it.[45] Of course, corrupt Roman officials like Felix can hamper it. But even Felix did not deliver Paul into the hands of the Jews or outlaw the preaching of the gospel, but treated him rather decently (Acts 24:23). His corruption may have delayed Paul's journey to Rome, but the sovereign Lord Jesus Christ made use of Felix, Festus, and the imperial army, as well as the imperial justice system, to bring Paul safely to Rome and provide him an opportunity to preach the gospel before Caesar. So, when Luke ends his book with the picture of Paul in Rome preaching the gospel of the Kingdom of God and the Lord Jesus Christ "with all boldness and without hindrance" (Acts 28:30-31), Luke seems confident about the further progress of the gospel within the Roman Empire.

All the kingdoms of the world including the Roman Empire will be replaced by the Kingdom of God at the *parousia* of the Lord Jesus Christ in a not-too-distant future. However, during the short interim period, fortunately the Roman Empire is providing an environment for the church to carry out her mission.[46] Therefore, instead of trying to bring about a revolution, it is better for the church to concentrate on preaching the gospel, taking advantage of the positive side of the *pax Romana,* and so hasten the day of Christ's *parousia* and the restoration of all things (cf. Acts 3:19-21).

---

44. In the nativity story of Luke 2:1-14, Luke specifically singles out the Augustan *pax Romana* or imperial order in contrast to the *pax Christi,* of course, because at that time Judea was subordinated to the Roman Empire and Jesus was born during the reign of Caesar Augustus, the founder of the empire and bearer of the *pax Romana.* By singling it out, is Luke then implying that it is the most diabolic of all heathen kingdoms and therefore the greatest target of Christ's campaign? Rather, he seems to imply that it may be the best order that human beings can achieve on earth but even that is diabolic and needs to be replaced by the Kingdom of God and the *pax Christi.*

45. Cf. Bryan, *Render to Caesar,* 101.

46. Cf. Origen, *Against Celsus* 2.30, cited p. 54, n. 53, above.

## Not Yet the Situation of the Revelation of John

It is likely that Luke wrote Acts after Paul's martyrdom in the Neronian persecution (A.D. 64). But then why does Luke end his book without any reference to Paul's actual trial before Caesar or his death, but with the positive note of Paul preaching in Rome the gospel of the Kingdom of God and the Lord Jesus Christ "with all boldness and without hindrance" (Acts 28:30-31)? On this question we can do no more than speculate. Does Luke want to leave his readers with a strong impression that the church must go on preaching the gospel courageously in full conviction of its ultimate triumph? He may be thinking that in spite of the occasional failures of the imperial justice and even its monumental failures in the cases of Jesus and Paul (the former has to be reported because it constitutes the saving event together with his resurrection and ascension; but the latter, being well known, need not be stressed), it is still possible to preach the gospel in the Roman Empire, as it is not outlawed and there is no state-wide persecution of the church. Therefore, he may think that if the church goes on preaching the gospel in spite of occasional persecutions, the gospel of the Kingdom of God and the Lord Jesus Christ will ultimately triumph. Perhaps Luke wants to leave this thought with his readers.

At any rate, Luke wrote with an optimistic prospect about Christian mission as well as with a relative appreciation of *pax Romana*, probably because he was not yet facing the situation of the Revelation of John at the end of the reign of Domitian (A.D. 81-96), in which Christians were pressured to participate in emperor worship (Rev 13:4-8, 15-16; 14:9-11; 15:2; 16:2; 19:20; 20:4) and a broad-scale persecution was looming large for those who would resist it (e.g., Rev 2:2-3, 10, 13; 6:9-11; 7:9-17; 11:7-10; 12:13-17; 13:7, 10, 16-18; 17:6; 18:24; 20:4).[47] Luke did not refer to the imperial cult. Nor did

---

47. Even if the Emperor Domitian did not himself promote his own cult and persecute Christians for their resistance to it, as many modern commentators (e.g., D. E. Aune, *Revelation 1–5*, WBC 52A [Nashville: Thomas Nelson, 1997], lxiii-lxix) now tend to believe against the traditional view (cautiously restated by G. K. Beale, *The Book of Revelation: A Commentary on the Greek Text*, NIGTC [Grand Rapids: Eerdmans/Carlisle: Paternoster, 1999], 5-17), it is not excluded that in some provinces the local priesthoods of the imperial cult promoted his cult to court his favor for their provinces. In fact, S. R. F. Price points to "the establishment of the provincial cult of Domitian at Ephesus, with its colossal cult statue" as the direct background of Revelation 13 (*Rituals and Power: The Roman Imperial Cult in Asia Minor*

he refer to state or provincial persecution of Christians. So it seems that he wrote before a large-scale persecution was feared. Therefore, writing a couple of decades after the Neronian persecution, which was limited to the city of Rome and was not related to the imperial cult, he was not forced to be so pessimistic about Christian relationships to the state authorities as the John of Revelation was.[48] It is noteworthy that even when Luke introduces in his narrative the *Asiarchs* of Ephesus, who are often supposed to have functioned also as the high priests of the imperial cult,[49] he does not refer to their raising any concern with Paul about the imperial cult. On the

---

[Cambridge: Cambridge University Press, 1984], 197; this view is accepted by Beale, *Revelation*, 14-15). Price plausibly argues: "It is in principle quite likely that the establishment of the cult of Domitian at Ephesus, which involved participation of the whole province [of Asia], as attested by the series of dedications by numerous cities, led to unusually great pressure on the Christians for conformity. John might well be worried about his flock" (*Rituals and Power*, 198). Then, even if by the time Revelation was written Antipas of Pergamon had been the only martyr in Asia (Rev 2:13) and the souls crying for vengeance under the altar (Rev 6:9-11; cf. also 17:6) were those who had been martyred elsewhere, the seer John could see the ominous prospect of the imperial cult for Christians in Asia with severe persecution breaking out for them. So he felt it necessary to prepare them theologically to stand firm in their faith and hope and resist the imperial cult, unto martyrdom.

48. For the limited nature of the Neronian persecution and the nature of the Domitian persecution at the end of his reign, cf. R. M. Grant, *Augustus to Constantine: The Thrust of the Christian Movement into the Roman World* (New York: Harper & Row, 1970; repr. Louisville, Ky.: Westminster John Knox, 2004), 79-80.

49. So, e.g., Bruce, *Acts of the Apostles*, 418; Barrett, *Acts*, 2:930; Witherington, *Acts*, 595; but against it, cf. R. A. Kearsley, "The Asiarchs," in *The Book of Acts in Its First Century Setting*, vol. 2: *Graeco-Roman Setting*, ed. D. W. J. Gill and C. Gempf (Grand Rapids: Eerdmans/Carlisle: Paternoster, 1994), 363-76. As we have seen, it is possible that with the reference to Naaman (Luke 4:27) Luke tries to assure converted Roman soldiers and administrators like Cornelius and Sergius Paulus that as Christians they might take part in the imperial ceremonies in a passive way. For the possibility of such a passive participation, Esler (*Community and Gospel in Luke-Acts*, 219) appeals to A. D. Nock's study which has shown that Roman officers and soldiers could easily avoid any active role in the pagan cult ("The Roman Army and the Roman Religious Year," *HTR* 45 [1952]: 187-252). If we see such an intention in Luke 4:27, then perhaps we should see in Acts 10:36 (see above, pp. 81-84) an intention to make sure that the converted Roman officers and officials do indeed participate in the imperial cult only in a passive way, without compromising their ultimate allegiance to the Lord Jesus Christ. If this interpretation of Luke 4:27 and Acts 10:36 is right, these verses may be taken as allusions to the imperial cult in Luke-Acts. But still they would confirm that at Luke's time the imperial cult was not yet so serious a problem as at the time of the Revelation of John.

contrary, he presents them as Paul's "friends" who try to protect him (Acts 19:31). As seen above, Acts 10:36 comes the closest to what may be regarded as an indirect allusion to the problem of the imperial cult, and even there it is understood that the Roman military officer Cornelius can profess Jesus as the only Lord and still serve his Caesar, or that he can serve his emperor while professing Jesus as his only *kyrios*.[50]

In Acts 4:19; 5:29 Luke shows how the Jerusalem apostles defied the Sanhedrin's ban on preaching the gospel, maintaining the fundamental principle that they must obey God rather than human beings. Does this suggest that if Luke was facing a situation of forced imperial cult and broad and severe persecution of the church, he would also take the position of the John of Revelation? We have seen above that Luke is not unaware of the diabolic nature of the Roman Empire and the parody character of the imperial claims and especially propaganda of *pax Romana*. Given this perspective, it is not out of the question that, in the situation of Revelation, Luke would come close to the stance of John, who highlights the diabolic and beastly nature of the Roman Empire, exposes the sham of *pax Romana,* and prophesies destruction through God's judgment, on the one hand, and on the other hand calls for the church to resist the imperial cult without compromise and discharge faithfully "the testimony of Jesus" (Rev 1:2, 9; 12:17; 19:10; 20:4; cf. also 6:9; 11:7; 12:11), i.e., preaching the gospel of the Kingdom of God and the Lord Jesus Christ, unto martyrdom, in the certain hope of the consummation of God's Kingdom and their salvation at the imminent *parousia* of the Lord.[51]

However, Klaus Wengst presents the Lucan perspective as quite pro-Roman, similar to Clement of Rome.[52] He also finds Paul's attitude to *pax*

50. Thus the allusion to the imperial cult in Acts 10:36 cannot be compared, in the degree of its negative bearing, even with that in 1 Clement 59:4 ("Let all the nations know that you are the only God, and Jesus Christ is your child/servant [παῖς]") and 61:2 ("For you, heavenly Master, King of the ages, give to the sons of men [= the Roman rulers] glory and honor and authority over those upon the earth"), let alone the numerous allusions in Revelation (e.g., Rev 13:5-8, 11-15).

51. Contra A. Brent, *The Imperial Cult and the Development of Church Order: Concepts and Images of Authority in Paganism and Early Christianity before the Age of Cyprian,* VCSup 45 (Leiden: Brill, 1999), who claims to see many parallels between the developing imperial cult in Asia Minor and the theology of Luke-Acts and argues that Luke presents Christianity as the fulfillment of Judaism in parallel to Augustus's fulfillment of the republican cult (see esp. pp. 75-77).

52. Wengst, *Pax Romana*, 89-105, 137. But see n. 43 above.

*Romana* not much different from that of Clement, either.[53] Then, regarding the Lucan writings, the Revelation of John, and Clement's letter to the Corinthians (1 Clement) as contemporaneous works written at the end of the reign of Domitian,[54] Wengst argues that the difference between the seer John's critical perception of *pax Romana* and Luke's and Clement's positive perception of it, or the difference between Rev 13 and Rom 13, cannot be attributed to a different time of composition.[55] Wengst suggests it should be explained rather in terms of the difference in those authors' "experiences of reality" and their interests. For the experiences and interests determined their particular standpoints and perspectives, which in turn determined their different perceptions and evaluations of *pax Romana*.[56] This is a quite helpful explanation of the differences among these authors.

It is clear that the difference between Clement and the seer John in their attitudes to the Roman Empire was determined by their respective interests (or purposes) as well as by their respective experiences of persecutions. Of course, they shared the common interest in the welfare of the church of Christ. But whereas John was interested in preventing the church from compromising her faith with the imperial cult and ideology (cf. Rev 2:14-15, 20-21; 3:4; 18:4; 21:8), Clement was interested in preventing her from collapsing not only because of internal disorder but also because of persecutions. The rebellion of some young people against their presbyters in the Corinthian church is Clement's main concern. However, his concern for the vulnerability of the church before state persecution is also evident. He refers not only to the past Neronian persecution and the martyrdom of Peter and Paul (1 Clement 5:1-7), but also to the present one, "the sudden and repeated calamities and misfortunes which have befallen us" (1 Clement 1:1). Then, towards the end of the epistle, Clement specifically prays:

> "direct our steps to walk in holiness and righteousness and purity of heart," and "to do what is good and pleasing in your sight" and in the sight of our rulers. Yes, Lord, "let your face shine upon us" in peace "for

---

53. Wengst, *Pax Romana*, 137. This summary statement is in some tension with his exposition of Paul's attitude to *pax Romana* in the earlier pages of his book (72-89), where he stressed that having suffered from numerous persecutions from imperial and local authorities Paul had a rather critical view of Roman justice and propaganda of "peace and security."

54. Wengst, *Pax Romana*, 106.

55. Wengst, *Pax Romana*, 138.

56. Wengst, *Pax Romana*, 139.

our good," that we may be sheltered "by your mighty hand" and delivered from every sin "by your uplifted arm"; and deliver us from those who hate us unjustly. Give harmony and peace to us and to all who dwell on the earth, just as you did to our fathers when they reverently "called upon you in faith and truth," that we may be saved, while we render obedience to your almighty and most excellent name, and to our rulers and governors on earth. You, Master, have given them the power of sovereignty through your majestic and inexpressible might, so that we, acknowledging the glory and honor which you have given them, may be subject to them, resisting your will in nothing. Grant to them, Lord, health, peace, harmony, and stability, that they may blamelessly administer the government which you have given them. For you, heavenly Master, King of the ages, give to the sons of men glory and honor and authority over those upon the earth. Lord, direct their plans according to what is good and pleasing in your sight, so that by devoutly administering in peace and gentleness the authority which you have given them they may experience your mercy. You, who alone are able to do these and even greater good things for us, we praise through the high priest and guardian of our souls, Jesus Christ. . . . (1 Clement 60:2–61:3)[57]

Earlier we examined this prayer to see how much Clement is concerned for *pax Romana* and how he uses the exhortations in Rom 13:1-7 and the related passages of the New Testament for it.[58] Now here we need to appreciate that his whole prayer for *pax Romana* is motivated by his concern for the church's existence in peace, free from persecution, rather than by his patriotism, his pride in the Roman imperial order, his general concern for world peace, or any other such thing. This fact is clearly expressed by the specific petition, "and deliver us from those who hate us unjustly" (1 Clement 60:3). The whole prayer is indeed based on the understanding of the state authorities as instituted by God as is taught in Rom 13:1-7; Tit 3:1; 1 Pet 2:13-17 (cf. also 1 Tim 2:1-2). But note how, on the basis of this theological understanding, Clement does not just exhort Christians to be subject to the authorities, but also stresses that the earthly rulers should "devoutly administer in peace and gentleness" the authority they

---

57. The translation is from M. W. Holmes, *The Apostolic Fathers: Greek Texts and English Translations*, updated ed. (Grand Rapids: Baker Books, 1999), 98-99, with only a minor modification to make it clear that 1 Clement 60:3 is one sentence.

58. See above, pp. 61-62.

have received from God. Clement and other Christians have been experiencing unjust persecution because the rulers have failed to administer their God-given government in a way that is pleasing to God. Therefore, Clement is praying that the rulers should exercise their God-given power for the God-given purpose and in the God-pleasing way, which would result in concord and peace for all, including Christians. On the basis of the same theological understanding of the state authorities as instituted by God, Clement also strongly exhorts Christians to lead a holy and righteous life in obedience to the rulers as well as to God. But note again how he links such a life to Christians' obtaining peace:

> . . . "direct our steps to walk in holiness and righteousness and purity of heart," and "to do what is good and pleasing in your sight" and in the sight of our rulers. Yes, Lord, "let your face shine upon us" in peace "for our good," that we may be sheltered "by your mighty hand" and delivered from every sin "by your uplifted arm"; and deliver us from those who hate us unjustly. *Give harmony and peace to us,* . . . just as you did to our fathers when they reverently "called upon you in faith and truth," that we may be saved, *while we render obedience to your almighty and most excellent name, and to our rulers and governors on earth.* (1 Clement 60:2-4)

Here it is quite noticeable that Clement is concerned that Christians lead a blameless life lest they give state authorities any pretext for persecution. Even when they cause no offense, Christians are hated "unjustly." This is the reason Clement prays for God's direction of the rulers to govern their subjects "devoutly, in peace and gentleness," as well as for God's help for Christians to live a holy and righteous life in obedience to the rulers as well as to God. Naturally the former is the more crucial for Christians to avoid persecution. But the latter is also essential since without it they cannot avoid persecution even from good rulers. Therefore, living an impeccable life is an absolute requirement for Christians to avoid persecution. Hence Clement equates God's deliverance of Christians from sin with his sheltering of them in the petition for God to grant peace to them and to deliver them from unjust persecution (60:3).[59]

---

59. Note that v. 3 is one long sentence, where the petition "and deliver us from those who hate us unjustly" (καὶ ῥῦσαι ἡμᾶς ἀπὸ τῶν μισούντων ἡμᾶς ἀδίκως) is closely attached to God's providing Christians with shelters and delivering them from sins, and so granting them the grace of peace:

Thus there is clearly a difference of interest between the seer John and Clement. This is based on their different judgments of the seriousness of the situation as well as their theological acumen. For John, the situation is so desperate that mere prayer for the rulers to rule "devoutly, in peace and gentleness" and mere blameless submission to them on the part of Christians would not be sufficient for the church to escape persecution. In fact, the rulers are so Satanic and their ideology so contrary to the Kingdom of God (esp. Rev 13; 17; 18) that submission to them is nothing but a betrayal of the Christian faith (Rev 2:14-15, 20-21; 3:4; 18:4; 21:8). Therefore, for John, there is no alternative to resisting the imperial cult and ideology and proclaiming the truth of the Kingdom of God, patiently bearing persecution unto martyrdom in hope for the consummation of God's Kingdom and salvation at the imminent *parousia* of the Lord Jesus Christ.[60] But apparently Clement judges the situation not so desperately. For him, there is still the possibility that at least some rulers would exercise their power "devoutly, in peace and gentleness." So, he judges that if Christians lead a blameless life in obedience to the rulers (except the imperial cult), it is possible for the church to survive, in spite of occasional persecutions like the one he has just experienced (1 Clement 1:1).[61] Apparently, besides the narrowly perceived emperor worship itself, he is not as troubled as John about the whole ethos and method of the Roman Empire.

This difference between the seer John and Clement in their perceptions of the situation and in theological judgments may be related to their different experiences of *pax Romana* in general and persecution in particular. Their different experiences may be due, in turn, to their different geographical location (Clement in Rome versus John in Asia), and also to their social location (Clement a well-positioned Roman citizen versus John a member of a subjugated nation). Clement's geographical and social location at the "center" may have led him not only to have a fundamentally

---

ναί, δέσποτα, ἐπίφανον τὸ πρόσωπόν σου ἐφ᾽ ἡμᾶς εἰς ἀγαθὰ ἐν εἰρήνῃ, εἰς τὸ σκεπασθῆναι ἡμᾶς τῇ χειρί σου τῇ κραταιᾷ καὶ ῥυσθῆναι ἀπὸ πάσης ἁμαρτίας τῷ βραχίονί σου τῷ ὑψηλῷ, καὶ ῥῦσαι ἡμᾶς ἀπὸ τῶν μισούντων ἡμᾶς ἀδίκως.

The text is cited from Holmes, *Apostolic Fathers*, 96, and the translation is printed above.

60. Contrast between the fervent eschatological hope in Revelation and the virtual absence of it in 1 Clement.

61. By saying there that because of "the sudden and repeated calamities and misfortunes which have befallen us" (1 Clement 1:1) he has come to write this letter to the Corinthians only now, Clement gives the impression that the persecution has either ceased or at least abated.

positive view of the Roman imperial order and an interest in its continued stability,[62] but also to suffer from state persecution relatively lightly,[63] whereas John's geographical and social location at the "periphery" or "margin" led him to suffer from state (or provincial) persecution severely and therefore to long to see the demise of the Roman Empire.

Whether or not Clement's higher social station and interest in preserving the Roman imperial order also affected his perception of the situation, he chose resisting emperor worship itself but otherwise honoring the rulers and loyally supporting the imperial order as the church's *modus vivendi* in the Roman Empire. This solution was adopted by Tertullian (*Apology* 28-37) and the early church as a whole. It may be unsatisfactory insofar as it narrowly focused on the imperial cult as the only objectionable feature of the Roman imperial system, and it failed to adequately draw the consequences for their political existence from the antithesis between the whole ethos and method of the empire and the way of the self-emptying God, the *theologia crucis,* the way of "the Lamb who was slain" sitting on the throne, as did the seer John. But when Tertullian, the jurist as well as the sharp theologian and critic of paganism, adopted this solution, he must have found it the only viable option for the survival of the church.

It may be debatable whether this recipe should be evaluated positively

---

62. From the language and thoughts of 1 Clement 37:2-4; 38:2; 55:2-5; 60:4; etc., Wengst describes Clement as "a Roman in a good position," who "in that position . . . experienced the Pax Romana as a good thing" (*Pax Romana,* 110), and therefore, naturally identified himself with the Roman Empire and was interested in the preservation of *pax Romana* (pp. 106-12). But cf. the praescript of 1 Clement for his understanding of the Roman and Corinthian churches as aliens in this world. On the terms the "center" versus the "periphery" or the "margin," see Wengst, *Pax Romana,* 140.

63. Clement makes only brief references to the Neronian persecution, in which Peter and Paul were martyred (1 Clement 5:1-6:2), and to the Domitian persecution (1 Clement 1:1; cf. also 59:4). As said above (n. 61), the wording of 1 Clement 1:1 suggests that the Roman church has just come out of the worst of the Domitian persecution. From the wording of "the sudden and repeated calamities and misfortunes which have befallen us" (διὰ τὰς αἰφνιδίους καὶ ἐπαλλήλους γενομένας ἡμῖν συμφορὰς καὶ περιπτώσεις) in 1:1, Wengst further notes that Clement regards the persecutions as mere misfortunes and accidents (*Pax Romana,* 111-12). James Bradley, my church historian colleague at Fuller Theological Seminary, has pointed out to me that although in the period right up to about A.D. 250 the Roman Empire was always menacing to the church, her persecution was not consistent but intermittent. In such a situation, it is understandable that some Christian leaders such as Clement and Tertullian entertained the hope of securing the Empire's toleration of the church, and so sought a way of securing it.

as having contributed to the survival of the church during the periods of repeated state persecution, or negatively as having paved the way for the post-Constantinian corruption of the church by the amalgamation of the church and the empire. We cannot enter into this debate here. We may just point out that the situation where the tiny budding church was facing the totalitarian religio-political complex of the mighty Roman Empire was quite unlike the situation of Nazi Germany where a large and strong church was facing the quasi-religious totalitarian ideology, or that of Korea during the 1970s and 1980s where a large and strong church was facing a secular military dictatorship, and that in the situation they faced, the way Clement and Tertullian chose could well have been the only realistic one.[64]

The dialectical perception of *pax Romana* in Paul and Luke is also to be explained in terms of their experiences of *pax Romana* in general and Roman persecution in particular, as well as their interests or purposes. The attitudes of Paul and Luke to *pax Romana* are here called dialectical because, as we have seen, they are neither so one-sidedly pro-Roman as Clement's, nor so one-sidedly anti-Roman as the seer John's. When they still see possibilities for Christian acquittal by Roman courts and for use of the facilities of *pax Romana* in the interest of Christian mission, both Paul and Luke must not have been experiencing the threats of the imperial cult and state persecution so severely as the seer John. If so, time may also be a factor in the difference between Paul and Luke, on the one hand, and the seer John, on the other. This is obvious in the case of Paul, who wrote in the 50s and early 60s, i.e., before the Neronian persecution. But even Luke's relative appreciation of *pax Romana* will have to be explained in a similar way: writing in the early part of the reign of Domitian in a place other than Asia, Luke did not see the threats of the imperial cult and state (province) persecution as seriously as John did.

---

64. The situation of the small fledgling church of Korea during the Japanese occupation of the land (1910-45) was similar to that of the early church in the Roman Empire (the Protestant mission in Korea began in 1885). At first Korean Christians resisted the Japanese imperial cult, but when the totalitarian religio-politico-military machinery of the Japanese Empire intensified the requirement of the imperial cult with the threats of severe persecution during the 1930s and early 1940s, all but a small minority of Korean Christian leaders gave in, performing rituals for the emperor worship as well as complying with the imperial rule in general. Therefore, on the whole, the early church was more faithful to the Christian faith than the Korean church, as it resisted at least the imperial cult consistently whereas the Korean church failed to do even that.

It is out of the question that both Paul and Luke show a relative appreciation of *pax Romana* because they have a fundamentally positive view of the Roman imperial order as such. For, as we have seen, they both see it as diabolic and as doomed to destruction or replacement by the Kingdom of God at the *parousia* of the Lord Jesus Christ, and they both (as members of the periphery like the seer John) identify themselves with the oppressed of the empire. See how, in the name of Christ crucified, Paul vehemently criticizes the imperialistic values of power and wisdom for the sake of the weak, uneducated, and low-born (e.g., 1 Cor 1:18-31; 11:17-22), and how strongly Luke shows his sympathy and solidarity with the poor and oppressed (e.g., Luke 1:46-55; 4:18-19; 6:20-26). Unlike Clement, Tertullian, and others in the early church, even Luke, not to mention Paul, does not have any idea of praying for the emperor or the empire. Therefore, it is wrong for Wengst to regard the attitude of Paul and Luke to *pax Romana* more or less the same as that of Clement.[65] The relative appreciation of *pax Romana* by Paul and Luke should be seen as motivated by their interest not in the stability of the empire but rather in the progress of Christian mission and the welfare of the church. Only because the order, peace, and stability of the world is a precondition for a rapid missionary movement, which they seek with their eschatological vision, do they appreciate *pax Romana* and does Paul even advise Christians to comply with imperial administration.[66]

Therefore, if the empire had been perceived as threatening the very existence of the church and making her mission impossible, Paul and Luke, with their overriding interest in the welfare and mission of the church as well as their fundamental understanding of earthly rulers as instruments of Satan, might well have found no alternative but to resist the imperial order. In such a case, they would have invoked the principle that Christians must obey God rather than human beings (cf. Acts 4:19). If the imperial cult had been forced upon Christians and the threat of persecution had been so severe that some Christians tried to survive by compromising with the imperial cult and ideology, surely Paul would have fought their com-

---

65. See pp. 182-83.

66. It is true that the heir(s) to Paul's theological legacy responsible for 1 Tim 2:1-4 urge the readers to pray "for all human beings, for kings and all who are in high positions." But even they are motivated for this not by concern for the stability of the empire, but rather by their concerns for securing a peaceable life for the church and advancing her mission of saving all human beings through earning the good will and respect of the pagan world for her "godly and respectful" lifestyle.

promise as hard as he fought the compromise of the gospel with the requirements of the law in Galatians or with the Hellenistic spirituality in the Corinthian correspondence. He would have done that precisely in order to preserve "the truth of the gospel" (Gal 2:5), or to preserve the church as the church of the Lord Jesus Christ. But this was precisely the position of the John of Revelation (cf. Rev 2:14-15, 20-21; 3:4; 18:4; 21:8). Even if Luke was theologically less sharp than Paul and was more willing to accommodate the law-abiding Jewish Christian wing of the primitive church, he would hardly have been different from Paul when it came to compromising the gospel with imperial *idolatry* (cf. Acts 15:29; 17:16, 22-31; 19:21-41). Or, would Luke also have opted for the solution of Clement, Tertullian, and the early church: no emperor worship, but otherwise loyal submission to the imperial order? Luke does not shy away from making many negative references, explicitly or implicitly, to the Roman imperial order in his two-volume work, as we have seen, whereas Clement hardly makes any (unless 1 Clement 59:4 and 60:3 are seen as pale references). In view of this fact, we may presume that Luke would not have promoted such a one-sidedly submissive attitude to the Roman imperial order as Clement did.

At any rate, we have so far compared the three different attitudes of the early church to the Roman imperial order: (1) the completely negative attitude of John the seer, which views it only as Satanic and therefore advises Christians only to resist it and withdraw from it (Rev 18:4: "come out of [Babylon]"); (2) the attitude of Clement of Rome and the later early church, which resists emperor worship itself but otherwise is loyal to the empire; and (3) the dialectical attitude of Paul and Luke, which recognizes the fundamentally diabolic nature of the empire and yet, for the sake of Christian mission, is willing to cooperate with it and use its facilities. We have argued that Paul and Luke were able to maintain their dialectical attitude without being forced to take up a position like that of John the seer because they had not yet experienced the threats of the imperial cult and state or province persecution as severely as John did, and they did not judge the situation as desperate as John did. Here we may only add that even the John of Revelation advocates merely passive resistance to the imperial cult and order but no active revolutionary uprising.[67]

---

67. See below, pp. 195-96.

# Summary and Conclusion

Luke is convinced that Jesus is the Messiah and he has wrought the messianic work of redemption of Israel as prophesied in the Scriptures. However, unlike many of the first-century Jews, Luke fully appreciates Jesus' understanding of his Messiahship and the Kingdom of God. As the Son or viceroy of God, the Messiah is to deliver God's people not by subjugating the nations by military might but by overcoming the reign of Satan and resolving the problem of sin that it causes, i.e., by restoring human beings to God, their creator, and bringing healing to the ills of sin.

The fundamental problem for human beings and the world is the reign of Satan in sin and death (Luke 11:14-23; 13:16; Acts 10:38; 26:18; etc.). It alienates human beings from God, their rich and loving Father, and leaves them in destitution or inflicts them with various forms of suffering (Luke 15:11-32). It manifests itself also in the form of the self-aggrandizing and oppressive rule of worldly kingdoms (Luke 4:1-13; 22:24-27). The Roman Empire is another embodiment of the reign of Satan, and therefore the *pax Augusta/Romana* achieved through military conquest and political suppression is no real peace. Hence God made his Son be born of Mary to bring the universal peace and so become the true *sōtēr* ("Yeshua/Jesus," Luke 1:31) and *kyrios* of the whole world (Luke 1:30-35; 2:1-14). By narrating the Messiah Jesus' birth in conscious contrast to the reign of Caesar Augustus in the beginning of his two-volume work (Luke 2:1-14) and by reporting the bold proclamation of the Kingdom of God and the Lord Jesus Christ by Paul, the apostle of Jesus Christ, at the close of his work (Acts 28:31), Luke makes it clear that the Empire of Rome and the lordship of Caesar are to be replaced by the Kingdom of God and the Lordship of Jesus Christ.

Yet precisely because in the Kingdom of God kingship or lordship is not lording it over others as in the kingdoms of the world, which are under the control of Satan, but rather serving others (Luke 22:24-27), the Messiah Jesus did not redeem Israel by a military struggle against the Roman Empire and the establishment of a nationalistic kingdom of Israel that could practice vengeance upon the nations, as many of his contemporaries wanted. The Messiah Jesus fought the empire of Satan itself (Luke 11:14-23) rather than the Empire of Rome, a mere manifestation of it, and he did that not by the Satanic way but by God's way (Luke 4:1-13). Therefore, with a clear appreciation of the true nature of the Messiahship that Jesus embodied, Luke shows how Jesus went the way of love and service as the king of peace in opposition to many contemporary Jewish revolutionaries (Luke 6:27-36; 19:41-44), and how therefore he has brought the real peace of the Kingdom of God in contrast to the sham peace of the Roman Empire. Concretely Luke presents Jesus as focusing upon redeeming people from the reign of Satan by materializing the saving reign of God in the form of physical and spiritual healings, restoring sinners to God, and building a community of love and service, shunning subversive political activities in spite of his critical view of the political conditions of the day.

Nevertheless, Jesus was accused of being a revolutionary, and Pilate, the representative of the Roman Empire, crucified him, although he knew well that the accusation was false (Luke 23:2-4, 13-14, 22). With this report, Luke points to the danger of misunderstanding inherent in Jesus' messianic proclamation of the gospel of the Kingdom of God, and, at the same time, defuses the suspicion of Jesus as an anti-Roman revolutionary that could naturally arise from the fact of his crucifixion.

God vindicated Jesus by raising him from the dead and exalted him to his right hand to confirm him as the Messiah and universal Lord (Acts 2:32-36). Then, on behalf of God, the Lord Jesus Christ poured out his Spirit upon his people, confirming the dawn of the eschaton, the age of salvation (Acts 2:17-21, 33). And the universal Lord Jesus Christ commissioned his apostles to proclaim the gospel of the Kingdom of God that he had ushered in to all the nations — to wit, to the ends of the earth — by the power of the Spirit (Acts 1:8), and to avail them of the forgiveness of sins that he had wrought (Luke 24:47; Acts 10:42-43; 26:18; etc.), so that they might also participate in the salvation of "Israel," the people of God, together with the believing Jews (Acts 15:17). So, appending, uniquely among the Evangelists, the history of the apostolic preaching of the gospel to the history of Jesus' proclamation of it, Luke shows how the apostles continued the work of Jesus, or how the exalted Lord Jesus Christ continued his work of redemption through them in the power of his Spirit. Hence, Luke shows that the apostles continued bringing about Christ's redemption precisely in three areas: healing the sick, restoring sinners to God, and building a community of love and service. Yet Luke holds these forms of the actualization of Christ's redemption to be only anticipating the ultimate salvation, the renewal and restoration of the whole creation, which will come about at the *parousia* of the Lord Jesus Christ (Acts 3:19-21).

Like his Master, the apostle Paul also was sometimes accused of proclaiming a message treasonous to Caesar (Acts 17:7; etc.). But the Roman officials repeatedly found him and his gospel innocent (Acts 23:29; 25:25; 26:31-32; etc.), so that, having arrived in Rome for the ultimate defense of the gospel, Paul was able to proclaim boldly the gospel of the Kingdom of God and the Lord Jesus Christ, confidently anticipating its ultimate vindication (Acts 28:31).

So we have been struck by the absence of Luke's concern for the materialization of the saving reign of God and the Lord Jesus Christ in the political sphere of life. Luke's especially strong concern for the poor and the oppressed and his strong emphasis on Jesus' Messiahship as the deliverer of Israel or the poor and the oppressed against the stark backdrop of Roman imperial rule in the opening chapters of his Gospel (Luke 1–4) have made that absence all the more glaring. In spite of his conscious contrast of Jesus' Lordship with Caesar's lordship and all his critical hints about the ills of the Roman imperial system, why does Luke refrain, in the remaining chapters of his Gospel and throughout Acts, from showing what practical implications the proclamation of the gospel of the Kingdom of God and the Lord Jesus Christ should entail in the political sphere?

Our examination of the evidence in Luke's two-volume work has led to this conclusion: in a situation where the Roman Empire is not yet imposing the imperial cult and systematically persecuting the church, Luke is apparently led  not to highlight the political implications of the gospel here and now by the interplay of various factors, such as his expectation of the *parousia* and consummation of the Kingdom of God (renewal and restoration of the whole creation) in a not-too-distant future; his understanding of the Satanic reign in sin as the fundamental human predicament and his comprehensive appreciation of its various ills; his primary concern about preaching the gospel to the end of the earth before the *parousia;* his political realism and relative appreciation of the *pax Romana;* his desire to assure Roman believers and attract more of them by affirming the compatibility of Christianity with their imperial allegiance; and his respect for Jesus' example and Paul's ministry. Thus, Luke limits his concern for the proleptic realization of the Kingdom of God and the Lordship of Jesus Christ here and now to healing, restoring sinners, and creating the community of love and service, without thinking through further to the changes that can be brought to the political, economic, and social system of the Roman Empire.

However, it is perhaps necessary to recognize that with his ascension Christology that appreciates Christ's present reign and implementation of the redemption of God's Kingdom in the power of the Holy Spirit through the church, Luke has provided the future church with a theological model so that under new circumstances where some other factors than the above-mentioned are in operation the church can extend the perspective of the present saving work of the Lord Jesus Christ to the political sphere, beyond the physical, spiritual, and social spheres.

## Excursus: Revelation, Paul, Hebrews

We see this extension into the political sphere happening at least partially in the Revelation of John, although probably independently of Luke. Facing the desperate situation of the forced imperial cult and threats of severe persecution, the seer John presents Christ as the exalted Lord who is presently engaged in saving work that has a political dimension. As the bearer of God's names ("the First and the Last," "the Alpha and the Omega," "the Beginning and the End"), Jesus Christ is the agent of God who establishes God's kingship on earth. He is the one who turns "the kingdom of the world" into "the Kingdom of our Lord and his Christ" (Rev 11:15). Jesus, as the Davidic Messiah (5:5; 22:16), has overcome the rebellious nations (1:16; 2:12, 16; 19:11, 15, 21; cf. Ps 2:8-9) and is now enthroned on the throne of God in heaven (Rev 3:21; 5:1-14). As the Passover Lamb slaughtered, Jesus Christ has also ransomed by his blood a people from all the nations of the world and "made them a kingdom and priests to serve God" (5:6, 9-10; cf. Exod 19:5-6). Now the enthroned Messiah Jesus commands this people (the church) as his army of 144,000 in battle (Rev 5:5; 7:4-8; 13:5-7; 14:1-5; 17:14; 19:11–20:15) against the "Beast," the Roman Empire, which blasphemes

God by the imperial cult and deceives, oppresses, exploits, and corrupts nations (esp. Rev 13; 17–18). He leads his church to fight the messianic war by empowering her with the Holy Spirit, which is his power operating in the world (3:1; 5:6). Through the messianic war, which consists in his Spirit-empowered church's faithfully bearing "the testimony of Jesus" (1:2, 9; 12:17; 19:10; 20:4; cf. also 6:9; 11:7; 12:11) — witnessing to the kingship of the true God and the Lamb slaughtered (i.e., God's rule by way of self-sacrificing love) — unto death among all the nations (11:1-13; 12:11, 17; 19:10), the Messiah Jesus is to convert the nations from idolatry to worship of the true God (11:13; 15:2-4). This present saving work of the exalted Christ will be consummated at his *parousia* as "King of kings and Lord of lords" (17:14; 19:16), when the Kingdom of God will be consummated with "a new heaven and a new earth," or "the Holy City, the New Jerusalem, coming down out of heaven from God" (21:1–22:5).

Thus the seer John presents basically the same Christology within the Trinitarian framework as Luke: an understanding of the exalted Christ presently working out God's redemption of the world through his church in the power of his Holy Spirit. But to meet the needs of his situation John advances beyond Luke in applying the present saving work of the exalted Lord Jesus Christ explicitly to the struggle with the Roman imperial politics and thus developing a truly "political" Christology. However, in spite of his fervent critique of the beastly Roman Empire and his explicit interpretation of Christ's work in the category of the messianic war, the seer John does not envisage the church as actively engaged in political subversion and military campaign. Nor does he show what concrete political changes in the present are entailed in the conversion of the nations to be brought about by the Spirit-empowered church's faithful witness to the true God and the Lamb slaughtered. Instead, John prophesies the conversion of the nations as constituting the ultimate victory of Jesus Christ and ushering in the consummation of the Kingdom of God, and therefore as something that will take place at the *parousia* of the Lord Jesus Christ. With this apocalyptic prophecy, John is interested only in assuring the believers of the victory of Jesus Christ and his imminent *parousia* for the eschatological judgment and redemption and calling them to "conquer" (Rev 2:7, 11; 12:11, etc.) the "Beast," the Roman Empire, in the same way that Jesus Christ, the Lamb slaughtered but now enthroned on God's throne, conquered (Rev 5:5): namely, by maintaining faithfully "the testimony of Jesus" unto martyrdom.

Clearly the seer John's fundamental apocalyptic dualism and imminent eschatology are the basic reasons for this lack of interest in the practical changes that the exalted Lord Jesus Christ brings to the present political order before his *parousia*. However, there are two more reasons for this. First, apparently the invincible might of Rome and her totalitarian rule (Rev 13:4), as well as the urgent situation of the mighty empire's persecution of the tiny church, leave John no room to contemplate how the church might draw strength from the exalted Lord Jesus Christ to bring about positive changes to the imperial system, let alone fight it politically and militarily. He can only advise the believers to resist the idolatry of the imperial cult unto death, faithfully bearing witness to the Kingdom of God in full confidence that *God himself* will *imminently* destroy the Satanic regime and consummate his Kingdom through the Lord Jesus Christ. But more importantly, John is convinced that the church, the army of the Messiah, can truly conquer the Roman Empire, the Satanic incarnation, by fighting it not in the Roman (i.e., Satanic) way but only in Jesus' way — that is, by proclaiming his gospel of the Kingdom of God and by following his example of self-sacrificing love (Rev 11:1-13; 12:11, 17). It is remarkable that even the author of Revelation, which appears most "belligerent" among the books of the New Testament, faithfully represents the way of Jesus, as do Paul, Luke, the author of 1 Peter, and the other authors of the New Testament.

Thus, by applying the present Lordship of Jesus Christ directly to the struggle with Roman imperial politics, the seer John does advance beyond Luke's mere contrast between the Kingdom of God represented by Jesus Christ and the Empire of Rome as well as his limited affirmation of the present saving work of the Lord Jesus Christ in relation to physical and spiritual illness and material and social needs. Yet, insofar as John envisages the present Lordship of Jesus not as bringing about concrete changes in the politics of the present but as fighting to replace the kingdom of the Beast with the Kingdom of God at the *parousia,* that advance amounts to little beyond formally affirming that the present Lordship of Jesus may (or must) be applied to the political as well as other spheres of existence.

This being so, the political Christology of Revelation may be seen as little more than the unfolding and application to the Roman Empire of Paul's affirmation in 1 Cor 15:24-28 that in the present (i.e., during the period between Christ's resurrection and his *parousia*) Jesus Christ as the exalted Lord and Son of God goes on destroying every rebellious "rule and authority and power," or subjecting all things to his Lordship, so that the whole creation may be restored to God, the Father — their creator and only rightful ruler — at the end of the End. Paul affirms the present saving activity of the exalted Lord Jesus Christ also in Rom 15:17-25: "For I will not venture to speak of anything except *what Christ has accomplished through me to win obedience from the Gentiles, by word and deed, by the power of signs and wonders, by the power of the Spirit of God . . ."* (vv. 18-19). We have already noted that this could easily be taken as a summary of the second half of Acts. (So, while 1 Cor 15:24-28 may be seen as unfolded in Revelation, Rom 15:17-25 may be seen as unfolded in the second half of Acts.) Thus, Paul also affirms the present saving activity of the exalted Lord Jesus Christ,[1] and, in 1 Cor 15:24-28, he even hints at its political applicability. Yet it is unmistakable that in his gospel proclamation Paul focuses more on Christ's atoning sacrifice on the cross and his future *parousia* for the consummation of salvation than on Christ's present saving reign, and that even where Paul affirms the present saving work of the exalted Christ, he does not make a real political application of it beyond the mere hint.

The author of the Epistle to the Hebrews stresses Christ's ascension as much as his atoning death. However, in view of the needs of his addressees, the author of Hebrews expounds the present work of the exalted Christ only in terms of his high-priestly intercession for his people at the right hand of God. Nevertheless, his creative way of developing out of the traditional kergyma a new doctrine of the exalted Christ's present saving work as the heavenly high priest in the light of the Scriptures, in order to meet the new needs of his situation, could provide a model here. Consider how the author expands the traditional kerygma of Christ, God's Son, as having offered himself as the eschatological atoning sacrifice and having been exalted at the right hand of God (Heb 1:3), which was affirmed on the basis of such Scriptures as Pss 2:7; 110:1; Isa 53:10-12; etc., by drawing further light from those passages: the Scriptures say that the Servant who offered himself as an atoning sacrifice for the sins of many (Isa 53:10-12e) made also "intercession for the transgressors" (v. 12f), and that the Lord who has been exalted at the right hand of God (Ps 110:1) has also been installed as "the eternal high priest after the order of Melchizedek" (Ps 110:4). Therefore, Christ, God's Son (Ps 2:7), who has offered himself as the eschatological atonement for sins (Isa 53:10-12e) must be understood as functioning as the high priest (Ps 110:4) at the right hand of God (Ps 110:1), also making

---

1. See further p. 69, above.

intercession for sinners (Isa 53:12f), at present. Thus the author of Hebrews develops a new doctrine of Christ's high-priestly ministry: Christ fulfilled this ministry by offering himself up as the sacrifice of the eschatological atonement and new covenant on the cross (Heb 9:11–10:18), but he is continuing at present his saving work as the eternal high priest at the right hand of God the Father, making intercession for those who draw near to God through him (Heb 7:25). This new doctrine developed out of the traditional kerygma with illumination drawn from further reflections on the Scriptures (Heb 1:3d [Ps 110:1] + Heb 5:6 [Ps 110:4] + Heb 1:3c; 9:14, 26, 28 [Isa 53:10-12e] + Heb 7:25b [Isa 53:12f] = the thesis in Heb 4:14-16) is then employed to meet the needs of those Diaspora Jewish Christians who were troubled by their post-baptismal sins and trying to return to Jewish cultic practice for their resolution.[2]

Unlike Luke (or Paul, or the seer John), the author of Hebrews does not contrast the Lordship of Christ to that of Caesar or other rulers of the world, and therefore his high-priestly Christology does not have a political dimension. So the author does not make any polemic against the Roman imperial cult or the notion of the Roman emperor as *pontifex maximus,* while presenting Jesus Christ as the Son of God and the High Priest.[3] Nor does he reflect on the socio-political effects of his high-priestly Christology on the Sadducean priesthood of Jerusalem (which was in collusion with the Roman imperial masters) when he argues that Christ's eschatological high-priesthood has made the old Aaronic priesthood of the Jerusalem temple obsolete. Nevertheless, the author's model of developing that Christology out of the traditional kerygma to affirm the present saving work of the exalted Lord Jesus Christ for the needs of his audience would serve as a useful analogy for an attempt to develop a Christology that affirms the present saving work of the Lord Jesus Christ in the political realm on the basis of the Lucan theological model.

---

2. Cf. B. Lindars, *The Theology of the Letter to the Hebrews,* NTT (Cambridge: Cambridge University Press, 1991).

3. This would be remarkable if the imperial cult was so great a burden on Christians during the second half of the first century A.D. as the so-called political interpreters of Pauline and other New Testament writings insist. It would be all the more so, if Hebrews was written from or to Rome, as often suggested (cf. Heb 13:24).

## Comparison between Paul and Luke

This study has affirmed a remarkable degree of agreement between Paul and Luke in their dialectical attitude to the Roman Empire or *pax Romana* and in their avoidance of expounding the political implications of the gospel and formulating it in an anti-imperial way, as well as in their comprehensive understanding of the human predicament and of Christ's redemption; their personalization of sin and salvation, or their stress on the priority of personal change (forgiveness of sins, or justification, and life in obedience to God's reign or Christ's Lordship — the double command of love) over against institutional change; their common vision of the imminent *parousia* of the Lord Jesus Christ for the consummation of salvation; and, above all, their concentration on the missionary work of proclaiming the gospel to all nations before the *parousia*. Also, both Paul and Luke consciously follow Jesus' way of nonretaliation, enemy love, and peace. So we can conclude that with his report of the Pauline mission Luke not only confirms much of the conclusion that we have derived from our study of Pauline epistles in Part One, but with his two-volume work as a whole he also takes a stance very similar to Paul's on the question of Christ versus Caesar. Luke does affirm more concretely than Paul the exalted Lord Jesus Christ's present redemptive work through the church in the power of the Holy Spirit, but even that does not constitute any fundamental difference between them, as Paul also presents the same Christology, though he does not unfold it as much as Luke.

# Epilogue: Some Implications for Today

What are the implications of our study for today's church? I would (or could) not presume to develop as adequate a discussion on this question as colleagues specializing in systematic theology, ethics, or practical theology might do. I would content myself just with pointing out some salient lessons of this study that need to be considered in any serious discussion of Christian political ethics. For many, the lessons drawn here may be only too obvious and familiar. But since there are also many who question or deny some of these lessons, they have to be stated again at least for confirmation.

First of all, it has to be recognized that in many countries still negligibly small churches have to struggle to survive in very hostile and intolerant societies, just as the early church had to in the Roman Empire. Often the religious and political situations make it difficult for the church worldwide to show solidarity with those national churches and help them. In those countries, many Christians may think that it is too risky to show any critical attitude toward the oppressive state authorities and hostile environment, and that for the survival of the church it is necessary to take a stance similar to that of Clement and Tertullian. Some Christians may take the risk of preaching on the Pauline and Lucan texts that are critical of pagan rulers and environments. A small minority may be inspired by the apocalyptic message of Revelation to refuse to adjust to the ethos and ways of their governments and societies that are contrary to their Christian faith. It will require some degree of freedom and tolerance in a society for Christians to have even a discussion as to which of the three options is the right one for them to take. I suppose that no responsible theologian in the West today would be so presumptuous as to criticize the small bands of Christians struggling to survive in such hostile environments for not waging a political revolution against their oppressive regimes. Then, is it right for us modern theologians to criticize Jesus, Paul, Luke, and even Clement and Tertullian for having failed to fight the Roman Empire as the Jewish revolutionaries did? Or is it wise to try to force Jesus and Paul to put on the uniform of a political revolutionary in order to overcome the "scandal" of a Messiah and an apostle who were not political revolutionaries?

However, it is also necessary to recognize that in many Western and non-Western countries our changed situation demands a more active Christian engagement in political processes than Paul and Luke exemplify. We have pointed out that both in Paul and Luke an imminent eschatology and political realism played their parts, along with other factors, in discouraging them from thinking about the present materialization of God's reign or Christ's Lordship in the political sphere. Even today, there are, of course, some Christians who are caught up in the vision of an imminent *parousia* of the Lord Jesus Christ. They generally abandon this "doomed" world more or less completely, awaiting their heavenward deliverance. But most Christians today no longer feel the pressure of an imminent eschatology so greatly, and they therefore naturally are concerned about the present materialization of God's reign or Christ's Lordship, however tentative it may be. Another change in today's situation is that in many parts of the world the church is no longer such a speck as it was at the time of Paul and Luke, but rather a real force by virtue of its numerical strength as well as the weight of its history and tradition. Therefore Christians are conscious that they can bring about changes to the political, economic, social, and cultural systems. Furthermore, in many countries they are quite free to be politically engaged and to seek such changes. These three new factors make us free from the inhibition that an imminent eschatology and political realism laid on Paul and Luke. So we should actively seek what changes need to be brought about in the political sphere in obedience to Christ's Lordship and thus help materialize the redemption of the Kingdom of God politically as well as in other spheres of existence.

For this endeavor, Luke's ascension Christology that appreciates Jesus Christ's present reign and implementation of the redemption of God's Kingdom in the power of the Spirit and through his church can effectively be extended to the political sphere beyond the physical, spiritual, and social spheres. As Paul also affirms the exalted Lord Jesus Christ's redemptive activities in the Spirit and through the church in the present (Rom 15:17-25) and speaks of his destroying "every rule and authority and power" (1 Cor 15:24-28), he too could support the efforts to articulate the demand of Christ's present Lordship in the political sphere. As we have seen, for this purpose, the model of Revelation can be particularly important. For in this book the seer John not only has the same understanding as Luke of the exalted Christ presently working out God's redemption through his church in the power of his Holy Spirit, but, in fact, also applies that Christology directly to the political realm. So John's presentation of the exalted Christ as waging the messianic war through his church against the kingdom of Satan that is incarnate in the Roman Empire provides a powerful warrant as well as a model for an attempt to develop a "political" Christology.

However, as we have seen, with his focus on the ultimate destruction of the kingdom of Satan and its replacement by the Kingdom of God at the *parousia* of the Lord Jesus Christ, the seer John does not show any interest in affirming concrete changes in the form of greater justice, peace, freedom, and so forth that the Lord Jesus Christ brings about through his church to the political existence of the present. Therefore, in developing an effective political Christology for the present, we will need to loosen John's apocalyptic concentration and extend Luke's stress on the Lord Jesus Christ's present work of delivering people from their concrete needs, so as to see his present redemptive work in relation to political problems as well as physical and spiritual illness and material and social needs. For such a development, support can also be drawn by way of analogy from the example of the author of Hebrews, from his way of meeting the needs of his situation by presenting the exalted Christ as carrying on his work of redemption as the high priest in the heavenly sanctuary, through a fresh interpretation of the Christ event, the kerygmatic tradition of the church, and the Old Testament. Finally, we may add that a political Christology developed in this way needs to be supplemented or deepened by the Pauline soteriology of justification (restoration to the right relationship with God in order to live in dependence upon and obedience to him or his Son, the Lord Jesus Christ) and walking according to the Spirit (who enables that life of dependence and obedience).

In developing such a political Christology/soteriology within the Trinitarian framework, the church, if she is to remain the church of the Lord Jesus Christ, will have to abide by some important principles that her Lord taught and demonstrated according to the witnesses of the New Testament. She will need to maintain a comprehensive view of evil and suffering, or of sin and death. Precisely a comprehensive view of evil and suffering, of course, requires the church to be conscious of structural or systemic evil as well as personal evil. But it should also help her properly locate political engagement within the framework of her total struggle with the evil forces operating in all spheres of existence, rather than making it the sole issue of her ministry. Further, while seeking to materialize the salvation of the Kingdom of God in terms of promotion of justice, freedom, peace, environmental health, and so on, the church must acknowledge the proleptic or provisionary character of such materialization in history, and maintain the eschatological vision for the consummation of salvation in terms of a trans-historical and transcendental reality. Thus the church should avoid reducing salvation to an immanent reality and thereby reducing Christianity to a variety of mere this-worldly ideology.

Furthermore, the church should not belittle Jesus' and the apostles' stress on the proclamation of the gospel and personal change, or "conversion" from the power of sin and entry into the Kingdom of God. She should indeed try to bring the political, economic, and social systems to reflect the values, ideals, and principles of the Kingdom of God as much as possible in order to materialize justice, freedom, peace, and environmental health even more. But precisely in order to bring about real changes to those systems, the church should not neglect proclaiming the gospel of the Kingdom of God and the Lord Jesus Christ and calling for change of the heart, attitudes, and relationships in obedience to Christ's Lordship. Above all, she should clearly present the truth that divine reign comes to us with the double command of love: love of God (exclusion of idolatry, especially that of Mammon) and love of neighbors, i.e., that Jesus Christ concretely exercises his Lordship by demanding that we obey this double command of love in all the moments of value judgment, ethical choice, and political decision.

So it is clear that the church cannot pursue a political soteriology in the way that Jesus shunned as Satanic or worldly, with a self-seeking motive and violent method, but only in the way of love — the self-sacrificing love that Jesus taught and demonstrated and that his apostle Paul and even the seer John propounded. The church can fight the principalities and powers in heaven and their representatives on earth only by proclaiming Jesus' gospel of the Kingdom of God and by following his example of self-sacrifice, or by putting on the "the whole armor of God," which consists of truth, righteousness, faith, love, hope, salvation, the gospel of peace, the word and Spirit of God, prayer, and perseverance (Eph 6:10-18; 1 Thess 5:8).

# Select Bibliography

Agosto, Efrain. "Patronage and Commendation, Imperial and Anti-Imperial." In *Paul and the Roman Imperial Order,* edited by Richard A. Horsley, pp. 103-23. Harrisburg, Pa.: Trinity Press International, 2004.

Alexander, Loveday. "The Acts of the Apostles as an Apologetic Text." In *Apologetics in the Roman Empire: Pagans, Jews, and Christians,* edited by M. Edwards, M. Goodman, and S. Price, pp. 15-44. Oxford: Oxford University Press, 1999.

Aune, David E. *Revelation 1–5.* Word Biblical Commentary 52A. Nashville: Thomas Nelson, 1997.

Aus, Roger D. *My Name Is "Legion": Palestinian Judaic Traditions in Mark 5:1-20 and Other Gospel Texts.* Studies in Judaism. Lanham, Md.: University Press of America, 2003.

Bammel, E. "Romans 13." In *Jesus and the Politics of His Day,* edited by E. Bammel and C. F. D. Moule, pp. 365-83. Cambridge: Cambridge University Press, 1984.

Barnes, Timothy D. *Tertullian: A Historical and Literary Study.* Oxford: Clarendon, 1971.

Barrett, C. K. *A Critical and Exegetical Commentary on the Acts of the Apostles.* 2 vols. International Critical Commentary. Edinburgh: T&T Clark, 1994, 1998.

———. *Luke the Historian in Recent Study.* London: Epworth, 1961. Repr. Facet Books: Biblical Series 24. Philadelphia: Fortress, 1970.

Beale, G. K. *The Book of Revelation: A Commentary on the Greek Text.* New International Greek Testament Commentary. Grand Rapids, Mich.: Eerdmans/Carlisle: Paternoster, 1999.

Beker, J. Christiaan. *Paul the Apostle: The Triumph of God in Life and Thought.* Philadelphia: Fortress, 1980.

Bergsma, John S. *The Jubilee from Leviticus to Qumran: A History of Interpretation.* Supplements to *Vetus Testamentum* 115. Leiden: Brill, 2007.

Blumenfeld, Bruno. *The Political Paul: Justice, Democracy and Kingship in a Hellenistic Framework.* Journal for the Study of the New Testament Supplement Series 210. Sheffield: Sheffield Academic Press, 2001.

Borg, Marcus. "A New Context for Romans XIII." *New Testament Studies* 19 (1972-73): 205-18.

Bornkamm, Günther. *Jesus of Nazareth.* Translated by Irene and Fraser McLuskey with James M. Robinson. London: Hodder & Stoughton/New York: Harper & Row, 1960. Repr. Minneapolis: Fortress, 1995.

Bovon, François. "Das Heil in den Schriften des Lukas." In *Lukas in neuer Sicht: Gesammelte Aufsätze.* Translated by E. Hartmann, A. Frey, and P. Strauss, pp. 61-74. Biblisch-Theologische Studien 8. Neukirchen-Vluyn: Neukirchener Verlag, 1985.

———. *Luke the Theologian: Fifty-Five Years of Research (1950-2005).* 2nd rev. ed. Waco: Baylor University Press, 2006.

Brandon, S. G. F. *Jesus and the Zealots: A Study of the Political Factor in Primitive Christianity.* New York: Charles Scribner's Sons/Manchester: Manchester University Press, 1967.

Braund, David C. *Augustus to Nero: A Sourcebook on Roman History, 31 BC–AD 68.* Totowa, N.J.: Barnes and Noble, 1985.

Brent, A. *The Imperial Cult and the Development of Church Order: Concepts and Images of Authority in Paganism and Early Christianity before the Age of Cyprian.* Supplements to Vigiliae Christianae 45. Leiden: Brill, 1999.

Brown, Raymond E. *The Birth of the Messiah: A Commentary on the Infancy Narratives in the Gospels of Matthew and Luke.* New updated ed. Anchor Bible Reference Library. New York: Doubleday, 1993.

Bruce, F. F. *The Acts of the Apostles: The Greek Text with Introduction and Commentary.* 3rd rev. and enlarged ed. Grand Rapids, Mich.: Eerdmans/Leicester: Apollos, 1990.

———. *Paul: Apostle of the Heart Set Free.* Grand Rapids, Mich.: Eerdmans, 1977.

Bryan, Christopher. *Render to Caesar: Jesus, the Early Church, and the Roman Superpower.* Oxford: Oxford University Press, 2005.

Burchard, Christoph. "A Note on 'PHMA in JosAs 17:1f.; Luke 2:15, 17; Acts 10:37." *Novum Testamentum* 27 (1985): 281-95.

Cadbury, H. J. *The Making of Luke-Acts.* New York and London: Macmillan, 1927. Repr. London: SPCK, 1958.

Carter, W. *Matthew and Empire: Initial Explorations.* Harrisburg, Pa.: Trinity Press International, 2001.

Cassidy, Richard J. *Jesus, Politics, and Society: A Study of Luke's Gospel.* Maryknoll, N.Y.: Orbis, 1978.

———. *Paul in Chains: Roman Imprisonment and the Letters of Paul.* New York: Crossroad, 2001.

————. *Society and Politics in the Acts of the Apostles.* Maryknoll, N.Y.: Orbis, 1987.

Caulley, T. S. "Rereading 1 Peter in Light of the Roman Imperial Cult." Paper presented at the Kolloquium für Graduierte, University of Tübingen, October 24, 2005.

Conzelmann, Hans. *The Theology of St. Luke.* Translated by Geoffrey Buswell. London: Faber and Faber/New York: Harper & Row, 1960. Translation of *Die Mitte der Zeit.* 2nd ed. Beiträge zur historischen Theologie 17. Tübingen: Mohr Siebeck, 1957.

Cramer, Frederick H. *Astrology in Roman Law and Politics.* Memoirs of the American Philosophical Society 37. Philadelphia: American Philosophical Society, 1954. Repr. Chicago: Ares, 1996.

Crossan, J. D., and J. L. Reed. *In Search of Paul: How Jesus' Apostle Opposed Rome's Empire with God's Kingdom.* San Francisco: HarperSanFrancisco, 2004.

Dahl, Nils Alstrup. "The Messiahship of Jesus in Paul." In *Jesus the Christ: The Historical Origins of Christological Doctrine,* edited by Donald H. Juel, pp. 15-25. Minneapolis: Fortress, 1991.

Davies, W. D., and D. C. Allison. *A Critical and Exegetical Commentary on the Gospel according to Saint Matthew.* 3 vols. ICC. Edinburgh: T&T Clark, 1988-97.

Deissmann, Adolf. *Light from the Ancient East: The New Testament Illustrated by Recently Discovered Texts of the Graeco-Roman World.* Translated by L. R. M. Strachan. New York: George H. Doran, 1927. Translation of *Licht vom Osten: Das Neue Testament und die neuentdeckten Texte der hellenistisch-römischen Welt.* 4th rev. ed. Tübingen: Mohr Siebeck, 1923.

De Vos, Craig Steven. *Church and Community Conflicts: The Relationships of the Thessalonian, Corinthian, and Philippian Churches with Their Wider Civic Communities.* Society of Biblical Literature Dissertation Series 168. Atlanta: Scholars Press, 1999.

Dietzfelbinger, Christian. "Vom Sinn der Sabbatheilungen Jesu." *Evangelische Theologie* 38 (1978): 281-98.

Donfried, Karl P. "The Imperial Cults of Thessalonica and Political Conflict in 1 Thessalonians." In *Paul and Empire: Religion and Power in Roman Imperial Society,* edited by R. A. Horsley, pp. 215-23. Harrisburg, Pa.: Trinity Press International, 1997.

Dunn, James D. G. *Romans 9–16.* Word Biblical Commentary 38B. Dallas: Word, 1988.

Edwards, M., M. Goodman, and S. Price, eds. *Apologetics in the Roman Empire: Pagans, Jews, and Christians.* Oxford: Oxford University Press, 1999.

Ehrenberg, Victor, and A. H. M. Jones. *Documents Illustrating the Reigns of Augustus and Tiberius.* 2nd enlarged ed. Oxford: Clarendon, 1976.

Ehrman, Bart D. *The New Testament: A Historical Introduction to the Early Christian Writings.* 2nd ed. New York and Oxford: Oxford University Press, 2000.

Elliott, Neil. "The Anti-Imperial Message of the Cross." In *Paul and Empire: Religion and Power in Roman Imperial Society,* edited by R. A. Horsley, pp. 167-83. Harrisburg, Pa.: Trinity Press International, 1997.

———. *Liberating Paul: The Justice of God and the Politics of the Apostle.* Bible and Liberation Series. Maryknoll, N.Y.: Orbis, 1994. Repr. Biblical Seminar 27. Sheffield: Sheffield Academic Press, 1995.

———. "Romans 13:1-7 in the Context of Imperial Propaganda." In *Paul and Empire: Religion and Power in Roman Imperial Society,* edited by R. A. Horsley, pp. 184-204. Harrisburg, Pa.: Trinity Press International, 1997.

Esler, Philip F. *Community and Gospel in Luke-Acts: The Social and Political Motivations of Lucan Theology.* Society for New Testament Studies Monograph Series 57. Cambridge: Cambridge University Press, 1987.

Fee, Gordon D. *Paul's Letter to the Philippians.* New International Commentary on the New Testament. Grand Rapids, Mich.: Eerdmans, 1995.

Fishwick, D. *The Imperial Cult in the Latin West.* Vol. 2: *Studies in the Ruler Cult of the Western Provinces of the Roman Empire,* Part 1. Études préliminaires aux religions orientales dans l'Empire Romain 108.2. Leiden: Brill, 1991.

Fitzmyer, Joseph A. *The Gospel according to Luke I–IX: A New Translation with Introduction and Commentary.* Anchor Bible 28. New York: Doubleday, 1981.

———. *Romans.* Anchor Bible 33. New York: Doubleday, 1993.

France, R. T. "God and Mammon." *Evangelical Quarterly* 51 (1979): 3-21.

———. "Liberation in the New Testament." *Evangelical Quarterly* 58 (1986): 3-23.

Freyne, Seán. *Galilee from Alexander the Great to Hadrian, 323 B.C.E. to 135 C.E.: A Study of Second Temple Judaism.* Studies in Judaism and Christianity in Antiquity 5. Wilmington: Michael Glazier/Notre Dame, Ind.: University of Notre Dame Press, 1980.

———. *Jesus, a Jewish Galilean: A New Reading of the Jesus-Story.* London and New York: T&T Clark International, 2004.

Gaca, Kathy L., and L. L. Welborn. "Introduction: Romans in Light of Early Patristic Reception." In *Early Patristic Readings of Romans,* edited by K. L. Gaca and L. L. Welborn, pp. i-vi. Romans through History and Cultures. New York and London: T&T Clark, 2005.

Gaca, Kathy L., and L. L. Welborn, eds. *Early Patristic Readings of Romans.* New York and London: T&T Clark, 2005.

Georgi, Dieter. "God Turned Upside Down." In *Paul and Empire: Religion and Power in Roman Imperial Society,* edited by R. A. Horsley, pp. 148-57. Harrisburg, Pa.: Trinity Press International, 1997.

Gerhardsson, Birger. "Einige Bemerkungen zu Apg 4, 32." *Studia Theologica* 24 (1970): 142-49.

Grant, Robert M. *Augustus to Constantine: The Thrust of the Christian Movement into the Roman World.* New York: Harper & Row, 1970. Repr. as *Augustus to*

*Constantine: The Rise and Triumph of Christianity in the Roman World.* Louisville, Ky.: Westminster John Knox, 2004.

————. *Greek Apologists of the Second Century.* Philadelphia: Westminster Press, 1988.

Grimm, W. *Der Ruhetag: Sinngehalte einer fast vergessenen Gottesgabe.* Arbeiten zum Neuen Testament und Judentum 4. Frankfurt: Lang, 1980.

Gundry, Robert H. *Mark: A Commentary on His Apology for the Cross.* Grand Rapids, Mich.: Eerdmans, 1993.

Haenchen, Ernst. *The Acts of the Apostles: A Commentary.* Translated by B. Noble and G. Shinn. Translation revised and updated by R. McL. Wilson. Oxford: Blackwell/Philadelphia: Westminster Press, 1971.

Hardin, Justin. "Decrees and Drachmas at Thessalonica: An Illegal Assembly in Jason's House (Acts 17.1-10a)." *New Testament Studies* 52 (2006): 29-49.

Harnack, Adolf von. *The Expansion of Christianity in the First Three Centuries.* 2 vols. Theological Translation Library 19, 20. Translated and edited by James Moffatt. London: Williams & Norgate/New York: Putnam's Sons, 1904-5.

Harrison, J. R. "Paul and the Imperial Gospel at Thessaloniki." *Journal for the Study of the New Testament* 25 (2002): 71-96.

Hawthorne, Gerald F. *Philippians.* Revised and expanded by R. P. Martin. Word Biblical Commentary 43. Rev. ed. Nashville: Nelson Reference & Electronic, 2004.

Hays, Richard B. "The Liberation of Israel in Luke-Acts: Intertextual Readings as Resistance." Paper presented at Fuller Theological Seminary, Pasadena, Calif., January 26, 2006.

Hendrix, Holland Lee. "Beyond 'The Imperial Cult' and 'Cults of Magistrates.'" In *SBL Seminar Papers, 1986,* edited by K. H. Richards, pp. 301-8. Society of Biblical Literature Seminar Papers 25. Atlanta: Scholars Press, 1986.

————. "Thessalonicans Honor Romans." Th.D. diss., Harvard University, 1984.

Hengel, Martin. *Property and Riches in the Early Church: Aspects of a Social History of Early Christianity.* Translated by John Bowden. London: SCM Press/Philadelphia: Fortress, 1974.

————. *The Zealots: Investigations into the Jewish Freedom Movement in the Period from Herod I until 70 A.D.* Translated by David Smith. Edinburgh: T&T Clark, 1989. Translation of *Die Zeloten: Untersuchungen zur jüdischen Freiheitsbewegung in der Zeit von Herodes I. bis 70 n. Chr.* 2nd ed. Leiden: Brill, 1976.

Holmes, Michael W. *The Apostolic Fathers: Greek Texts and English Translations.* Updated ed. Grand Rapids, Mich.: Baker Books, 1999.

Horrell, David G. Introduction [to issue devoted to the New Testament and the Roman Imperial Cult]. *Journal for the Study of the New Testament* 27 (2005): 251-55.

Horsley, G. H. R. *New Documents Illustrating Early Christianity.* Vol. 4: *A Review of the Greek Inscriptions and Papyri Published in 1979.* Macquarie University: Ancient Documentary Research Centre, 1987.

Horsley, Richard A. "'By the Finger of God': Jesus and Imperial Violence." In *Violence in the New Testament,* edited by Shelly Matthews and E. Leigh Gibson, pp. 51-80. New York and London: T&T Clark, 2005.

————. "1 Corinthians: A Case Study of Paul's Assembly as an Alternative Society." In *Paul and Empire: Religion and Power in Roman Imperial Society,* edited by R. A. Horsley, pp. 242-52. Harrisburg, Pa.: Trinity Press International, 1997.

————. General Introduction to *Paul and Empire: Religion and Power in Roman Imperial Society,* edited by R. A. Horsley, pp. 1-8. Harrisburg, Pa.: Trinity Press International, 1997.

————. Introduction to section on "The Gospel of Imperial Salvation." In *Paul and Empire: Religion and Power in Roman Imperial Society,* edited by R. A. Horsley, pp. 10-24. Harrisburg, Pa.: Trinity Press International, 1997.

————. Introduction to section on "Paul's Counter-Imperial Gospel." In *Paul and Empire: Religion and Power in Roman Imperial Society,* edited by R. A. Horsley, pp. 140-47. Harrisburg, Pa.: Trinity Press International, 1997.

————. *Jesus and Empire: The Kingdom of God and the New World Disorder.* Minneapolis: Fortress, 2003.

————. *Jesus and the Spiral of Violence: Popular Jewish Resistance in Roman Palestine.* San Francisco: Harper & Row, 1987. Repr. Minneapolis: Fortress, 1993.

————. "Rhetoric and Empire — and 1 Corinthians." In *Paul and Politics: Ekklesia, Israel, Imperium, Interpretation: Essays in Honor of Krister Stendahl,* edited by Richard A. Horsley, pp. 72-102. Harrisburg, Pa.: Trinity Press International, 2000.

Horsley, Richard A., ed. *Paul and Empire: Religion and Power in Roman Imperial Society.* Harrisburg, Pa.: Trinity Press International, 1997.

————. *Paul and Politics: Ekklesia, Israel, Imperium, Interpretation: Essays in Honor of Krister Stendahl.* Harrisburg, Pa.: Trinity Press International, 2000.

————. *Paul and the Roman Imperial Order.* Harrisburg, Pa.: Trinity Press International, 2004.

Hultgren, Arland J. *Paul's Gospel and Mission: The Outlook from His Letter to the Romans.* Philadelphia: Fortress, 1985.

*Inscriptiones graecae.* Editio minor. Berlin: de Gruyter, 1924-.

Jefford, Clayton N. *The Apostolic Fathers and the New Testament.* Peabody, Mass.: Hendrickson, 2006.

Jervell, Jacob. *Luke and the People of God: A New Look at Luke-Acts.* Minneapolis: Augsburg, 1972.

————. *The Theology of the Acts of the Apostles.* New Testament Theology. Cambridge: Cambridge University Press, 1996.

Jewett, Robert, assisted by Roy D. Kotansky. *Romans: A Commentary.* Edited by Eldon Jay Epp. Hermeneia. Minneapolis: Fortress, 2007.

Judge, E. A. "The Decrees of Caesar at Thessalonica." *Reformed Theological Review* 30 (1971): 1-7.

Kearsley, R. A. "The Asiarchs." In *The Book of Acts in Its First Century Setting,* Vol. 2: *Graeco-Roman Setting,* edited by D. W. J. Gill and C. Gempf, pp. 363-76. Grand Rapids, Mich.: Eerdmans/Carlisle: Paternoster, 1994.

Kelber, Werner H. "Roman Imperialism and Early Christian Scribality." In *Orality, Literacy, and Colonialism in Antiquity,* edited by J. A. Draper, pp. 135-53. Semeia Studies 47. Atlanta: Society of Biblical Literature, 2004. Repr. in *The Postcolonial Biblical Reader,* edited by R. S. Sugirtharajah, pp. 96-111. Oxford: Blackwell, 2005.

Kim, Seyoon. "Isaiah 42 and Paul's Call." In *Paul and the New Perspective: Second Thoughts on the Origin of Paul's Gospel,* pp. 101-27. Grand Rapids, Mich.: Eerdmans/Tübingen: Mohr Siebeck, 2002.

———. "Jesus, Sayings of." In *Dictionary of Paul and His Letters,* edited by Gerald F. Hawthorne, Ralph P. Martin, and Daniel G. Reid, pp. 474-92. Downers Grove, Ill.: InterVarsity Press, 1993. Repr. as "The Jesus Tradition in Paul." In *Paul and the New Perspective,* pp. 259-92. Grand Rapids, Mich.: Eerdmans/Tübingen: Mohr Siebeck, 2002.

———. "Jesus — The Son of God, the Stone, the Son of Man, and the Servant: The Role of Zechariah in the Self-Identification of Jesus." In *Tradition and Interpretation in the New Testament: Essays in Honor of E. Earle Ellis,* edited by Gerald F. Hawthorne and Otto Betz, pp. 134-48. Grand Rapids, Mich.: Eerdmans/Tübingen: Mohr Siebeck, 1987.

———. "The Jesus Tradition in 1 Thess 4.13–5.11." *New Testament Studies* 48 (2002): 225-42.

———. "Kingdom of God." In *Dictionary of the Later New Testament and Its Developments,* edited by Ralph P. Martin and Peter H. Davids, pp. 629-38. Downers Grove, Ill.: InterVarsity Press, 1997.

———. *The Origin of Paul's Gospel.* Wissenschaftliche Untersuchungen zum Neuen Testament 2.4. Tübingen: Mohr Siebeck, 1981, 1984/Grand Rapids, Mich.: Eerdmans, 1982.

———. *Paul and the New Perspective: Second Thoughts on the Origin of Paul's Gospel.* Grand Rapids, Mich.: Eerdmans/Tübingen: Mohr Siebeck, 2002.

———. "Paul's Entry (εἴσοδος) and the Thessalonians' Faith (1 Thessalonians 1–3)." *New Testament Studies* 51 (2005): 519-42.

———. "2 Corinthians 5:11-21 and the Origin of Paul's Concept of Reconciliation." In *Paul and the New Perspective: Second Thoughts on the Origin of Paul's Gospel,* pp. 214-38. Grand Rapids, Mich.: Eerdmans/Tübingen: Mohr Siebeck, 2002.

————. "The Structure and Function of 1 Thessalonians 1–3." In *History and Exegesis: New Testament Essays in Honor of Dr. E. Earle Ellis for His 80th Birthday,* edited by Sang-Won (Aaron) Son, pp. 170-88. New York and London: T&T Clark, 2006.

————. "To Win Caesar: A Lesson from the Missionary Strategy of the Apostle Paul." In *Theology and Higher Education in a Global Era: Festschrift for Professor Doctor Sang Chang,* edited by S. J. Kim and K. S. Lee, pp. 218-29. Seoul: Theological Study Institute, 2005.

————. "Die Vollmacht Jesu und der Tempel — Der Sinn der 'Tempelreinigung' und der geschichtliche und theologische Kontext des Prozesses Jesu." [In Korean.] In *Jesus and Paul,* pp. 119-65. Seoul: Chammal, 1993.

————. "Die Vollmacht Jesu und der Tempel — Der Sinn der 'Tempelreinigung' und der geschichtliche und theologische Kontext des Prozesses Jesu." In *Aufstieg und Niedergang der römischen Welt,* edited by H. Temporini and W. Haase. New York: de Gruyter, forthcoming.

Knox, John. "Rom 15:14-33 and Paul's Conception of His Apostolic Mission." *Journal of Biblical Literature* 83 (1964): 1-11.

Koester, Helmut. "Imperial Ideology and Paul's Eschatology in 1 Thessalonians." In *Paul and Empire: Religion and Power in Roman Imperial Society,* edited by R. A. Horsley, pp. 158-66. Harrisburg, Pa.: Trinity Press International, 1997.

Lindars, Barnabas. *The Theology of the Letter to the Hebrews.* New Testament Theology. Cambridge: Cambridge University Press, 1991.

Lindemann, Andreas. *Paulus im ältesten Christentum: Das Bild des Apostels und die Rezeption der paulinischen Theologie in der frühchristlichen Literatur bis Marcion.* Beiträge zur historischen Theologie 58. Tübingen: Mohr Siebeck, 1979.

Lohfink, Gerhard. *Jesus and Community: The Social Dimension of Christian Faith.* Translated by J. P. Galvin. Philadelphia: Fortress/New York: Paulist, 1984.

MacMullen, Ramsay. *Enemies of the Roman Order: Treason, Unrest, and Alienation in the Empire.* Cambridge, Mass.: Harvard University Press, 1966. Repr. London and New York: Routledge, 1992.

Maddox, Robert. *The Purpose of Luke-Acts.* Forschungen zur Religion und Literatur des Alten und Neuen Testaments 126. Göttingen: Vandenhoeck & Ruprecht, 1982.

Marshall, I. Howard. *The Gospel of Luke: A Commentary on the Greek Text.* New International Greek Testament Commentary. Grand Rapids, Mich.: Eerdmans, 1978.

————. *Luke: Historian and Theologian.* Enlarged ed. Grand Rapids, Mich.: Zondervan, 1989. Repr. New Testament Profiles. Downers Grove, Ill.: InterVarsity Press, 1998.

McLaren, James S. "Jews and the Imperial Cult: From Augustus to Domitian." *Journal for the Study of the New Testament* 27 (2005): 257-78.

Merklein, H. "μετανοέω/μετάνοια." In *Exegetical Dictionary of the New Testament*, 2:415-19, edited by Horst Balz and Gerhard Schneider. 3 vols. Grand Rapids, Mich.: Eerdmans, 1990-93.

Moiser, J. "Rethinking Romans 12–15." *New Testament Studies* 36 (1990): 571-82.

Moore, Stephen D. "Mark and Empire: 'Zealot' and 'Postcolonial' Readings." In *The Postcolonial Biblical Reader*, edited by R. S. Sugirtharajah, pp. 193-205. Oxford: Blackwell, 2005.

Munck, Johannes. *Paul and the Salvation of Mankind*. Translated by Frank Clarke. London: SCM Press/Richmond, Va.: John Knox, 1959.

Neagoe, Alexander. *The Trial of the Gospel: An Apologetic Reading of Luke's Trial Narratives*. Society for New Testament Studies Monograph Series 116. Cambridge: Cambridge University Press, 2002.

Nock, Arthur Darby. "The Roman Army and the Roman Religious Year." *Harvard Theological Review* 45 (1952): 187-252.

Noormann, Rolf. *Irenäus als Paulusinterpret: Zur Rezeption und Wirkung der paulinischen und deuteropaulinischen Briefe im Werk des Irenäus von Lyon*. Wissenschaftliche Untersuchungen zum Neuen Testament 2.66. Tübingen: Mohr Siebeck, 1994.

*Novum Testamentum Graece*. Edited by E. and E. Nestle, B. and K. Aland, et al. 27th ed. Stuttgart: Deutsche Bibelgesellschaft, 1993.

Oakes, Peter. *Philippians: From People to Letter*. Society for New Testament Studies Monograph Series 110. Cambridge: Cambridge University Press, 2001.

———. "Re-mapping the Universe: Paul and the Emperor in 1 Thessalonians and Philippians." *Journal for the Study of the New Testament* 27 (2005): 301-22.

O'Toole, Robert F. "Luke's Position on Politics and Society in Luke-Acts." In *Political Issues in Luke-Acts*, edited by R. J. Cassidy and P. J. Scharper, pp. 1-17. Maryknoll, N.Y.: Orbis, 1983.

Price, S. R. F. "Response." In *Paul and the Roman Imperial Order*, edited by Richard A. Horsley, pp. 175-83. Harrisburg, Pa.: Trinity Press International, 2004.

———. *Rituals and Power: The Roman Imperial Cult in Asia Minor*. Cambridge: Cambridge University Press, 1984.

Rathke, Heinrich. *Ignatius von Antiochien und die Paulusbriefe*. Texte und Untersuchungen zur Geschichte der altchristlichen Literatur 99. Berlin: Akademie-Verlag, 1967.

Riches, J. K., and D. C. Sim, eds. *The Gospel of Matthew in Its Roman Imperial Context*. Early Christianity in Context/Journal for the Study of the New Testament Supplement Series 276. London and New York: T&T Clark, 2005.

Riesner, Rainer. *Paul's Early Period: Chronology, Mission Strategy, Theology*. Translated by Doug Stott. Grand Rapids, Mich.: Eerdmans, 1998.

Roetzel, Calvin J. "Response: How Anti-Imperial Was the Collection and How Emancipatory Was Paul's Project?" In *Paul and Politics: Ekklesia, Israel, Imperium, Interpretation: Essays in Honor of Krister Stendahl,* edited by Richard A. Horsley, pp. 227-30. Harrisburg, Pa.: Trinity Press International, 2000.

Rowe, C. Kavin. "Luke-Acts and the Imperial Cult: A Way Through the Conundrum?" *Journal for the Study of the New Testament* 27 (2005): 279-300.

Sandmel, Samuel. "Parallelomania." *Journal of Biblical Literature* 81 (1962): 1-13.

Schlueter, C. J. *Filling Up the Measure: Polemical Hyperbole in 1 Thessalonians 2.14-16.* Journal for the Study of the New Testament Supplement Series 98. Sheffield: Sheffield Academic Press, 1994.

Smith, Abraham. "'Unmasking the Powers': Toward a Postcolonial Analysis of 1 Thessalonians." In *Paul and the Roman Imperial Order,* edited by Richard A. Horsley, pp. 47-66. Harrisburg, Pa.: Trinity Press International, 2004.

Stanton, Graham N. *Jesus and Gospel.* Cambridge and New York: Cambridge University Press, 2004.

Strathmann, H. "μάρτυς, κτλ." In *Theological Dictionary of the New Testament,* 4:474-514, edited by Gerhard Kittel and Gerhard Friedrich, translated by Geoffrey W. Bromiley. 10 vols. Grand Rapids, Mich.: Eerdmans, 1964-76.

Stuhlmacher, Peter. *Paul's Letter to the Romans: A Commentary.* Translated by Scott J. Hafemann. Louisville, Ky.: Westminster John Knox, 1994.

Sugirtharajah, R. S. *Postcolonial Criticism and Biblical Interpretation.* Oxford and New York: Oxford University Press, 2002.

Tajra, H. W. *The Trial of St. Paul: A Juridical Exegesis of the Second Half of the Acts of the Apostles.* Wissenschaftliche Untersuchungen zum Neuen Testament 2.35. Tübingen: Mohr Siebeck, 1989.

Tannehill, Robert C. *The Narrative Unity of Luke-Acts: A Literary Interpretation.* 2 vols. Foundations and Facets. Philadelphia: Fortress, 1986, 1990.

Tellba, Mikael. *Paul between Synagogue and State: Christians, Jews, and Civic Authorities in 1 Thessalonians, Romans, and Philippians.* Coniectanea Biblica: New Testament 34. Stockholm: Almqvist & Wiksell International, 2001.

Theissen, Gerd. *The Miracle Stories of the Early Christian Tradition.* Edited by John Riches. Translated by Francis McDonagh. Studies of the New Testament and Its World. Edinburgh: T&T Clark/Philadelphia: Fortress, 1983.

————. "The Political Dimension of Jesus' Activities." In *The Social Setting of Jesus and the Gospels,* edited by Wolfgang Stegemann, Bruce J. Malina, and Gerd Theissen, pp. 225-50. Minneapolis: Fortress, 2002.

————. *Sociology of Early Palestinian Christianity.* Translated by John Bowden. Philadelphia: Fortress, 1978.

Trocmé, A. *Jesus and the Nonviolent Revolution.* Translated by M. H. Shank and M. E. Miller. The Christian Peace Shelf. Scottdale, Pa.: Herald, 1974.

Walaskay, Paul W. *'And So We Came to Rome': The Political Perspective of St. Luke.*

Society for New Testament Studies Monograph Series 49. Cambridge: Cambridge University Press, 1983.

Walter, Nikolaus. "Paul and the Early Christian Jesus-Tradition." In *Paul and Jesus: Collected Essays*, edited by A. J. M. Wedderburn, pp. 51-80. Journal for the Study of the New Testament Supplement Series 37. Sheffield: JSOT Press, 1989.

Walton, Steve. "The State They Were In: Luke's View of the Roman Empire." In *Rome in the Bible and the Early Church*, edited by Peter Oakes, pp. 1-41. Carlisle: Paternoster/Grand Rapids, Mich.: Baker, 2002.

Wan, Sze-kar. "Collection for the Saints as Anticolonial Act: Implications of Paul's Ethnic Reconstruction." In *Paul and Politics: Ekklesia, Israel, Imperium, Interpretation: Essays in Honor of Krister Stendahl*, edited by Richard A. Horsley, pp. 191-215. Harrisburg, Pa.: Trinity Press International, 2000.

Wengst, Klaus. *Pax Romana and the Peace of Jesus Christ*. Translated by John Bowden. Philadelphia: Fortress, 1987.

Wilckens, Ulrich. *Der Brief an die Römer*. 3 vols. Evangelisch-katholischer Kommentar zum Neuen Testament 6. Neukirchen: Benziger and Neukirchener, 1978-82.

Wiles, Maurice F. *The Divine Apostle: The Interpretation of St Paul's Epistles in the Early Church*. Cambridge: Cambridge University Press, 1967.

Wilson, Stephen G. *The Gentiles and the Gentile Mission in Luke-Acts*. Society for New Testament Studies Monograph Series 23. Cambridge: Cambridge University Press, 1973.

Winter, Bruce W. "The Entries and Ethics of Orators and Paul (1 Thessalonians 2.1-12)." *Tyndale Bulletin* 44 (1993): 55-74.

Witherington, Ben, III. *The Acts of the Apostles: A Socio-Rhetorical Commentary*. Grand Rapids, Mich.: Eerdmans/Carlisle: Paternoster, 1998.

Wright, N. T. *Christian Origins and the Question of God*. Vol. 2: *Jesus and the Victory of God*. Minneapolis: Fortress, 1996.

————. *Paul: In Fresh Perspective*. Minneapolis: Fortress, 2005.

————. "Paul's Gospel and Caesar's Empire." In *Paul and Politics: Ekklesia, Israel, Imperium, Interpretation: Essays in Honor of Krister Stendahl*, edited by Richard A. Horsley, pp. 160-83. Harrisburg, Pa.: Trinity Press International, 2000.

Yoder, John Howard. *The Politics of Jesus: Vicit Agnus Noster*. 2nd ed. Grand Rapids, Mich.: Eerdmans/Carlisle: Paternoster, 1994.

# Index of Modern Authors

# Index of Scripture and Other Ancient Texts